I0660645

The Literatures of Spanish America and Brazil

NEW WORLD STUDIES
Marlene L. Daut, Editor

The Literatures of
Spanish America and Brazil

Volume I

FROM THEIR ORIGINS THROUGH
THE NINETEENTH CENTURY

Earl E. Fitz

University of Virginia Press

Charlottesville and London

University of Virginia Press
© 2023 by the Rector and Visitors of the University of Virginia
All rights reserved
Printed in the United States of America on acid-free paper

First published 2023

9 8 7 6 5 4 3 2 1

Library of Congress Cataloging-in-Publication Data

Names: Fitz, Earl E., author.
Title: The literatures of Spanish America and Brazil : from their origins through the
  nineteenth century / Earl E. Fitz.
Description: Charlottesville : University of Virginia Press, 2023. | Series: New World
  studies | Includes bibliographical references and index.
Identifiers: LCCN 2023012261 (print) | LCCN 2023012262 (ebook) |
  ISBN 9780813950006 (hardcover ; acid-free paper) | ISBN 9780813950013
  (paperback ; acid-free paper) | ISBN 9780813950020 (ebook)
Subjects: LCSH: Latin American literature—History and criticism. | Spanish
  American literature—History and criticism. | Brazilian literature—History and
  criticism. | LCGFT: Literary criticism.
Classification: LCC PN849.L29 F58 2023 (print) | LCC PN849.L29 (ebook) |
  DDC 860.9/98—dc23/eng/20230503
LC record available at https://lccn.loc.gov/2023012261
LC ebook record available at https://lccn.loc.gov/2023012262

Cover art: Detail from *Amerique,* Pierre Du Val, 1682. (David Rumsey Map
Collection, David Rumsey Map Center, Stanford Libraries)

Despite their common peninsular origins, Spanish America and Brazil have always been separate and apart, since the first days of the discovery and conquest of the New World. . . . In general, Spanish American and Brazilian literature progressed in parallel but separate lines of development.

—Emir Rodríguez Monegal, *The Borzoi Anthology of Latin American Literature,* volume 1

Contents

The Literatures of Spanish America and Brazil

Introduction

THIS BOOK is for students and scholars who want to examine Spanish American and Brazilian literature together in a systematic, integrated, and comparative fashion, from their origins to the end of the nineteenth century. It does not discuss every work by every author; this type of information can be easily gleaned from any number of excellent literary histories currently in existence that focus on Spanish America or Brazil separately. In contrast to these more traditional studies, my project here, comparative and integrative in design, looks at the evolution of creative writing in Brazil and Spanish America as a whole. It examines those authors, texts, and issues that, though given different expression and coming from two different traditions, deal with similar issues.

Historically, Latin Americanists have tended to emphasize Spanish America and treat Brazil as an add-on. I propose to deviate from that approach and establish an equal presence for Brazilian letters. To do so allows us to see the richness of *both* of Latin America's two great traditions. When the editors of the *Cambridge History of Latin American Literature* declare Brazilian literature to be perhaps the "most independent" and "most original" of all New World literatures, we need to take them seriously (González Echevarría, Pupo-Walker, and Haberly 1). Differing slightly in my focus, then, I hope the result will be a new and unified but not homogenized view of early Latin American literature. My intention is to explore the commonalities that tie Spanish America and Brazil together while maintaining the very real differences that distinguish them. For as many commentators, including Emir Rodríguez Monegal and Afrânio Cândido, have shown, they are far from identical (see Cândido 130–39).

Focusing on specific and representative texts, I look at five major topics: the political and cultural situation in 1492 Spain and in 1500 Portugal;[1] the indigenous American cultures encountered by the Spanish

and Portuguese and the effects these had on their future national literatures; Colón's discovery document versus that of Caminha; the colonial
poetry of Mexico's Sor Juana Inés de la Cruz and that of Brazil's Gregório
de Matos; and, in the book's longest section, the poetry of Rubén Darío
and the prose fiction of Brazil's Machado de Assis. In that final chapter,
I argue that at the end of the nineteenth century Latin America produced
not one but two great literary revolutions, both of which were unique in
the Americas. One, as just indicated, manifested itself in the new poetry of
Darío and Spanish American *Modernismo,* but the other, finding expression in his post-1880 stories and novels, stems from Machado de Assis
and his creation of a new kind of narrative. Experience has shown me
that these five topics can form the heart of a successful comparative course
on the development of literature in Brazil and Spanish America from their
beginnings through the end of the nineteenth century.

Several other topics are touched on in less detail (Bartolomé de Las
Casas and Antônio Vieira; Sor Juana and Vieira; and Romanticism in
Spanish America and Brazil), while yet others (the eighteenth century
in Spanish American and Brazilian literature; literature and politics in
nineteenth-century Spanish America and Brazil; and the contrasting
nature of Spanish American and Brazilian Naturalism) are broached in
the hope that an enterprising Latin American comparatist will one day
find herself interested in pursuing them in greater depth. The comparative
methodology, based on a careful examination of both similarities and differences, is crucial to the future of Latin American literature, and any of
these topics, or others yet to be yoked, are capable of forming the basis
of useful and illuminating courses.

While we will always need specialists, in either Spanish American or
Brazilian literature, history, and culture, the future for experts in Latin
Americanists seems destined to involve both Spanish America and Brazil.
Brazil has long been ignored, but its importance—to Latin America, to
the Americas, and to our ever more integrated global culture—is simply
too great to be ignored, minimized, or shunted aside any longer. To be a
Latin Americanist today, in the third decade of the twenty-first century,
requires that one understand not merely how Spanish America and giant
Brazil relate to and contrast with each other but how they, constituting
what we imagine as Latin America, relate to the United States, to the rest
of the Americas, and beyond. Like the rest of the world, North, Central,
and South America are today so interconnected that to disregard their
historically based relationships is to undermine our efforts to understand
them. We in the Americas have to know more about one another if we

are to have a more harmonious and a more just future together. This is our task. And literary study is part of it.

But the current study is also intended for friends and colleagues in departments of comparative literature, English, French, American studies, and American history who are interested in reading American literature from a comparative and hemispheric perspective. To that end, I have included references to US writers and texts that bear on the Latin American issues being discussed. I do something similar with respect to certain Canadian and Canadien authors who are especially important to the inter-American project. Indeed, just as Canada divides into its English- and French-speaking parts, so too does Latin America divide into its Spanish- and Portuguese-speaking parts. Spanish America, however, remains even today a clutch of culturally different regions and nations united by a single language but roiled by a variety of social, political, and economic conflicts. Yet even on this score there is a parallel with Canada and the United States.

The already mentioned points of contact are intended to inspire the reader to pursue more in-depth studies herself. In 2023, critical thinking about the Americas has changed. Today we are seeing a field that is newly comparative and plural in nature and "variously referred to as *Americas* studies, transamerican studies, interamerican studies, hemispheric studies, or Latin American subaltern studies," depending on the program or perspective involved (Spitta and Zamora 192). Although we can be cheered by this less nationalistic and more comprehensive approach to what it means to be "American," "we must," as Spitta and Zamora warn, "avoid paying lip service to a more inclusive vision of the Americas while reinscribing U.S. hegemony" (193). As Claudia Sadowski-Smith, Claire F. Fox, Vera Kutzinski, and Antonio Barrenechea have shown, this remains a challenge for many US-based inter-Americanists (see Sadowski-Smith and Fox 23; Kutzinski, *Worlds of Langston Hughes* 230; and Barrenechea, *America Unbound* 6–7, 147–48, 154–56). Unless and until US-based inter-Americanists learn the requisite languages, study the primary texts in their original languages, and read the essential critical studies, they will remain limited in terms of their contributions to this field. But foreign-language enrollment figures in the United States are falling, not rising, and this does not auger well, at least in the immediate future, for US-based inter-American scholarship. The Canadian scholar Robert K. Martin, of the Université de Montréal, points to the problem: if, he writes, US readers are not willing to learn enough Spanish to read even Chicana and Chicano texts, why would one ever expect them to learn enough French "to read

Québécois or Acadian texts?" (359). Or, thinking of Brazil, texts written in Portuguese?

Speaking as English professors interested in a more hemispheric approach to American literature, Sadowski-Smith and Fox sum it up this way: "We fear that an Americanist-led [i.e., US-led] hemispherism will only promote a vision of the Americas in which all academic disciplinary configurations are subordinate to those of the United States and in which every region outside the United States is collapsed into a monolithic order" (23). Martin concurs, observing that the US approach to comparative inter-American study maintains the literature and culture of the United States at what its scholars and critics regard, without justification, as its rightful ("predestined," à la the Puritans?) place in the "hegemonic center" of the entire American paradigm (359).

And yet, as Barrenechea reports, most inter-American or hemispheric American literature programs today are housed in US departments of English and American literature (*America Unbound* 147–49). Perhaps this is because English departments here in the United States are driving the World Literature movement and arrogating unto themselves authors and texts from other parts of the world, including Latin America. Or perhaps it is because, after having their languages and literatures judged for so many years to be inferior or second rate, departments of Spanish and Portuguese are reluctant to now assert themselves and demand the respect they, their writers, and their texts deserve. Even in a field, comparative inter-American studies, in which they have formidable expertise, speak the essential languages (including English), and know the literary history of Brazil as well as those of the nations of Spanish America, scholars of literature written in Spanish and Portuguese are hesitant to assert their expertise. But a new generation is beginning to do so, and we can all regard this as a very positive development.

Interestingly enough, however, of Latin America's two grand traditions, the Spanish and the Portuguese, it is the Brazilianists who have long cultivated a more expansive inter-American perspective, one involving not merely the United States but the United States, Canada, the Caribbean, and Spanish America.[2] For those of us who work with Brazil, it was no surprise, therefore, that in 1958 the Brazilian historian Vicente Tapajós published his monumental *História da América*, which argued against always studying América, or America, only in terms of a single nation, the United States, and not in terms of its many nations, and in favor of remembering that for all the very real differences therein, America was, from the beginning, a vision that united us all. America existed as an idea in Latin America long before it did in English North America. Decrying the myriad ways scholars and political leaders had splintered that original unifying vision, Tapajós, in the midst of the Cold War, reminded us all of one important fact: "O homem separou as Américas, mas a América é uma só" (from the front matter; Men separated the Americas, but America remains one).[3]

The ignoring of Brazil as an American nation, even by well-intended colleagues, is a continuing problem. In Hortense Spillers's *Comparative American Identities,* for example, published by Routledge and the English Institute in 1991, there are no essays on either Brazil or English Canada. The collection does, however, include one essay on Caribbean literature, one on Québec, and one (plus part of a second) on Spanish America. This is laudable. But then the same tome gives us either five or six essays, depending on how one counts them, on the literature of the United States. When Spitta and Zamora urge us to expand our thinking about what constitutes America and American literature, but to do so without "reinscribing U.S. hegemony," this is what they are talking about. Three years earlier, in 1988, two eminent US literary scholars, Brian Wilkie and James Hurt, both professors of English, referred to pre-Boom Latin America as "a placid backwater of world literature" (2052). This was never the case, of course, as even a cursory understanding of Latin American literary history would show. From its beginnings, in 1492 and 1500, Latin American literature has been actively engaged with world literature and thought. More so, arguably, than the United States has been. While our two colleagues were undoubtedly trying to say something positive about writing from Latin America, to make this kind of wildly incorrect statement demonstrates, sadly, the level of disregard that critics in the United States have long shown to the literatures of Spanish America and Brazil. Attitudes here in the States are changing, however, though even now, in 2023, Canada and Brazil, the latter boasting one of the most fascinating American literatures, remain all but invisible for US-centered inter-Americanists.

While a potential danger, this kind of cultural blindness (not to say arrogance) need not remain a hemispheric reality. Nor the misinterpretations that go along with it. Latin Americanists know this. Most have spent their entire professional lives dealing with this type of neglect. Today, however, we in the Americas are more interrelated than ever, and it is high time we embraced this truth. It is also essential that we all do so as

Americans. But before we can take this step, we must replace ignorance with knowledge. We must learn the truth about *all* of "nuestra América," as Martí would say, and not just parts of it. As US-based scholars have come to the inter-American perspective, there has been a tendency for them to think first, and only, of Spanish America. For many, Martí's 1891 essay "Nuestra América," which has been translated into English, is the point of entry to the field. Its influence in the United States has thus been considerable. It is possible to think, however, that because Martí does not include Brazil (or Canada) in his vision of "our America," interested parties in the United States read the Cuban writer and are led to believe that Brazil is not part of Latin America or even of America in the hemispheric sense. It finds itself completely elided, even by well-intended scholars.[4] For comparative Latin Americanists especially, but also for inter-Americanists generally, the omission of giant, literarily rich Brazil is a serious mistake.[5]

Students and scholars of Spanish America and Brazil know they cannot adequately till their fields without seriously considering the literature, history, and culture of the United States. And more and more, that of Canada as well. The late Richard Morse deserves recognition as one of the first to make this point. But it is also true, as Morse argued, that students and scholars of the literature, history, and culture of the United States can no longer ignore their Latin American and Canadian neighbors or give short shrift to their artistic and intellectual achievements. To do so is not only insulting, it is dangerous; and, to invoke the voice of William Carlos Williams, it goes against the grain of American history. While narrow specializations will always be valuable and needed, today there is *also* a need for those who wish to conceive of America as a plurality, a sisterhood of nations and not the domain of a single nation. This is part of our collective hemispheric future. *E pluribus unum!*

Fortunately, things are changing, and for the better. The field of inter-American studies continues to grow and evolve, this being a sure sign of its vitality and potential. Younger scholars are combining forces with seasoned veterans to explore new and exciting facets of our shared American reality. Charles A. Perrone's *Brazil, Lyric, and the Americas* (2010), Luciano Tosta's *Confluence Narratives* (2016), and Antonio Barrenechea's *America Unbound* (2016) are examples of this, as is *Essays in Honor of Lois Parkinson Zamora: From the Americas to the World*, edited by Monika Kaup and John Ochoa (2021). These studies break new ground and illustrate vividly just how profoundly interdisciplinary the hemispheric project is and how effectively it gets departments and programs long isolated by subject matter and language talking with one another.

In assessing the state of the discipline today, Antonio Barrenechea divides academic inter-Americanism into two periods. The first, running from about 1980 to about 2000, sought to be inclusive and egalitarian in its approach to American literature. It focused on literary texts almost exclusively, and it stressed the utility of the comparative method. The second period, beginning in the late 1990s and centered in US departments of English and American studies (which were attempting to accept that the term America involved more than the United States alone), moved away from literary study and toward cultural studies (Barrenechea, "Hemispheric World of Differences"). In fact and in practice, if not in theory, it also defined the field in binary terms, with the English-speaking United States at its center and a vaguely understood entity known as Spanish-speaking America swirling around to the south and making contributions to US literature and culture. This second period, argues Barrenechea, led to the "less comparative" nature "of today's hemispherism" and to its much narrower vision (Kaup and Ochoa, introduction xiii). National literatures like those of Canada and Brazil are left out.

For the comparative approach to the literatures of America to succeed, either the student must be able to read sophisticated poems, novels, short narratives, plays, and criticism in all the languages that are involved in the inter-American project (Spanish, Portuguese, French, and English, plus the many Native American tongues) or translations must be used. Since very few of us are going to be sufficiently fluent in all these languages and their literatures, translation has its place in inter-American study. But translations, no matter how good, are not the same as the original text, and we must all understand this. The reading experience is never the same. Nor are the levels of historical and cultural awareness brought to the reading of translations. While most of us would, I suspect, agree that reading a work of literature in its original language is the best way to consume it, that is not always possible. Lacking the ability to read Sor Juana Inés de la Cruz in Spanish or Machado de Assis in Portuguese, the next best thing is to read them in translation. To be completely unaware of other great American writers because you cannot read them in their original language is no virtue. It is better for a scholar or student of hemispheric American literature to know American masters like Sor Juana, Machado, and the others from Latin America via even a less than perfect translation than not to know them at all. Ignorance is not a position most of us would wish to defend. But to think that only Spanish and English define inter-American literature is a mistake, and if such thinking continues, it will distort our understanding of American literature. At least three of the many American languages are necessary, and students, basing their decision on their own particular interests, should be advised to study them and their literatures as much as possible.

My goal with this book is, first of all, to show how Spanish American and Brazilian literature originated and evolved, comparatively speaking, through time to the end of the nineteenth century, a period of tremendous vitality, growth, and creativity. Secondly, however, and with the above warning in mind, I also argue for Latin American literature (meaning that of *both* Spanish America and Brazil) as the foundation of the field known today as inter-American, or hemispheric, literary study. I do not contend that Latin American literature is somehow the best of the several American literatures; only that, beginning as early as it does (1492 for Spanish America and 1500 for Brazil), it is the oldest American one. As such, it offers a historical and inherently comparative perspective on all things "American" that we would not otherwise have (see E. Fitz, "Spanish American and Brazilian Literature"; and McClennen, "Comparative Literature and Latin American Studies").

But more than this, as its authors and texts have consistently demonstrated through the years, Latin American literature also deals with the issues that define the greater American experience: the existence of fascinating and diverse pre-Columbian civilizations; the arrival of Europeans and the destruction of indigenous people; slavery and race, racial mixing, and racial violence; religious animosity; the quest for independence and an authentic American identity; political and economic exploitation; the struggle for human rights; the status of women in American societies; immigration; and the environment. Comparatively inclined Latin Americanists tend to know both Spanish and Portuguese, as well as English and French. This kind of language and literature training makes them ideally equipped to engage in inter-American work as well. So while I do not argue that the literatures of Spanish America and Brazil are necessarily the best in the Americas, I do maintain that because of their age, their thematic concerns (including the status of indigenous peoples and those of African descent), their passion for stylistic originality, their awareness of themselves as participants in a global system, and their commitment to our common fight against global warming, they are uniquely well suited to serve as platforms from which to observe the development of literature in the rest of the New World. Who, after all, knows more about the story of America—the good, the bad, and the ugly of it—than Latin Americanists?

But as already noted, my study is also directed at students and scholars in the United States, Canada, and the Caribbean who are interested in an integrated but not homogenized Latin American literary history and who also see it as a vital part of a larger, more inclusive view of America.[6] To that end, I reference, in each chapter, those comparisons with the literature of these other American cultures that might yield some revealing studies of American literature, understood, now, in its hemispheric sense. It is my hope that this additional information will make the current study useful to scholars who are not primarily focused on Spanish America and Brazil but who might well have an interest in them. Since the early years of the twentieth century, US historians have been aware of the "epic of Greater America," as Herbert Bolton, one of the earliest inter-Americanists, termed it. This comparative and hemispheric view of American history has persisted among professional historians up to the present day. Historians, in fact, must be credited with endorsing the inter-American project long before we literary scholars, who seem too mired in tired old issues of hegemony and stereotypes, did. But the times are changing, and for that we can all give thanks (see McClennen and Fitz, introduction).

In 1959, the historian Henry Parkes wrote that "the central theme in the history of the Americas can be stated very simply. During the four and a half centuries that have elapsed since the first voyage of Columbus, a stream of migration has been flowing from Europe westward across the Atlantic and into the two American continents. Relatively small during the first three hundred years, it increased during the nineteenth century and did not reach its peak until shortly before the First World War. In all between fifty and sixty million persons left their European homes and established themselves in the New World. During the same period, another five or ten millions were brought to the Americas by force from Africa. This is by far the largest movement of peoples in all history" (3). While Parkes's figures may be a bit off in terms of the exact number of African slaves brought, in chains, to the shores of America, North, Central, and South, his basic argument about the peopling of post-1492 America remains solid. Parkes, a specialist in the history of the United States, does not fail, especially in the first sixty-three pages, to compare and contrast the story of the United States with that of Spanish America, though the latter does not come off well. France, better known and more respected in the United States of the 1950s, gets eight listings in the index, plus a bit of commentary; giant Brazil gets two (pp. 16 and 57) and, merely mentioned, is not discussed at all. Still and all, Parkes does show that he is aware of how the term *America* might properly relate to New World nations other than the United States. This amounts to a retreat from Bolton's earlier, more egalitarian, and more comprehensive vision, but it is representative of the US-centric attitudes of the post–World War II period (the period in which the Boom occurred).

Here in the United States, of course, now as even in the 1950s, we know we can boast of a long and proud Hispanic tradition, one that predates the better-known and more venerated English tradition. I believe we should honor both, and part of this book seeks to do just that. But the case for Spain's presence in our early formation is strong. "Between 1513 and 1543," historian Bradford Burns argues, "the Spaniards explored and claimed the territory in North America between the Carolinas and Oregon. In fact, two-thirds of the territory of the continental United States was at one time claimed by Spain. By the time George Washington was inaugurated as President, Spain had colonized a far greater area, ranging from San Francisco to Santa Fé to San Antonio to St. Augustine, than that encompassed by the original thirteen states" (*Latin America* 16). In the United States we know this, but we have a tendency to minimize it or to forget about it entirely. In Canada too a new appreciation of Latin America is emerging, as is a new and exciting awareness of Canada's part in the growth and development of hemispheric American letters. Long appreciated as the crossroads of the Americas, the Caribbean is now coming into its own as a major force in inter-American letters as well. The times are indeed changing.

Although I do hope to bring all these issues into view, my primary concern here is a comparative assessment of early Spanish American and Brazilian letters through the end of the nineteenth century. Latin America, I contend, forms the foundation of the inter-American project.

Before we proceed any further, this is a propitious moment to summarize how the differing literary traditions of Spanish America and Brazil reflect "their dissimilar origins" as well as their "contrasting historical processes" (González Echevarría, Pupo-Walker, and Haberly 2). As the editors of the *Cambridge History of Latin American Literature* point out, there are several points of difference. First, the Portuguese who colonized Brazil tended to remain along the "coastal areas" and did not encounter "populous and complex indigenous cultures"; second, and in comparison with the political system erected by the Spanish in America, colonial Brazil was much less controlled and "less developed institutionally"; third, while Spain built universities in its American colonies as early as 1538 (in Santo

Domingo), then in 1551 (in Mexico City and Lima, Peru), and even more in later years, Brazilian "centers of higher learning" were not established until 1827, with the first Brazilian university not being founded until 1920; fourth, and to its great advantage, "colonial Brazil was a society receptive to the foreign intellectual currents that often came with trade." Because of this, the Brazilians and the Portuguese Crown "never developed the paranoid fear of foreigners displayed by the Spanish authorities" (González Echevarría, Pupo-Walker, and Haberly 2). In Brazil, conceivably a consequence of point 4, "tolerance and a penchant for compromise have held sway" (3). Fifth, Brazil did not suffer the Balkanization that afflicted Spanish America after its wars for independence, fought between 1810 and 1825, were over. A huge nation, and by the mid-eighteenth century one that was a bubbling "amalgamation of Indians, Africans, and Europeans," Brazil, a constitutional monarchy, remained intact during the Spanish American wars for independence and in fact actually became even more unified (3).

As we can surmise even from this quick look at its past, the future of Latin American literary study is going to be comparative in nature. It is as difficult to think of Spanish America without Brazil, or vice versa, as it is to think about France or England without thinking about Germany. Or of China without Japan. While we will always have our specific interests and areas of focus, the days of narrow specialization in either Spanish America or Brazil are over. Our future now turns on our ability to connect with the other languages and literatures of our hemisphere and world. While as Latin Americanists we have always done this, as have our writers, artists, and intellectuals, we have to do more of it, and we have to do it well. The question before us now is, How can we best proceed? How, exactly, do we integrate the complex literatures of Spanish America and Brazil? And how can we do this without homogenizing these two grand literary traditions, without making them seem the same? The answers lie in judicious application of the comparative method, which calls for studying literary texts in terms of the following categories: theme and motif; genre and form; period and movement; influence and reception; translation; literature and another discipline; literary history, theory, and criticism—and for doing so while remaining alert to issues of historical, cultural, and textual difference.

While some may find my methodology to be stodgy and old fashioned, I believe it is still useful. One can, I think, still learn something from it. In utilizing it, I do not intend it to replace, supplant, or in any way inhibit other approaches to comparative Latin American and inter-American study; only that it be considered as one possible methodology among many others, and one that can add to them and all they can teach us. It is still useful to know the centrality of race as a theme in hemispheric American literature, the history of the novel in the Americas, or the importance of nineteenth-century literature to nation building.

A note on translation is perhaps in order here. Except for those whose knowledge of both Spanish and Portuguese is sufficient to allow them to read complex literary texts in both languages, translation plays a role in any comparative discussion of literature from Spanish America and Brazil. And in its dissemination in the rest of the Americas and the world. In the global circulation of literary texts, the quality of the translation is of paramount importance. It can never be discounted or taken for granted. Ideally, a first-rate author gets a first-rate translator, and the result is felicitous, a near-perfect reproduction of the original in all respects. But that is not always the case. Given the vagaries of the publishing industry, sometimes the pairings go awry. A mediocre translator can transform a subtle, sophisticated, and nuanced writer into a very ordinary and pedestrian one. By the same token, however, a great translator can transform a mediocre writer into an outstanding one. Although in the ancient history of translation (which we would do well to think of as a vital form of human communication) not many translators have believed they had the right to improve an author's work, a few have taken this position, among them such illustrious figures as Schiller and Borges. Then, too, the translator will also add to or subtract from the original text. Or both, often at the same time. Inevitably, this happens for a variety of reasons, notable among which are those of political ideology, religious belief, or sexual orientation. This explains why a text works one way in its original language and other ways in its translations. More importantly, it also explains why a translation is never identical to its original text.

Whether or not the translator arrogates unto herself the right to make an existing text "better," the role of the translator is at least as important as that of the original author and very often more so. The reader who gets her *Dom Casmurro* via the English translation of R. L. Scott-Buccleuch, for example, will come away with a far different experience than the one offered by Helen Caldwell in her rendering of the same narrative. So while both translations percolate a great novel by Brazil's Machado de Assis through the hemispheric and global reading systems, they offer wildly divergent versions of the same original text. The reader must be aware of this. Something similar is true for the various translators we have of the poems of Pablo Neruda. When we read a translation, we are, quite literally, reading not the words of the original author but those of the translator. *Cien años de soledad,* written by Gabriel García Márquez, is a great novel; *One Hundred Years of Solitude,* translated by Gregory Rabassa, is another. And while they have much in common, and while both are great works of American literature, they are not the same text. And the reading experience is not the same.

Perhaps because the Spanish and the Portuguese arrived in the Americas before the French and the English and so were always aware of what their European competitors were doing, Latin Americanists have long imagined America in plural rather than in singular terms. And yet, as their earlier explorers and settlers understood, Spain and Portugal were longtime rivals and at times in Iberian history antagonists. When they arrived in the New World (which was, of course, already an ancient and complex world to the millions of people who lived here), in 1492 and 1500, respectively, Spain and Portugal brought singularly different ideas about how their new societies would be set up. And each was acutely aware of what the other was doing. This is why today we need to apply a comparative lens in thinking about early Latin America, one that considers not only the differences between Spain and Portugal but also the many and diverse indigenous cultures they encountered. Three of these cultures—the Aztec, the Mayan, and the Incan—would be more sophisticated than anything the Europeans had ever known. And their conquests would be both bloody and tragic. This point is made dramatically clear by Bernal Díaz del Castillo in his *Historia verdadera de la conquista de la Nueva España.*

And since at their core all successful comparative studies rely on two separate but closely interrelated steps, the establishing of what disparate texts have in common and then the elucidation of how they differ, how they illustrate their uniqueness, it seems clear that applying the comparative method to an integrated understanding of Spanish American and Brazilian literature can result in useful and illuminating insights. As Lúcia Helena Costigan and Leopoldo Bernucci put it, "Continuamos, portanto, nesse percurso cuja meta principal é a diminuição da grande distância que ainda separa os brasileiros dos demais povos latino-americanos. Que os trabalhos aqui incluídos sirvam como ponto de partida para novas veredas no campo do comparatismo latino-(e inter)Americano. Sejamos comparatistas!" (13; Let us continue, therefore, with this project, the principal goal of which is the diminution of the great distance that still separates the Brazilians from the other peoples of Latin America. May the works included here serve as a point of departure for new paths in the field of Latin [and inter-]American comparatism. Let us be comparatists!).

This is solid advice, and it serves the inter-American project exceedingly well. The inherently democratic comparative method, which holds that no text is superior to another simply because of its language or place of cultural origin, is perfectly suited to the study of the several American literatures. While most scholars of American literature would probably agree on the value of the comparative approach, for some of us there is an unforeseen and perhaps troubling complication in the process. By its nature, the comparative method can upend long-established notions of hierarchy and superiority. It can lead one to ask some serious questions. What if in applying the comparative optic to a now more hemispheric conception of American literature we find ourselves concluding that Mexico's Sor Juana Inés de la Cruz is our greatest colonial poet and intellectual? Greater than Anne Bradstreet, Jonathan Edwards, or even Edward Taylor? Or that at the end of the nineteenth century Brazil's Machado de Assis was a better novelist (however we wish to define this elusive term) and short story writer than Henry James? How would such conclusions be received in US-centered departments of American literature? What would happen to our sense of American (and, indeed, global) literature if, as Roberto González Echevarría suggests, we used certain Brazilian and Spanish American texts as the models against which other texts from other cultures must measure themselves (see González Echevarría, "Latin American and Comparative Literatures")? Are those US scholars who are committed to World Literature prepared to see their own texts, those that constitute the corpus of US American literature, sometimes displaced by other American texts, those from Brazil, Argentina, Mexico, or Peru, for example? What is acceptable in theory may not be so easy to swallow in actual fact, and yet this is what we must all be prepared to do if we truly wish to examine the literatures of the Americas without bias or prejudice.

1   The Iberian Origins

WE CANNOT understand the origins of Spanish American and Brazilian literature without first considering what was going on in 1492 Spain and in 1500 Portugal. They were far from identical. The distinctions between the two were brought to the New World. As the editors of the acclaimed *Cambridge History of Latin American Literature* write, "Differences between both literary traditions," that is, those of Spanish America and Brazil, "are due to their dissimilar origins, and are informed by contrasting historical processes" (González Echevarría, Pupo-Walker, and Haberly 2).

In Spain, the long-running Guerra de la Reconquista finally ended in 1492. The Moors were driven out, and Spain was unified—politically, religiously, and linguistically. Portugal had been a separate nation since about 1143, its culture leavened with both Jewish and Muslim customs and practices and its language enriched by many Moorish words. Its clergy exercised less power over the state than in any other European nation of the time (Seed 134, 135). In Spain, Antonio de Nebrija argued in his *Gramática* that empire and language went hand in hand. Tellingly, there was no Nebrija in Portugal to codify Portuguese as the language of power, dominion, and empire, this absence once again highlighting the differences between the Spanish outlook in 1492 and the Portuguese. We would do well to remember that at this pivotal juncture in European and American history, the official policy of commercial expansion of these same Portuguese was well under way down and around Africa, up to India, and then on to India and the East Indies, where the spice trade would, for a time, make them very wealthy. Drawing heavily on "Islamic and Hebrew mathematics and astronomy," at peace, and not controlled by the country's own "anti-Semitic" and anti-Muslim religious leaders, the Portuguese monarchs would invest more blood and treasure in overseas expansion (Seed 107, 135). For the Spanish, however, now that they had defeated the Moors, the question what to do next loomed large. Then came Colón with a daring proposal, one that would have the Spanish sail to the West and win the support of the "fanatically intolerant Catholic Kings of Spain" (Seed 135).

In the preceding years, however, both the Spanish (with their sense of *convivencia,* or living together) and the Portuguese (with their even more accommodating practice of *convivência*) had had their visions of what cultural and intellectual mixing could achieve, with the Portuguese version being the more aggressively (and strategically) synthesizing of the two. It must be noted, in this same context, that in Iberia, "Moslem rule proved surprisingly tolerant," so the concept of Christians, Jews, and Moslems living together in peace was not as outlandish as one might think. In fact, it was often the norm (Herring 65). During the Moorish occupation of Iberia (711–1492), Christians and Jews could worship freely and conduct their lives "without interference" (65). The Moorish occupation of the Iberian Peninsula was long, and the military violence aside, it proved to be quite beneficial, often to Muslims and Christians alike. "The first three centuries of Moslem rule," Herring writes, "were a decided success both for the invaders and for their victims. . . . The Moslems . . . extended irrigation, encouraged seed selection, fertilization, and stock breeding, and introduced rice, sugar, and other crops to the peninsula. They were skilled metallurgists, with improved methods for mining and processing of ores. They promoted industry. The Moslems built new cities and expanded old ones. . . . They brought intellectual ardor to the peninsula, organized schools, and won credit as preservers and transmitters of Greek and Roman culture. They were intellectually co-operative; Arabic, Christian, and Jewish scholars worked side by side. They produced scientists and mathematicians. They introduced paper to the peninsula long before it reached the rest of Europe, and books multiplied" (65–66). "Unlike most medieval Christian science, Islamic science openly allowed people of other religious faiths to participate in scientific discussions and dialogue" (Seed 117). Through translation and commentary on it, Jewish scholarship on mathematics and astronomy made its way into the store of Iberian knowledge. After 1492, however, the religious zealotry of the conquering Christian forces would destroy this social, political, economic, and intellectual progress and comity. There is a lesson to be learned here about the need for religious tolerance. And for the strict separation of religion and politics.

But by 1492, and after finally winning the bloody, eight-hundred-year-long War of the Reconquest, which ran from 732 and the Battle of Tours, in the north, to 1492 and the fall of the Moorish stronghold, Granada, in the south, Spain had begun to look inward and to purge itself of what it considered "impure" elements. Except for its American adventure, Spain, about to lose more than it had gained in the Reconquista, was seeking to isolate itself from the rest of the world so as not to be "contaminated" by it. After hundreds of years of more or less constant warfare, Spain was not in the mood to be conciliatory toward people or cultures who did not see things as it did. For the Catholic monarchs of Spain, the age of *convivencia* was over.

In Portugal, which became an independent country in 1143, things were different. To begin with, Portuguese law, the "most liberal" legal code in Europe, protected the rights of minority groups, most notably "the Moors and the Jews" (Freyre 193, 194). In late fifteenth-century Portugal, the at least nominally Catholic majority was, considering its time and place, surprisingly tolerant of other religious groups. This was partly, as Seed points out, because of a rift between the church and Portugal's more secular leaders about how the nation should be run, where its best interests lay, and how to attain them (134). Payne too makes note of the conflict that existed in Portugal "between the church and crown" (124). In Spain, the church and the government were one and the same. Freyre contends that even the Portuguese middle class, thoroughly "impregnated with Moorish and Jewish blood," was doing relatively well and that few wanted to rock the boat (210). Knowing this, the government was loath to turn control over to the more fanatically religious factions for fear that they would begin to persecute the Jews and Moors, as was happening in Spain, and by so doing move the nation backward.[1] By the late fifteenth century, Portugal could boast an uncommon level of tolerance for non-Christian peoples and, surprisingly, an at least partial, if tenuous, separation of church and state. We cannot say this about 1492 Spain, and it would not be said of the Puritans in 1610 and 1620.

These facts help explain why, in colonial Brazil, and more than in colonial Spanish America, it was not uncommon for even prominent families to have Jewish, Moorish, and Indian blood coursing through their veins. More miscible with respect to other cultures, and able to learn from them, the Portuguese of 1500, one can conclude, brought fewer social, political, and religious rigidities to the New World than did the Spanish, the French, or the English.

By 1250 Portugal had established a kind of de facto peace with the Moors,[2] and in contrast to Spain (which was tied down by its seemingly endless war with the Moors), it began, around 1400, to open itself up to the world. This cessation of hostilities with the Moors allowed the Portuguese to invest in activities other than warfare. Agriculture benefitted, as did other socially beneficial sectors, including science and astronomy. Importantly, three additional professions received new government funding: mathematics, navigation, and naval engineering. Thanks largely to work done by Moorish and Jewish scholars, the Portuguese were learning how to build bigger and better ships and how to sail them wherever they wished. The oceans were no longer obstacles for the Portuguese but their great global highways. New investments in navigation, nautical equipment, and shipbuilding thus enabled the Portuguese to begin their maritime global expansion, which they did, albeit on a modest scale, before the end of the fourteenth century. By 1400 the Portuguese were skilled mariners, and their marvelously seaworthy ships, the caravels, were beginning to move south from the strategically critical African port city of Ceuta, which the Portuguese, aware of what they needed, captured. In the meantime Spain, Portugal's old rival, was still slugging it out with the Moors on the battlefield.

By 1419 Portugal was seriously committed to overseas exploration and commerce, and by 1460 it had explored nearly all of the western coast of Africa. In 1488 Bartolomeu Dias rounded the Cape of Good Hope, and ten years after that, in 1498, Vasco da Gama arrived in India; settlements there and in China, Japan, and the Indies quickly followed. Rather like the Phoenicians of the Ancient World, the Portuguese of the second half of the fifteenth century were fast becoming a seafaring and a trading people. As Burns puts it, "Along the coasts of South America, Africa, and Asia, the Portuguese eagerly established their commercial—not colonial—empires" (*Latin America* 13). Spain, slowly but surely winning out in its protracted land war with the Moors, was not concerned with honing its maritime expertise. It was, moreover, winning its costly religious war with Islam, a religion it knew it could live with if it wished to. But it did not. And so it persisted. And upon discovering the New World, it would be keenly interested in colonization. Then as now, religious fanaticism functioned as a powerful motivator but also as a dangerous and sometimes fatal problem.

With the surrender of Granada, the last Moorish citadel, to Spanish forces in 1492, the long struggle finally came to an end. But what to do then? Concentrating more and more on issues of purity in bloodlines and in religious orthodoxy, Spain moved to consolidate itself nationally, to seal itself off from the outside world, and to concentrate on what it hoped would prove to be its profitable New World discoveries (see Herring 71, also 67–74). The decision to exile the Moorish "infidels" and the Jews, who would not "accept Catholicism," would, however, prove disastrous for Spain, though in 1492 it was not apparent that this would be the outcome (Herring 72, also 73). For those who wish to live in a democracy, which requires that all its citizens have equal rights and responsibilities and that dissent is protected, there is a lesson to be learned here.

Seeing an opportunity to benefit from a mistake on the part of their Iberian neighbor, the Portuguese monarchs orchestrated a different response to the people being thrown out of newly unified Spain. A major part of Portugal's growth during this period was owing to its acceptance of Jews and Moors exiled from Spain and its investment in scientific pursuits (notably mathematics, navigation, and shipbuilding) and in agriculture. Portugal eagerly accepted the help of Jewish and Moorish intellectuals and continued its long-standing program of cultural assimilation, a kind of biological and cultural *mestiçagem* that we do not see in a xenophobic Spain increasingly obsessed with purity in all things. This flexible, more tolerant attitude would carry over to Portugal's American colony. While Bosi wonders whether too much has been made of this Portuguese malleability, it should not be dismissed, as it could be invaluable in terms of social and political cohesion (Bosi 40–43, 45–51). As a result, Henríquez-Ureña notes, the "absence of deep social and racial prejudices" in colonial Brazil is even more striking than that in early Spanish America, which suffered from Spain's imposition of a rigid, largely inflexible, and deeply class-conscious society (37; see also Herring 187–88). Putnam, interested in comparisons between Brazil and the United States, chimes in with this: "In contrast to the racially unprejudiced Portuguese, the Puritans and other North American colonists cherished a feeling of superiority to colored peoples" (143; see also 8–18).[3]

This attitude of contemptuousness so many in the United States have had toward non-white peoples and their cultural production reveals just how applicable Edward Said's landmark 1978 study, *Orientalism,* has been to the reception of Latin American literature and thought in the United States. Even during the 1960s, the relatively positive era of the Boom, this deeply rooted prejudice against writers and thinkers working in Spanish and Portuguese was the major obstacle advocates of Latin American literature in the United States, such as the esteemed scholar and translator Gregory Rabassa, would have to overcome. While the main focus of Said's thesis was on the Middle East and its skewed representation in the West, the point he makes about non-white, non-Christian cultures tending to be regarded in the WASPish English-speaking world as more exotic than substantive rang true for Latin Americanists as well. Indeed, there existed among Latin Americanists a substantial bibliography that concerned itself with exactly the issues that Said wrote about in 1978. But they were ignored by him, as they were by most others outside the Latin American ken.[4] As far as Latin American literature was concerned, even by the late 1980s the US academy, rife with problems of disdain, devaluation, and misrepresentation, was dismissive (Wilkie and Hurt 2052).[5] And for the Spanish Americans and the Brazilians (who had long prided themselves on being a racially and culturally mixed people), no issue, with the possible exception of miscegenation (which is not really a separate issue), was more fraught in the United States than "race."[6] Inter-"racial" marriage was not even legal in most of the United States until 1967 and the *Loving v. Virginia* Supreme Court ruling.

This was a far cry from the situation in Brazil, which, with its Portuguese roots, offered a very different take on "race" relations. The Portuguese, writes Herring, were "well equipped" because of their "long experience with Negro and Moslem" peoples to form "a colony," Brazil, "that would prove a gigantic melting pot of Indian, Negro, and white" (88). The result was that in Portugal's American colony, from the very beginning, "the intermingling of white, Indian, and Negro was rapid," and "slight stigma was attached to miscegenation" (Herring 230–31). Comparing the Brazilian colonial experience with those of Spain, England, and France, Gilberto Freyre arrived at the same conclusion: Brazil was different because its Portuguese heritage was different—different from that of Spain in the New World but also from that of the English, the French, and the rest of Europe as well. "The Portuguese," he wrote, were "less ardent in their orthodoxy than the Spaniards and less narrow than the English in their color prejudices and Christian morality" and had no reservations about biological or cultural mixing (81). "Hybrid from the beginning," the Brazilian inter-Americanist famously averred, "Brazilian society is, of all those in the Americas, the one most harmoniously constituted so far as racial relations are concerned" (Freyre 83).

While certain of Freyre's ideas have been challenged since the 1970s,[7] his basic argument, that here in the Americas and in comparison with the Spanish, the French, and most especially English America, Brazil's experience has been notably distinct, remains solid. For those scholars who interpret his words as meaning that Brazil had somehow achieved a racial democracy, clearly Freyre was wrong. Although race relations in

Brazil are different, they have never constituted a true racial democracy. But at no point does Freyre actually claim that they did. He does believe that Brazil's racial experience can and should be distinguished from those of our American neighbors, for it is not the same. On this point American history bears him out. For those who believe Freyre was seeking to differentiate Brazil's racial experience from that of Brazil's American neighbors, and most notably that of the United States (a place Freyre knew well, having spent a lengthy sojourn here), the Brazilian scholar's thesis becomes much more palatable and useful (see, e.g., 11–13, 18, 40, 185, 190).

In his masterwork, *Casa-grande e senzala* (1933; *The Masters and the Slaves*), Freyre gives us a study that should be required reading for comparative Latin Americanists and for all inter-Americanists. His landmark opus, coming after years of travel and study in the United States (where he would work with Franz Boas at Columbia University), focuses on Brazil by integrating considerations of its unique Portuguese heritage, its indigenous heritage, and its African component. It also discusses the cultures of the United States and Brazil as being profoundly patriarchal in nature. All in all, Freyre's study is valuable to inter-Americanists because it examines, in a consistent and systematic fashion, the formation of Brazil in comparison with that of Spanish America, the United States, and French America. Although some of its conclusions have been challenged, it remains an indispensable text for anyone interested in a comprehensive view of the hemispheric American experience.

In both Spanish America and Brazil, native cultures mingled from the very beginning with the culture of the Iberians. This mixing was especially prevalent in Brazil, where not even the church objected too strenuously to sexual relations between Portuguese men and native women or, a few years later, African women. As Freyre saw it, Catholic Portugal's sense of "sexual morality," which he believed was "Mozarabic in character," had been "rendered supple by contact with the Mohammedan, and more easy-going, more relaxed, than among the northern people. Nor was [Portugal's] religion the hard and rigid system of the Reformed countries of the north, or even the dramatic Catholicism of Castile itself; theirs was a liturgy social rather than religious, a softened, lyric Christianity with many phallic and animistic reminiscences of pagan cults" (30).

Other forms of coupling, involving Native Americans and Africans, also ensued. In Brazil in its formative years, sexual activity between colonizer and colonized was the norm, this in contrast to what took place in the religiously and politically more tightly controlled Spanish America and in French America, and in sharp contrast to the norm in

Puritan America. In Canada, for example, the story of Louis Riel and the Métis people is woven into the national fabric, as is the entire concept of *métissage* (see Braz, *False Traitor*). And yet, as Monica Kaup and Debra Rosenthal argue in *Mixing Race, Mixing Culture: Inter-American Literary Dialogues* (2002), this same kind of hybridity has characterized the Americas, North, Central, and South, from the moment the Europeans arrived in the New World, especially if one considers cultural mixing as well as biological. Here in the Americas, which were indigenous long before they were white and Christian, we have been characterized, and we are continuing to be characterized, by the not always harmonious blending of both blood and culture (see also E. Fitz, *Rediscovering the New World* 70–94). America has never been exclusively white, though even today there are some Americans who want to define it as such.

The US scholar Thomas E. Skidmore devotes an entire essay to outlining how Brazilian intellectuals have grappled with the question of Brazil's racial makeup and cultural identity for many decades and, in more recent years, how they have dealt with Freyre's important but controversial argument (see Skidmore).[8] One of these, the anthropologist, author, and statesman Darcy Ribeiro, has issues with Freyre but concludes that "we Brazilians . . . are a mixed-blood people in flesh and spirit, for miscegenation here was never a crime or a sin" (321). Like Freyre and so many other Brazilian scholars through the years, Ribeiro employs a comparative and inter-American optic to try to understand more clearly the true nature of Brazilian society and culture. And although he differs from Freyre on other points, Ribeiro is like Freyre in finding the case of Brazil unique.

The historian Patricia Seed, like Skidmore, Freyre, and Herring before her, is especially perceptive about the Portuguese Crown's ability to see how it could benefit from Spain's fateful decision to isolate itself, to avoid contamination by only guardedly dealing with "the other," and to cultivate "purity" in religion and politics (which, for the Spanish, we can think of as one and the same) and blood. Something similar could be said of the Puritan agenda in North America. But it could not be said of Brazil. As Seed suggests, the Portuguese Crown and the Portuguese clergy were not as in step as were the Spanish monarchs and the Spanish clergy, which wielded much more power in Spain and in its American colonies than did the Portuguese church. There was friction between Portugal's political leaders and its religious leaders, and the former maneuvered constantly to ensure that religious positions did not prevent Portugal from achieving the most desirable political outcomes. It appears that there was a degree of secularism and political practicality in the Portuguese approach to governance that did not exist in 1492 Spain and its American colonies.

When transferred to Spanish America and Brazil, this pattern would have a tremendous impact on how the colonies were organized and run; Spanish America would be on a very short leash, controlled closely by Ferdinand and Isabela, while Brazil would not be. With respect to religion, "The first settlement plans for Brazil contained no mention of any role for clerics," and, indeed, "the first time that clerics became involved in a political role in Brazil was in the middle of the sixteenth century, when the first governor-general, Tomé de Sousa, was sent with a contingent of Jesuits" (Seed 134). In the years immediately following 1500, Portugal would have its eye not on Brazil but on its revenue-generating possessions in India and the East Indies (Pagden 4). It could not have escaped the attention of the Portuguese Crown that the cargo Vasco da Gama brought back to Portugal from his first trip to India (1497–99) netted sixty times what it had cost to finance the original voyage (Burns, *Latin America* 13). It is probably not wrong to conclude that from that point on, Portugal's main interests, in Brazil but even more so in its Asian outposts, were economic rather than religious. "Along the coasts of South America, Africa, and Asia, the Portuguese eagerly established their commercial—not colonial—empire," and in just a few years Brazil would be exporting brazilwood, dye, cotton, and sugar to European markets. But the relative lack of interest the Portuguese showed in Brazil because it was not as robust a revenue producer as East Indian spice growers, would lead first to a kind of neglect and then, in 1822, to official independence, all without loss of life, unlike in the United States and in Spanish America, nor even a shot being fired. The giant Brazilian tail came very soon to wag the Portuguese dog.

From the beginning, Portugal was more liberal in allowing foreign ideas to enter and circulate in its American colony than Spain was. In matters of administration, Brazil "enjoyed a lax control which left the colony free to develop in its own haphazard fashion" (Herring 239). And it did. Even the colonial Brazilian church, which happily absorbed Native American and African influences, became "infinitely more elastic" than the Spanish Catholic church in Mexico and Peru (239). In early Brazilian literature we can see this budding sense of nationalism first in the boastfulness about Brazil's abundance and its coming greatness that characterizes much of *Prosopopéia* and other early texts. This spirit of *ufanismo* was unifying to the Brazilians, as they early on sensed that they were something new, and it reached its maximum expression in the eighteenth century with Sebastião da Rocha Pita's ebullient *História da América Portuguesa* (1730). These two forces, then, *brasilidade,* a sense of being Brazilian rather than Portuguese, and *ufanismo,* a desire to boast about it, served to weaken Brazil's ties to Portugal and to spur nationalistic feelings. In Spanish America, such sentiments were nipped in the bud by Spanish authorities, who were determined not to allow this to happen there. Much about Spanish America could be lauded, of course, and it often was, as with Bernardo de Balbuena's *La grandeza mexicana* (1604), but it could not be done in such a way as to generate a taste for independence.

Yet there was a deeper difference, one more ontological in nature. "Unlike Isabel of Castile, who founded Spanish domination upon the imposition of a foreign religion, Portuguese rulers initiated their claims to the New World through science, which had been created for them by Jewish astronomers based upon the heritage of the Islamic era" (Seed 135). Tolerance and flexibility, then, along with "*hybridization* and *miscegenation,*" begin to mark early Brazilian society in ways they did not apply in early Spanish America (Monteiro, "Dialectic of Resistance" 14). Although this open-mindedness was a matter of degree and not kind, as in the Puritan United States, it is a valid point and important for comparative Latin Americanists to keep in mind.

Two contrasting theories of sociopolitical organization were thus brought to the New World and implanted. From this we can posit that colonial Spanish America would, as a result, be fundamentally different from colonial Brazil. We can further propose that these two radically different ideas—mix with the rest of the world (Portugal and Brazil) or resist contact with it (Spain and Spanish America)—would mark the social, political, economic, and literary development of colonial Latin America. In Brazil, the ports remained open to global traffic, but in Spanish America they were closed to it. This meant that new ideas, international in nature, could more easily enter and circulate in Brazilian intellectual circles. As González Echevarría puts it, "Brazil," in comparison with colonial Spanish America, "was much more receptive and active in the commerce of ideas with the rest of the world" (introduction 15). In terms of the creation of a new culture and national literature, this position was of incalculable importance.

For both 1492 Spain and 1500 Portugal, the Baroque was the prevailing artistic and intellectual system. In sharp contrast to that of Puritanism, "the essence of the baroque spirit was . . . the dualism, the oppositions, contrasts and contradictions, the state of conflict and tension that arose out of the duel between the Christian spirit, anti-worldly, theocentric, and the secular spirit, rationalist and worldly" (A. Coutinho 84). As a result, we find in early Spanish American and Brazilian literature "a series of antitheses—asceticism and worldliness, flesh and spirit, sensualism and mysticism, religiosity and eroticism, realism and idealism, naturalism and illusionism, heaven and earth. . . . The baroque soul is formed by this dualism, by this state of tension and conflict" (84).

We do not see this same dualism, this same tension between, say, "religiosity and eroticism," or religiosity and worldliness, in Puritan literature, which, to be fair, comes from a different literary heritage. The English literary tradition simply did not look with favor on the kind of writing we associate with the Baroque. In addition, the Puritans, a product of the Protestant Reformation, appear in the New World more than one hundred years after the Spanish and Portuguese, who, infused with a deep appreciation of literature, arrive in the Americas and begin to produce creative writing almost immediately. This work, in all its elegance and complexity, was the opposite of the Puritan plain style. At the same time, some of the most interesting work of Edward Taylor, commonly regarded as the "most outstanding" writer of literature in the colonial United States, strikes one as being eminently comparable to the Spanish American and Brazilian Baroque writers (Scheick 94). Taylor's "wilderness Baroque," which demonstrates a very Latin American "fascination with language, . . . rich imagery and subtleties of nuance and argument," has "disturbed" some US critics, who suspect him of being tainted by "Roman Catholic influences" and so led astray from "mainstream . . . Puritan orthodoxy" (96). Then, too, the English literary establishment, never fully at ease with the work of John Donne and the Metaphysical poets, could not warm to Baroque poetry, which, the product of Catholic cultures, was judged to be excessive, extreme, and imbalanced. In reading such criticism of Taylor, one wonders whether his detractors are more worried about Catholicism than they are about his style. Either way, it is intriguing to read Taylor while being cognizant of the specifics of Góngora's brand of the Iberian Baroque. Pursuing Scheick's concerns about Taylor would highlight one of the fundamental differences between the colonial United States and colonial Latin America—the tension between Protestantism and Catholicism.

From the colonial literature of the United States, it is Taylor, and not Anne Bradstreet, who merits comparison with Mexico's Sor Juana Inés de la Cruz. Of their many and varied works, moreover, Sor Juana's *Primero sueño* (1692) and Taylor's *Preparatory Meditations* (1682–1725) are the two that most merit being read together. Sor Juana's poem, written in *silvas,* differs from Taylor's in several important ways: though religiously inspired, the *Primero sueño* specifies neither God nor Christianity, it is more unabashedly a quest for knowledge, it concerns itself more with the intellect than with belief, and its conclusion strikes many readers as more skeptical than one would expect from a seventeenth-century nun. At the same time, several qualities tie these two texts together: both exude an intensely personal ethos; both reflect a restless, inquisitive mind contemplating the human relationship to God; and both employ vivid metaphors, images, and figures of speech. The *Primero sueño* may also be the more radical of the two in that it suggests at the end that we will never gain the kind of understanding we seek and that frustration is our lot. While doubt also creeps into Taylor's text, it does not have the sense of modernity, the unsettling sense that we will never possess what we want, that pervades Sor Juana's poem. Although Matos wrote a great many religious poems, many of them deeply moving, nowhere in his oeuvre do we find an equivalent to either the *Primero sueño* or the *Preparatory Meditations*.

One can conclude that while the Spanish Americans and the Brazilians prized literature and practiced it avidly, the Puritans were deeply suspicious of it, fearing that it might lead its writers and readers away from what they took to be the proper task of life, namely, a closer relationship with their conception of God. The southern colonies, though differing from the New England colonies in many ways, could also look askance at books and learning. As Virginia's governor, Sir William Berkeley, expressed it, "I thank God we have not free schools nor printing, and I hope we shall not have these three hundred years. For learning has brought disobedience and heresy and sects into the World and printing has divulged them, and libels against the Government" (Hallewell 1). Neither Matos nor Sor Juana, one thinks, would have gained the approval of the Puritans or the southern Protestants. For both these groups, literature was to be didactic rather than imaginative, which could lead one to do the devil's work. It was for that reason suspect. Another useful distinction comes from Spitta and Zamora:

> In the Spanish New World, Counter-Reformation writers surveyed the horizon of the visible, sending their written texts, along with vast quantities of natural objects and artifacts, across the Atlantic. They described the material world in the service of spiritual conquest, political domination, and economic gain. In contrast one immediately senses the more abstract purposes of texts from the English New World. William Bradford's characterizations of faceless savages

in *History of Plymouth Plantation: 1620–1647*—"savage, and brutish men, which range up and downe, little otherwise than the wild beasts of the same" (56)—are a far cry from Franciscan friar Bernardino de Sahagún's richly detailed descriptions of Nahua cultural practices in his twelve-volume *Historia general de las cosas de la Nueva España* [completed in 1569]. (198)

Too often, Latin Americanists think that their cultures and their literatures began in 1492 and 1500. They did not. Their distinctive roots go back to Iberia. The natures of early Spanish America and Brazil were determined by events in Spain and Portugal. And in those nations, contrary to what many simply assume to be the case, things were far from the same. The worldview the militaristic Spanish brought to what was for them a "new world" differed markedly from the one the already more global, more flexible, and more commercially oriented Portuguese brought. The Spain that came ashore on a Caribbean island in October of 1492 was a far cry from the Portugal that dropped anchor off the coast of Brazil in early 1500. The American colonies Spain set up would be more closed to the outside world, more closely monitored and administered, and more rigidly controlled, intellectually and artistically, than the one claimed by the Portuguese. Thus would Spanish America and Brazil begin their histories of parallel but separate lines of development. To understand how and why colonial Spanish America differed from colonial Brazil, one must look to Spain and Portugal.

2 Indigenous America

In 1492 AND 1500, when the first Europeans arrived in the New World, it was far from empty. Quite the opposite. The Americas were thoroughly populated, from their icy northernmost reaches to the cold and windswept Tierra del Fuego and from the sun-splashed beaches of the Caribbean and Brazil to the towering Andes Mountains running along the western coast. Total population numbers vary widely, with some experts suggesting that the number might be as high as 112 million. Although the estimates change constantly, as anthropologists have learned more, most have come to believe that the first Americans crossed the Bering Strait somewhere between twenty thousand and forty thousand years ago. Then they began to fan out in the rest of the Americas, moving to the east, west, and south. By 1492 and 1500, and the arrival of the Spanish and the Portuguese, the Americas could claim a great variety of human populations. And many of them had been here for eons. For the Europeans it may have been a new world, but for the millions of people that lived here, and whose ancestors had lived here, it was already an ancient world. As one thinks about the European conquest of America, and how momentous it was, how life changing, it is critical to keep this most salient fact in mind.

Mexico and Spanish America alone are estimated to have been home to some fifteen to twenty million people who would have spoken around sixteen hundred different languages. And Latin America's diverse cultural tableaux ran the gamut, from the Stone Age to the highly sophisticated, from jungle dwellers to the great builders and farmers of the Andes, and from those who made their homes on America's great, grassy plains to those who lived along its warm beaches. Some of these preconquest American cultures, most notably the Aztec, the Mayan, and the Incan, were superior in political organization, architecture, and city planning to anything the invading Europeans had known.

Bernal Díaz, who took part in the Spanish invasion of Mexico, wrote of the Spanish reaction to their entrance into the fabulous Aztec citadel of Tenochtitlán, which, connected with the surrounding shore by causeways, was situated in the middle of a lake: "We were astounded. These great towns and cues and buildings rising from the water, all made of stone, seemed like an enchanted tale of Amadís. Indeed, some of our soldiers asked whether it was not all a dream. . . . It was all so wonderful that I do not know how to describe this first glimpse of things never heard of, seen or dreamed of before" (214). And Mee writes that "the Aztec capital had been built up atop mudbanks and islands until, like Venice, it was a wonder of human artifice, laced with canals and bridges. Three long and wide causeways connected it to the mainland. An aqueduct brought fresh water from a hillside spring into the middle of the city" (63). By all accounts, it was a thriving metropolis of clean, well-ordered streets, abundant parks and flower gardens, bustling marketplaces, beautiful public buildings, and open spaces. Tenochtitlán was indeed a marvel of pre-Columbian America.

The term *Indian* came into our lexicon because of a mistake. Colón, thinking he had found the offshore islands of Japan or India, the gateway to fabulous Asia, which was his goal, immediately began to refer to the people with whom he came into contact that fateful day in the Caribbean as "Indians," and the name stuck, much to everyone's confusion. Later, further explorations would reveal that the "'Indians' of the New World belonged to a large number of cultural groups of which the most important were the Aztecs and Mayas of Mexico and Central America, the Carib of the Caribbean area, the Chibcha of Colombia, the Inca of Ecuador, Peru, and Bolivia, the Araucanian of Chile, the Guaraní of Paraguay, and the Tupí [*sic*] of Brazil. Of these, the Aztec, Maya, and Inca exemplify the most complex cultural achievements" (Burns, *Latin America* 7).

For the Latin Americanist Rolena Adorno, the most significant "colonial native cultural traditions" at the time of the conquest are "the Nahua of Central Mexico, the Yucatec Maya of the lowland Maya area, the Quiche Maya of the Maya highlands, and the Quechua of the South American Andes" (44; see also 45–57). All these Native American culture groups produced literature that, though oral in nature, was nevertheless sophisticated, philosophical, and varied. As such, it passed on to the

Spanish a powerful and vital tradition that would in some ways influence their Iberian traditions. In a sign of the richness of the native traditions involved, the cultural exchange, albeit between the conquerors and the conquered, would not be entirely one-sided.

The indigenous cultures encountered by the Spanish differed radically from those encountered by the Portuguese. And the consequences of this for Brazil's development would be deep and long lasting. Arriving only eight years after the Spanish, the Portuguese never came into contact with the advanced, sophisticated indigenous cultures that greeted the Spanish in Mexico, in Central America, and on the mountainous western coast of South America. Moreover, the Native Americans they did encounter were not plentiful, numbering only around 2–2.5 million persons. Of these, the Tupi most influenced the Portuguese, though it would have to be said that the influence of native America on the Portuguese colonists was not nearly as significant as that of the Spanish Americans, who remain today nearly as vitally connected to their indigenous roots as they were at the time of the conquest.

Burns puts it succinctly: "The cultures of the Brazilian Indians can, in no way, be compared to the remarkable civilizations of their contemporaries, the Aztecs of central Mexico, the Mayas of Yucatan and Guatemala, and the Incas of Peru. The Brazilian Indians possessed no well-established tribal organization; their agriculture was simple; they did not know how to use stone to build; they lacked any animal for transportation; they had no written means of communication. On the other hand, they had adapted well to their tropical environment, and they had much to teach the European invaders in the utilization of the land, its rivers, its forests, and their products" (*History of Brazil* 21). Also commenting on the extraordinary diversity of cultures that made up indigenous America at the time of the European conquest is Alistair Cooke, who, taking an inter-American stance, reminds us:

There were Indian societies that dwelt in permanent settlements, and others that wandered; some were wholly democratic, others had very rigid class systems based on property. Some were ruled by gods carried around on litters, some had judicial systems, to some the only known punishment was torture. Some lived in caves, others in tepees of bison skins, others in cabins. There were tribes ruled by warriors or by women, by sacred elders or by councils, or by fraternities whose rituals and membership were as unknown to the rest of the tribe as those of any college secret society. There were tribes that worshipped the bison or a matriarch or the maize they lived by. There were tribes that had never heard of war, and there were tribes debauched by centuries of fighting. In short, there was a great diversity of Indian nations, speaking over five hundred languages. (24–25)

What, in summary, can we say about indigenous America in 1492 and 1500? Millions of people lived here, forming cultures and ways of life that varied dramatically. Some lived in ice and snow, while others lived out their lives in hot jungles. Some lived in cold, dry mountains, while others resided on grassy plains. Thousands of different languages were spoken. One common denominator we have is that the Indian in America, in both North and South America, regarded the earth as sacred and a life-giving force that was not to be desecrated or despoiled. In an age of climate change and rampant pollution, this is a lesson that we can learn from our ancient American ancestors. There were also, as Cooke shows, social, political, and economic differences among pre-Columbian American people. More than a few were matriarchal in nature, as in the Iroquois Confederation. Matriarchy would also be a key factor in Brazilian Oswald de Andrade's concept of *antropofagia* in the 1920s. Pre-Columbian civilizations were far from uniform. And they were all very old, having arrived in the Americas thousands of years before the Europeans did. From the perspective of the people who lived out their lives here, the so-called New World was not new at all; it was ancient.

Although more germane to Spanish America, an additional point that needs to be commented on is that the indigenous cultures of Brazil in 1500 appear not to have produced the kind of creative language use we see so impressively developed in Spanish America. Indigenous Brazil cannot boast, for example, a philosopher-poet like Nezahualcoyotl. As a result, Brazilian literary historians do not begin their studies citing and describing the nature and continuing influence of their pre-Columbian literary history, their indigenous traditions. In the highly regarded *Cambridge History of Latin American Literature,* for example, a full chapter, in volume 1, is devoted to pre-1492 literary production in what would become Spanish America (see Adorno), but there is no such chapter, no equivalent chapter, for Brazilian literature, to which the entirety of volume 3 is devoted. This is not a mistake, and it is not a form of disrespect. Rather, it reflects a general consensus that either the several cultures of the Tupi-Guarani language family (among them the Tupi, the Tupinambá, the Gês, the Cariris, and the Caribas) did not cultivate what we today, and even giving full valence to the oral tradition, think of as literature or they did but we do not know about it. Either way, the difference, literarily speaking, between pre-Columbian Spanish America and pre-Columbian Brazil is striking. Other histories of Brazilian literature have taken the same position.

This is not to say that indigenous Brazil did not have cultures; it did, of course, and some of them have survived, especially in the form of folklore. It is impossible to believe that Brazil's native peoples did not enjoy singing and dancing, or that they did not gather together to tell stories about their origins or about events that affected them or their ancestors. But, assuming they did, these have not survived; they have not endured and been passed along, as living traditions, as they have in Spanish America. Beginning in the nineteenth century, Brazil has a strong tradition of writers who, like Gonçalves Dias, studied and then transformed into art Brazil's native traditions or, as with Alencar and others, used them, as glorified figures, for sociopolitical ends as emblems of national identity. Poti, the noble indigenous hero of Alencar's O *Guarani* (1852), is of this sort. The issue here has to do with the existence and transmission of what was itself Tupi-Guarani literary activity, as we have so vividly displayed in the still living traditions of the Aztecs, the Mayas, and the Incas. Does Brazilian literature have such a tradition? So far, it appears that the answer is no, and so this, a lacuna, is the glaring difference. Perhaps it was because Brazil did not have a literarily influential past that it later became so innovative and successful at creating one. Its creative spirit was less constrained by reality.

In thinking about this question—how and to what extent indigenous America influenced Spanish and Portuguese America—we need to consider the question of influence and reception. In the case of native America and its response to the arrival of the Europeans, the always complex question of influence and reception becomes even more so. In addition to the problems generated by the fact that powerful oral traditions were clashing with powerful written traditions, there was also the devastating pressure of violent colonization. Entire indigenous cultures would be wiped out, and others would be altered forever. Yet the process of influence and reception still plays out. The question for us today is, how did all the participants involved respond? What was taken, and what was not? What were the consequences? What are the issues that live on today, that still strain relations between native and nonnative America? In ways large and small, our consideration of indigenous America shows us that it is indeed the bedrock, the foundation, of all inter-American study. It is also a continuous, living tradition, one still very much with us.

When we speak of pre-Columbian literature, we are, of course, speaking of oral literature. And we must always remember to evaluate it in this context. In the Spanish American tradition, Chang-Rodríguez and Filer see two basic divisions as standing out: the Maya-Quiché and the Nahua-Quechua (13). Literary production in these zones was varied in form and highly valued, by its practitioners and by its audience. It was very much a part of life and a function not of the individual but of the group.

The rich and enduring Nahua tradition features three great poets: Nezahualcoyotl, the philosopher-king of Texcoco and one of the greatest pre-Columbian voices; Moctezuma, the Aztec ruler at the time of the conquest of Mexico; and Macuilxochitl, a talented woman whose importance is only now becoming known. Nahua poetry has several defining characteristics: its parallelisms, its recurrent images, tropes, and metaphors, and its use of certain established comparisons (Chang-Rodríguez and Filer 14). It also features some of humankind's timeless, most enduring themes: the inexorable passing of time, the transitory nature of life, the mysteries of birth and death, the meaning of life, and the prospect of the divine. These concerns match up well with those of the Iberian Baroque, a fact that would have greatly facilitated the intellectual exchange between the Mexican poems and their Spanish interpreters, inscribers, and translators.

In "Solo un breve instante" (Only a brief instant), the great poet-king Nezahualcoyotl ponders, through his Spanish translator, the nature of human existence:

Acaso es verdad que se vive en la tierra? Ay!
Acaso para siempre en la tierra
Hasta las piedras finas se resquebrajan,
hasta el oro se destroza, hasta las plumas preciosas se desgarran.
Acaso para siempre en la tierra?
Sólo un breve instante aquí!

(Is it true that one lives only on earth?
Not forever on earth: only a short while here.
Even jade will crack;
Even gold will break;
Even quetzal feathers will rend,
Not forever on earth; only a short while here.)

(trans. unknown; Von Hagen 196–97)

And from "A Song by Nezahualcoyotl," we have the following lines:

Toztliyan quechol nipa tlantinemia in tlallaicpac oquihuinti ye noyol ahua
 y yai.
Ni quetzaltototl niyecoya ye iquiapan ycelteotl yxochitic pac nihueloncuica
 oo nicuicaihtoa paqui ye noyol ahuay.

. . . .

Ninochoquilia niquinotlamati ayac in chan oo tlallicpac ahua.
Zan niquittoaya ye ni Mixicatl mani ya huiya nohtlatoca tequantepec ni
 yahui polihuin chittepehua a ya yechoca in tequantepehua o huaye.
Ma ca qualania nohueyotehua Mexicatli polihui chile.
Citlalin in popocaya ipan ye moteca y za ye polihui a zan ye xochitecatl
 ohuaye.
Zan ye chocaya amaxtecatl aya caye chocaya tequantepehua.

(The sweet-voiced *quetzal* there, ruling the earth, has intoxicated my soul.
I am like the quetzal bird, I am created in the one and only God; I sing sweet
 songs among the flowers; I chant songs and rejoice in my heart.

. . . .

I grieve to myself that ever this dwelling on earth should end.
I foresaw, being a Mexican, that our rule began to be destroyed. I went forth
 weeping that it was to bow down and to be destroyed.
Let me not be angry that the grandeur of Mexico is to be destroyed.
The smoking stars gather against it; the one who cares for flowers is about to
 be destroyed.
He who cared for book wept, he wept for the beginning of the destruction.)
 (trans. Brinton)

According to both Astrov and Brinton, the fall, or "destruction," of the
Mexican, or Aztec, state was foretold in a series of what were taken as
omens of their fate "during the ten years preceding the arrival of Cortés"
(Astrov 315). As part of this narrative, the poetic reference to the "smoking
stars" is thought to be a reference to "a comet that was visible for about
a year" (315). All in all, the reader gains here a sense of impending doom,
of the fall of a great civilization, one that prized learning and beauty.

This song by one of the outstanding poets of the pre-Columbian era
illustrates both the need for translation and its pitfalls. First, coming as it
does from the oral tradition, we do not know for certain what the exact
words of Nezahualcoyotl's song were. On this point, the case of Nezahualcoyotl is not unlike that of Homer and the oral roots of ancient Greek
literature. In moving from the oral to the written, there is always the problem of transcription. Second, we cannot know how well Brinton himself
knew Náhautl or how close the language he knew was to the language

spoken by Nezahualcoyotl. And finally, there is the debate that has long swirled around Brinton's own translation, which has been criticized for grammatical inaccuracy. Or was he exercising poetic license? For Astrov, a person possessed of some understanding of ancient Náhuatl "could come to the conclusion that Brinton—with the genius of a poet—must have caught the *atmosphere* of this unique literature almost to perfection, regardless of philological errors with which his translations might abound" (Astrov 311). So in an absolute sense, we cannot know these pre-Columbian poets and singers because we cannot know exactly what their language was like. Still, who would say we are not better off knowing something of what Nezahualcoyotl said rather than nothing at all?

Mayan culture, in eastern Mexico and what is today's Guatemala, was already flourishing by around 2000 BC. By the ninth century BC it had mysteriously disappeared. Anthropologists cannot say for certain what happened. What we do know, however, is that an advanced Mayan civilization existed before Stonehenge or the reign of Egypt's Tutankhamen. It is estimated that by AD 400 the largest Mayan city would likely have had a population twice that of Rome. Some believe it could have been home to perhaps one hundred thousand people. In addition to being great builders, the Mayas, sometimes referred to as "the Greeks of America," were also sophisticated astronomers and mathematicians. They worked with the concept of zero, and they developed a precise calendar. Although the Mayas are today more famous for their glyphs, they are also believed to have been moving toward a phonetic writing system (see Stuart and Stuart 26, 39ff., 50, 75, 106–7). "The temporal horizons of Mayan civilization," writes linguist George Steiner, "seem to have exceeded by far, and by deliberate expansion those available to other Central American cultures" (155).

The Mayan civilization the Spanish began to attack in 1526 was in decline, only a faint shadow of what it once had been. Years of conflict and internecine warfare had vitiated the once brilliant Mayan Empire and so enabled its defeat by the Spanish. The fighting was nevertheless bitter. But while there were pockets of isolated and determined resistance, the tribally splintered and fractious Mayas were not able to unite themselves against the invaders, and they fell quickly. For the modern reader, there is a sobering lesson to be learned from the Mayan experience.

Like their mighty neighbors to the north, the Quechua-speaking Incas, whose domain ran along the western coast of South America, also prized poetry. At its height, the Inca Empire was nearly three thousand miles long and, at its maximum point, some four hundred miles wide. It extended from southern Colombia into present-day Chile. Cuzco, the capital city, was held to be the center of the Incan universe. The empire was criss-crossed by a network of some ten to fifteen thousand miles of roadway, portions of which were so well engineered that they can still be seen today. Runners, known as chasquis, traversed these roads carrying information coded into strings of variously knotted cord.

The oldest and most organized of the pre-Columbian cultures, the Incan political structure would assimilate newly conquered people into its domain. All were required to learn Quechua and to observe Incan law. Although the rights of nonroyal Incas were limited, experts on Incan culture believe that the Incan government, which was highly central-ized, made certain that everyone had adequate food, shelter, and clothing. No one was to go hungry. Men and women were supposed to work the care-fully terraced and irrigated fields together. Some scholars regard the first Inca, Pachacuti, as "the greatest of American Indians" (McIntyre 66).

The ancient Incas are thought to have been particularly inclined toward music, especially that of pipes, flutes, and other wind instruments. In this regard, they stand, argues Astrov, "at the forefront of the pre-Spanish peoples of America" (343; see also D'Harcourt and D'Harcourt) . The socially and politically advanced Incas even had a special cast, the *hara-vicus,* who were charged with overseeing the dissemination of poetry throughout the empire. As with their Mexican counterparts, the Incan appreciation of poetry merged with music, song, dance, and dramatic presentations. There was a vibrant Incan theater, one from which two fascinating works still exist: *Ollantay* and *Rabinal Achí.* The first, long thought to be a hybrid text, one influenced by the Spanish *comedia,* has in recent years been reconsidered. Today, some scholars believe that *Ollan-tay* was likely conceived, as as indigenous art form and part of a grand oral tradition, long before the Spanish arrived, which, if true, would obvi-ate any possibility of direct influence. The second work, possibly even older, is a dance-drama, *Rabinal Achí.* Of the latter's importance, Tedlock writes that while many plays "are performed in contemporary Mayan communities," only *Rabinal Achí* "dramatizes a time when Europeans had yet to appear over the horizon of the Mayan world. This same play is one of the few whose dialogue is entirely in a Mayan language," a play that reaches back in time to "the fourth through the tenth centu-ries" (1, 2). What we can say for certain is that the Spanish, lacking the knowledge that would have allowed them to respond to this oral tradition as it was, could only react to it by means of what they knew, which was the Spanish theater and its creative and critical apparatus. This encounter between the Spanish and native America thus represents our first American experience with the complicated process of influence and reception, a process that defines the experience of the human race.

Also from the ancient Incas, and known to us because it was translated into Spanish early in the conquest, is this poem/song/prayer, a supplication to the creator god.

Viracocha,
poderoso cimiento del mundo,

. . . .

"Sea éste varón,
sea ésta mujer."
Óyeme,

. . . . .

Tú, que me mandaste
el cetro real,
óyeme
antes de que caiga
rendido o muerto.
(See Anderson Imbert and Florit 8–9)

(Viracocha, Lord of the Universe!
Whether male or female,

. . . .

Hear me! Oh! Hearken to me,
listen to me,
let it not befall
that I grow weary
and die.) (Means 437)

The translation history of this text is complicated. As part of the pre-conquest Incan tradition, it existed originally in Quechua and in oral form, so that it may well have changed with each telling or singing. At some point, it was translated into Spanish, by whom it is not known, though a few names have been advanced (Anderson Imbert and Florit 8). We do know that Dr. Miguel Mossi translated it from its original Quechua into English in 1892, and it was from this English translation that P. Ainsworth Means produced the version we have above (see Astrov 342). For the modern reader, it is interesting to note that for this translator of the

Incan singer-poet the supreme divinity is not necessarily male. Viracocha could well be female, and this is not presented as any kind of problem. The contrast with Christianity is sharp.

For the Incas, poetry also had a distinctly political dimension, a way of unifying the people and of inculcating in them a sense of identity and of the Incan past. Some have speculated that Incan poetry possessed a particularly strong religious and philosophical dimension (Chang-Rodríguez and Filer 15). What we in the Western tradition regard as lyrical poetry constitutes a high percentage of Incan poetry, which is traditionally characterized as being deeply contemplative but also as plaintive and exuding a sense of melancholy and even resignation about the human condition. And like ancient Greek lyric poetry, Incan poetry was regularly accompanied by music. What is certain is that like the Aztecs and the Mayas, the Incas produced literature of a sophisticated nature, and they held it in high regard. It was this thriving artistic and intellectual tradition that the Spanish would encounter from 1492 on.

Quechua and the Incan oral tradition live on in the works of many writers, including El Inca Garcilaso de la Vega, the "founding father" of Spanish American literature (Rodríguez Monegal, *Borzoi Anthology* 1:67); Mariano Melgar, from the early eighteenth century; and José María Arguedas, whose 1958 novel, *Los ríos profundos* (splendidly translated by Frances Horning Barraclough as *Deep Rivers*), is a monument to the importance of translation to the dissemination of Quechua literature and to keeping it and its ancient culture alive. "A half-caste and a bastard, Garcilaso Inca was the first American-born writer of real distinction," and "his masterpiece, *The Royal Commentaries* (I, 1609; II, 1617)," was "a historical work" but also "a defense of the Incan heritage and an exalted description of its originality and grandeur" (Rodríguez Monegal, *Borzoi Anthology* 1:66). But the more hemispheric Native American tradition also lives on, often as a form of resistance to disrespect and exploitation, in a host of American writers, which is why we can rightly regard our indigenous heritage as the foundation of inter-American study (see Brotherston 341–49).

Pre-Columbian Brazil cannot boast the rich literary heritage of pre-Columbian Spanish America. This likely owes in large part to its indigenous people not having civilizations as advanced as those of the Aztecs, the Maya-Quiché, and the Incas. Instead, the Portuguese found "tribes of extremely primitive people" who lived by means of "rudimentary agriculture, hunting, and fishing" and were "constantly warring among themselves" (Torres-Ríoseco 211). In Brazilian literary history there is no

Nezahaulcoyotl, or if there is, we have no record of it. One is struck by the dearth of equivalent, high-quality pre-Columbian literature there. While, as we have seen, its native peoples surely enjoyed song and dance, and while they would almost certainly have told stories, for pleasure and for edification, we have little to no evidence that gives us insight into it—as we do in Spanish America. Commenting on native responses to Caminha's discovery document in 1500 and to other early contacts between the Portuguese and the natives of Brazil, Sadlier finds that "no indigenous documents exist on this or any other encounter between the two groups" (10).

In terms of finding a comparable literary tradition, the situation in early Brazil was very different from that in Spanish America. Neither Moisés, Soares Amora, Nunes, nor Bosi mentions the importance of any pre-Columbian literary activity to the development of Brazilian literature. Coutinho, a comparative literary historian, makes no note of it. Neither does Haberly in his lengthy and detailed discussion of colonial Brazilian literature ("Colonial Brazilian Literature"). Merquior sums up the situation thusly: The early Portuguese colonizers, he writes, "never encountered Amerindians of a high material culture" (364), and while Tupi-Guarani and Tapuya influences were strong in other areas of cultural transfer, notably cooking, mythology, and language, they were not strong with respect to their cultures' literary production, at least not in comparison with pre-Columbian Spanish America. At the same time, as the social anthropologist Charles Wagley notes, it was the Tupi-Guarani tradition that "played the major role in the initial formation of Brazilian culture" (14). But literary expression was not a significant part of this "initial formation." We can conclude, therefore, that Brazil's Indian heritage made its presence known not in literary production but in legends, folklore, and popular culture.

For Moisés, as for most other commentators today, Brazilian literature began in May of 1500 with Caminha's *Carta de achamento* (*A literatura brasileira* 15). He goes on to write of Brazil's earliest literary production that it was of two great types: the writings of the Jesuits, which very quickly made use of the techniques of drama, fiction, and poetry to make their case, and the plethora of nonfiction reports sent back to the Portuguese court concerning the flora and fauna of Brazil, the new American colony, and the customs and languages of its people (15). This latter category, important to the Portuguese Crown for purposes of administration, was also coveted by the planters, who would need Indian labor for their *fazendas,* or plantations. Putnam comes to much the same conclusion but regards the two founding groups of Brazilian culture as the priests and the planters (51–52, 54). Writing much later, Bosi too would stress the origins of Brazil and its literature as emerging almost immediately from the antagonistic relationship between these same two groups, the planters and the Jesuits (41–49).

Because the Portuguese did not encounter Native American populations as sophisticated as those encountered by the Spanish, the question of literary influence and reception was, for them, quite distinct. Yet there were other differences too. The Indians found by the Lusitanians were also fewer in number, less organized, and less inclined to resist. Or to do so successfully. And they were able to slip away more easily into the forest. The Portuguese experiences with the Native Americans of Brazil differed considerably, then, from those of the Spanish Americans, who collided with pre-Columbian America's three most advanced indigenous cultures. Yet it is also true that as the conquest gave way to colonization and its aftermath, for both these Iberian invaders the demand for cheap native labor was paramount. This hard economic fact, at odds with religious interest, put both Las Casas and Vieira at odds with their respective planter classes. And for reasons of political expediency, it forced these two early American religious leaders to choose between defense of the native peoples and defense of the enslaved Africans, who were being imported into Spanish America and Brazil in ever larger numbers. Long before 1619, then, when African slaves were first brought to the United States, the moral blight of slavery was already bound up in the Americas with economic exploitation and political leaders who enabled it.

Like the crime of slavery, the destruction of native peoples and their cultures here in the Americas is another topic that binds us together. White Christian America has much to answer for. From events in the Caribbean in late 1492 to events in the western United States in the mid-nineteenth century, when "The only good Indian is a dead Indian" was a popular rallying cry for what amounted to genocide, the story of the postconquest American Indian is an appalling study in the racism, hypocrisy, and violence that supposedly moral men and women can direct at people not like them. In attempting to evaluate the treatment suffered by Native American peoples at the hands of the Spanish, the Portuguese, the French, and the English, it is useful to remember that this topic has been examined by scholars for at least a hundred years. It is not new. Although Herbert Priestly's *Coming of the White Man* (1929) focuses (in chapter 5) only on a comparison of how the English regarded the indigenous peoples they came across with how the Spanish regarded theirs, it stands as one of the earliest systematic examinations of this tragic inter-American theme.

The Iroquois Confederation, formed around 1400 (New, on p. 360, dates it from 1390) and reaching its peak in the early 1720s, was quite likely "the greatest indigenous polity north of the Rio Grande in the two centuries before Columbus and definitely the greatest in the two centuries after" (Mann, "Founding Sachems"). Held together by its remarkably democratic Great Law and its focus on government by the consent of the governed, it also influenced the framers of the US Constitution, including such key figures as John Adams and Benjamin Franklin, and such thinkers as the ethnographer Lewis Henry Morgan and the political theorist Friedrich Engels. And, with its emphasis on the rights of women, it would also inspire later reformists such as Elizabeth Cady Stanton and Matilda Joslyn Gage. Demos, citing the work of Father Lafitau as recorded in the *Jesuit Relations,* writes that women "played a central role in choosing the clan chiefs," in "the disposition of captives," and in "initiating wars of revenge" (165). Observing Iroquois social dynamics from close up, Lafitau was moved to conclude that "nothing is more real than the women's superiority. . . . It is they who really maintain the tribe"; and "in them . . . resides all the real authority; . . . they are the soul of the council, the arbiters of peace and war; they hold the taxes and the public treasure" (165). Some scholars have regarded Iroquois society as a matriarchy, and Demos himself notes that the records show that there were a "large number of captive" white "women who chose to remain with their captors" rather than be returned to their former culture (166; for more on the matriarchy question, see 292n92).

This question of how the different European settlers related to the Native Americans they encountered is one that ties colonial America, North and South, together. Indeed, it does so even today, when stark contrasts between native America and European America can still be seen. Much of Latin America's diversity stems from its indigenous past, this being especially apparent in Spanish America, with its rich pre-Columbian heritage. In Bolivia, Peru, Mexico, and Guatemala, for example, indigenous culture is still very much alive. And it continues to have a powerful effect on their national literatures. This is less true in Brazil, where, as we know, the indigenous heritage is less spectacular. Yet even there it has influenced the evolution of Brazilian literature, particularly at critical junctures in its development.

As Monteiro notes, for several generations now an ongoing effort among Brazilian intellectuals has been to understand how it is that a national literature as rich, as diverse, and as international in nature as Brazil's can still be allowed to languish, largely unappreciated, as "a peripheral experience," forced to "develop in the . . . shadows of models" not its own and only occasionally to be indulged by the global literary elites ("Dialectic of Resistance" 7). The standards of evaluation that emanate from the United States and, I would add, from Spanish America are not always appropriate for Brazilian literature. Borges, for example, is today a global name, as are those of Pablo Neruda and Carlos Fuentes. But Machado de Assis is not. Nor is Guimarães Rosa or Clarice Lispector.

But Brazil can say that a great many of its most canonical writers have actively cultivated its Native American heritage, one tied together by the Tupi-Guarani language family. From Father Anchieta and his Jesuit brethren, through Gregório de Matos in the colonial period to Basílio da Gama in the eighteenth century, and on to José de Alencar, Gonçalves Dias, and the other Indianistas of the nineteenth century, pivotal Brazilian novelists, poets, and dramatists have made extensive (Dias), if often quite imaginative and strategic (Alencar), use of their nation's autochthonous heritage. Although not as intellectually or artistically influential as the Aztecs, the Mayas, and the Incas were to Spanish America, Brazil's indigenous cultures became influential thanks to the efforts of writers, artists, and musicians working in a number of different fields. In Brazil, one might say, imagination and creativity provide the nation with what reality cannot.

Nevertheless, we have to conclude that in contrast to Spanish American literature, Brazilian literature "is without a native tradition that could serve as a useful past" (A. Coutinho 26). This lack of an indigenous past that could directly help build a national literature, as pre-Columbian Spanish America has so vitally enriched its national literatures, meant that Brazilian letters would have to depend heavily on imported forms and themes to invent national types, as they did during the Indianist phase of the nineteenth century, and then to develop its own, hybridized national writers. It was this long-standing tradition in Brazilian literary history (the blending of the national and the international) that powered Brazilian *Modernismo* and that today, as Damrosch notes, makes it so representative of the World Literature movement (17, 27). Hoyos, concentrating more on Spanish America but also considering Brazil, makes a similar point. What is interesting here is that while US-based scholars of American literature assert themselves as the leading advocates for World Literature, it seems clear, to Latin Americanists at least, that they, and not their US counterparts, represent the American cultures that have most ably represented the best principles of World Literature and continue to do so today.

While the Spanish conquistadores would encounter such advanced and sophisticated Native American societies as the Aztecs, the Mayas, and the Incas, the Portuguese would not. Instead, the Lusitanians came into contact with the less-developed Tupi-Guarani and the Tapuya, with the result that in the realm of creative writing, the indigenous heritage of Spanish America had, and continues to have, a greater impact. Although substantial in Brazil in other areas, the indigenous heritage is less so in the realm of literature. It is, however, a question of degree. Nevertheless, there is no "La noche boca arriba" ("The Night Face Up") in Brazilian literature. At the same time, the degree of racial mixing that took place in early Brazil appears to have been both deeper and more extensive than in Spanish America, where, to be sure, it also occurred. And occasionally, as with the work of Inca Garcilaso de la Vega, with brilliant results. On this same point, however, Latin American attitudes toward racial and cultural mixing stand in sharp contrast to the more segregationist stance taken, some one hundred years later, by the English Puritans, who abhorred the idea of mixing, racial or cultural.

Today, the brilliant literary and philosophical contributions of the Aztecs, the Mayas, and the Incas are a fundamental area of study in Spanish American literature. Their traditions gave rise to Spanish American letters. Brazil's indigenous heritage is too often passed over, disregarded as a topic of literary importance. This is a mistake, and the comparative Latin Americanist must not make it. Yet the record is clear: Brazil cannot boast the kind of brilliant pre-Columbian past that Spanish America has. And the consequences of its not having a native heritage as rich and complex as those stumbled upon by the Spanish conquistadores are profound. Nowhere is this more obvious than in the development of Spanish America's various national literatures. The lack of a powerful, sophisticated indigenous tradition ranks among the basic differences between colonial writing in Spanish America and in Brazil. For the Spanish Americans, the presence of a flourishing autochthonous past allowed them to graft their own themes and forms onto a vibrant tradition, one that endures to this day. Brazilian literature does not have this. For the Luso-Brazilians, lacking such a tradition, it would be necessary to invent one—and to look to the rest of the world for inspiration.

3 The Literature of Discovery and Conquest

Spain/Spanish America, 1492–1600, and Portugal/Brazil, 1500–1601

IN LATIN AMERICAN literature, we have two European "discovery" documents to consider, the famous Spanish one, from 1492, and the less well-known Portuguese one, from 1500. They are far from identical. Indeed, they reflect very different historical backgrounds. I enclose *discovery* in quotation marks to remind us that indigenous America—North, Central, and South—had existed for thousands of years before the arrival of the Europeans. Millions of people lived here and had for a very long time; many different languages were spoken in many different cultures. The so-called New World was, in truth, an ancient, diverse, and complicated world. How the Spanish and Portuguese choose to learn about it, and deal with it, would mark the differences between early Spanish America and Brazil.

Colón and Spain

The people with whom Colón made contact on October 12, 1492, were the peaceful Tainos.[1] From them he would learn that other people, the fierce Caribs, lived on the small islands to the south. The Caribs, later to be known as cannibals, were reputed to eat human flesh. This must have been quite sobering to Colón and his men. Importantly, however, the first Americans encountered by the Spanish were beguiling to the Europeans, who found their nudity, their peaceful behavior, and their demeanor to be problematic, if very attractive. As New puts it, "Amerindian nakedness was taken as a sign of an animal nature and . . . presumed European superiority in the world" (19). Much impressed, and seeming to have found concrete evidence of what had long been part of a European intellectual speculation, Colón wrote his sovereigns to praise all that he was finding and to confirm its worth to the Crown. But his exaggerated report also "contained the seed of the complex problem of 'natural man,'" which would engage European and American minds for the next "three hundred years" (Henríquez-Ureña 10).

But the more anthropophagous Caribs also would have their day, as would certain of the indigenous peoples of Brazil who, like their Carib counterparts, also partook of human flesh. The famous explorer and cartographer Amerigo Vespucci (whose first name gave us *America*) visited Brazil in 1501 and, in fact, is credited with being the first to employ the phrase *earthly paradise,* which would quickly come to define thinking about the green and fertile land that was Brazil. Vespucci's stay in Brazil also afforded him an opportunity to observe Brazilian natives, who impressed him with their grace and beauty (also their nudity), their athletic prowess, their sense of innocence and freedom, and their generosity. But also with their penchant for ritual cannibalism.

This debate about "natural man" versus "civilized man," set off by Colón's epic discovery, would reach its zenith in the hands of Montaigne, whose essays on coaches and on cannibals would defend the practices of the Native Americans by contrasting their conduct to that of their supposed "betters," the "civilized" Europeans, who, as the French sage points out, committed equally egregious if not worse crimes. In the essay on coaches, Montaigne argues that civilizations more advanced than those of Europe existed in the New World and that the conquest of America involved inferior cultures (those of Europe) destroying superior cultures; that the conquest was both morally unjust and illegal; and that the motivations propelling the conquest would lead to the decline and fall of European society. The gist of Montaigne's argument in his commentary on cannibals, which is based in part on interactions with the Brazilian "savages" whom he had observed at Rouen with King Charles IX, is that our horror at this particular practice blinds us to our own, truly horrific practices and allows us to feel morally superior to them. This self-deception, he suggests, will eventually make it impossible for us to rectify our own errors and faults. How much more barbaric is it, Montaigne challenged his compatriots, to consume the flesh of a person already dead than to burn a person alive? Who is the more "savage"? Then and now, the question is arresting.

Reading it today, we can appreciate how fantastic Colón's *Carta* was. Could we say that the roots of *realismo mágico* can be found here,[2] in Colón's rather fanciful *Carta?* It is possible to think so. And at least one writer has already cast this idea in the necessary language. Struck, apparently, by the fabulous New World that Colón's famous missive pointed to, the sixteenth-century French courtier and sonneteer Mellin de Saint-Gelais wrote that it all seemed to be "la merveille unie à vérité" (quoted in Henríquez-Ureña 8; the marvelous united with the true).[3] What Colón and the Spaniards had come upon truly existed, but it was all so fantastic that it could not be apprehended by the standard measures of their reality. Aesthetically speaking, the distance between Colón's epochal *Carta* and the world of Macondo may not be so great after all. This approach, moreover, sets up another comparison with the Brazilian text. Noting that Caminha's foundational *Carta* functions as an outline of what Brazil would eventually become by providing its reader with a perspective that comes from both "inside" and "outside," K. David Jackson contends that we could consider Caminha's text as "Brazil's first short story" ("Introduction" 6). It is intriguing that both Latin American discovery documents lend themselves so readily to literary readings, Colón's as an early form of *realismo mágico* and Caminha's as short fiction, a more realistic text but one full of contending forces, interests, and points of view.

The Spanish and the Portuguese had stumbled into a bewilderingly complex world, one they knew nothing about and were ill prepared to understand. Colón, for example, thought he had arrived on one of India's offshore islands. His imagination was already fired by Pliny's speculations in his *Natural History,* by the travel accounts of Marco Polo, and by Renaissance epics and romances of chivalry about what the New World might be like, and he was prepared to see it as he imagined it to be (Rodríguez Monegal, *Borzoi Anthology* 1:4). Colón's response as a reader of the New World had been thoroughly prepared; his expectations were set. He was primed to find a world of monstrosities, men with tails or with an eye in their foreheads, women with a single breast. Not surprisingly, then, a strong sense of wonder and amazement permeates his report to the Spanish monarchs. A mariner and not a man of letters, he lacked the language to accurately describe what he was feeling, seeing, hearing, touching, and tasting. His only points of reference were his faulty European models. And his own desires.

But Colón would have had at least a vague idea of what he wanted to find, and so he must have realized that what he found did not measure up to his expectations. Yet he was confident that eventually it would. As a result, a strong sense of futurity also marks his report, a sense that if this new American reality was not quite what he had anticipated, it would surely become so in the future. It is because of this desire on Colón's part, perhaps, that his *Carta* possesses such an inflated and hyperbolic style, with exaggeration and a strong sense of futurity—things that *would* happen or be the case in the future.

One of the things he wanted was a return trip to the New World. But for this to happen, he would need additional royal support. In addition to being a discovery document of tremendous value, therefore, Colón's *Carta* can also be thought of as the first example of "grantsmanship" that we have in the Americas. Colón needed to get funded, again, for an additional trip. And he was successful, though subsequent trips to the New World would yield more and more frustration. And in the end he was brought home in chains. Whatever else we wish to say about Colón and his 1492 *Carta,* we can say this: "America as a literary and poetic subject was invented by this hyperbolic Genoese" (Rodríguez Monegal, *Borzoi Anthology* 1:5).

In a general sense, 1500 Brazil was for Caminha and the Portuguese more real and less fantastic than Hispaniola was for Colón and the Spanish. Where Colón waxes rapturous about all he is seeing, Caminha is more objective and restrained, more reportorial. He was, after all, the official scribe of Cabral's fleet, and it was his job to record all that was seen and found and to do so without exaggeration or distortion. Both these qualities characterize Colón's *Carta.* If, wearing our inter-Americanist hat, we were to compare Caminha and Colón with John Smith, we might conclude that the embellished if not fanciful *True Relation of Such Occurrences and Accidents of Note as hath Happened in Virginia* (1608) places Smith closer to Colón than to Caminha. Because Caminha was, in a sense, a professional writer, it is no surprise that his 1500 *Carta* evinces, as Merquior puts it, "rhetorical skills worthy of the best humanist writing of the Renaissance" (363).

As we have seen, differences between Spain and Portugal abound, as do, in turn, differences between early Spanish America and Brazil. These two American civilizations were far from being the same. Haberly points to several issues as key. Beyond the several sociopolitical and historical differences already enumerated by him, González Echevarría, and Pupo-Walker, Haberly sees two more, each more literary in nature. First, there is the question of what he describes as Caminha's "implicit vision" of Brazil as "an American Eden," a vision he believes to be "much more" explicitly expressed by Colón ("Colonial Brazilian Literature" 48). Then, too, there is the assertion that there exists "an even more striking difference between the colonial literature of Brazil and that of Spanish America: the lack of a clear consensus among Portuguese and Brazilian intellectuals on the canon which comprises colonial Brazilian literature" (49). No such debate exists about Spain and Spanish America, where the list of canonical texts of colonial literature has long been established. Another in a long tradition of Brazilianists interested in comparative and inter-American perspectives, Haberly also opines that while the United States achieved some level of consensus about its basic colonial literary texts in the first half of the nineteenth century, this was not accomplished in Spanish America until some point after 1870 and has not yet been accomplished in Brazil even today, as the question remains a moot point (49–50). If Haberly is correct, then a comparative Latin Americanist might conclude that early Brazilian literature is less set, less established, than is Spanish American literature.

A final difference between our two great *cartas* of discovery is this: While Colón's letter was widely translated into other languages and disseminated all over Europe, thus exerting a tremendous influence over European thinking about the New World and all its possibilities, Caminha's was not. His did not become widely read until 1817, well into the nineteenth century. Always more secretive about their affairs, and especially so where the militarily more powerful Spanish were concerned, the Portuguese managed to keep their huge American colony developing under the hemispheric and global radar for many years. This was not just about the Portuguese wanting to keep their affairs hidden from the Spanish; it also allowed them to concentrate on what was fast becoming their very lucrative spice trade in the East Indies.

Caminha and Portugal

The less famous but equally important *Carta de achamento* of Pêro Vaz de Caminha has been the object of a reevaluation.[4] Lisa Voight has argued that while it is significantly distinct from Colón's rather overheated report, it is nevertheless a discovery document and demonstrates a similar interest in conquest and possession. More importantly, Caminha's *Carta* is not the benign document that too many scholars, motivated by a perhaps overly zealous desire to contrast it utterly with Colón's text, have taken it to be. Caminha's summation of the America he and his Portuguese shipmates had come upon is not that of Colón, but it is not its exact opposite either (see Voight). And we should not make the mistake of thinking it is. Given his use of the term *achamento,* as opposed to *descobrimento,* it is also possible to think that the Portuguese had been here before, that in 1500 they were not "discovering" Brazil but returning to it. Did the Portuguese already know that there was a large landmass somewhere in the south-western Atlantic? Although it has never been proven conclusively, there are some who believe they did and that they only had to find it, *achá-la,* again.

Rodríguez Monegal, who has drawn the contrast between these two Latin American discovery documents as well as anyone, has this to say about Caminha's 1500 *Carta:* "His account of the discovery of that new land . . . is as free of hyperbole and rhetoric as Columbus's is full of them. His is a matter-of-fact presentation of the natives and their life and habits. Even when he wrongly decoded some of the signs (there is a comic confusion about whether the natives have gold or not), his good sense finally took over" (*Borzoi Anthology* 1:11–12).

Funny though it is, the confusion over the gold points to a more serious aspect of the European conquest of the New World, one that, moreover, connects all its participants. I refer to the problem of interpretation, to how wholly new and unknown sets of signs, linguistic but also cultural, would be read. Literally and figuratively, the different participants could not understand each other. Yet decisions had to be made, and fatefully, these would affect everyone involved, some more negatively than others. In the case of Caminha and the gold, what is most striking is that, as his text unambiguously states, he and the Portuguese knew exactly what they were doing and why. They suffered from no delusions. Realizing that he was mistaken about what he thought the Indians had been telling him, that there was gold ashore and that they, the Portuguese, could have it, Caminha writes this most revealing entry about the Indians he had only just met:

> Viu um deles umas contas de rosário, brancas; acenou que lhas dessem, folgou muito com elas, e lançou-as ao pescoço. Depois tirou-as enrolou-as no braço e acenava para a terra e de novo para as contas e para o colar do Captão, como dizendo que dariam ouro por aquilo. Isto tomávamos nós assim por assim desejarmos. Mas se ele queria dizer que levaria as contas e mais o colar, isto não o queríamos nós entender, porque não lho havíamos de dar. (Moisés, *A literatura brasileira* 16)

> (One of them saw some white rosary beads, made signs for us to give them to him, and with these amused himself for quite a while, putting them around his neck and throwing them up in the air, getting them tangled around his arm. And he pointed to the land and then to the beads and the Captain's collar, as if to give gold for the beads. Or rather we took this to be his meaning because we wished it to be so, while he really meant to say that he would take the beads

and the collar together for himself; this we did not wish to understand because we did not have it to give.) (trans. Thomas Colchie, Rodríguez Monegal, *Borzoi Anthology* 1:13)

We do not see this level of self-awareness in Colón's *Carta* or in any other American discovery document. Caminha's perspective comes from experience, and likely from having been through this before. Already globalists, the Portuguese were well accustomed to dealing with other cultures and so could laugh at themselves for misinterpreting the signs here involving gold. Although it was certainly of interest to them, the Portuguese knew well that it was far from the only valuable commodity in their far-flung trading network. Spices from the East Indies would do for Portugal what American gold and silver would do for Spain. And what furs, acquired by the French *coureurs de bois,* would do for France.[5] Caminha and his Portuguese mates were also able to accept without rancor or insult the Native Americans' rejection of European food and drink, and while struck by their nudity and customs, they could record it all in detail and with objectivity. "His natives," as Rodríguez Monegal puts it, "are almost as noble as Columbus' but more real" (*Borzoi Anthology* 1:12).

Because the place they lived was hot and humid, the people the Spanish and Portuguese came upon in 1492 and 1500 went about nude. To the overdressed Europeans this would have been something of a shock. Perhaps also a source of delight. But it is their differing reactions that interest us today. Although the difference is slight, it is there: Colón was more bothered by the Indians' lack of clothing than was Caminha, who, invoking the Garden of Eden myth, comments in his *Carta* that the innocence of Adam himself could not have been greater than that of the naked people he and his comrades were meeting. Was Colón's more troubled response because of religious scruples on his part, or was he simply aware that his report would go directly to the Spanish monarchs, who were very devout Catholics? We cannot know, but Caminha and the Portuguese do appear to have had a different, less negative reaction to Indian nudity. It is also worth remembering, in this same context, that the Portuguese, thanks to their program of maritime expansion and trade, had been encountering people with different habits since at least 1400 and so had more experience dealing with "the other" than did the Spanish. The Portuguese of 1500, we might say, lived very much in the real world, whereas the Spanish of the same period lived in the rigid world of religious fanaticism and a fear of being polluted by foreign cultures and mores. Did the more traveled and flexible Portuguese deal with difference more easily than the Spanish did? It is possible to think so.

Other Documents Marking the Conquest of America

Bernal Díaz del Castillo's *Historia verdadera de la conquista de la Nueva España,* published long after the events depicted had passed and written to correct the many errors and distortions other chroniclers had committed about the Spanish conquest of the Aztec Empire, is the prime example of a genre Brazilian literature does not have. This is primarily because, as we have seen, the Portuguese did not encounter any indigenous cultures capable of resisting them as fiercely and resolutely as the Aztecs or the Incas. For Brazil, we have instead an abundance of letters and reports about the land, the climate, the food supply, and the native peoples, their languages, customs, political organizations, and belief systems. Of these documents, a great many were authored by the Jesuit fathers, who played a pivotal role in the formation of early Brazil, its literature, and its culture. Thinking of Latin America comparatively, we can say that while Spanish America was forged by military conquest, Brazil came into being more bureaucratically, the Portuguese being more interested in commerce than in conquest (Pagden 66). By no means pacific, as all conquests are by some measure violent, its birthing was nevertheless less dramatic than that of Spanish America, as evidenced by Bernal Díaz's still remarkable account and by the absence of such a text in early Brazilian literature.

The *Historia verdadera* is not the story of a detached, objective observer. Rather, it is told in the first person by a Spanish soldier, a man who actually participated in the fighting. As the now elderly Bernal Díaz tells us in his opening remarks, "What I myself saw, and the fighting in which I took part, with God's help I will describe quite plainly, as an honest eyewitness, without twisting the facts in any way" (*Conquest of New Spain* 14). What we have here, then, is a battlefield soldier's account of the conquest of the great Aztec Empire. The *Historia verdadera* gives us an infantryman's perspective on the epic events unfolding around him.

Bernal Díaz writes in a style that even in translation is direct, unvarnished, and honest. It makes for a gripping narrative. Its author, a man who actually battled the Aztec warriors, often in hand-to-hand combat, does not hesitate to praise his Indian adversaries for their bravery and military prowess. Nor does he hesitate to celebrate the wonders of Aztec civilization—or to condemn the Aztecs' practice of human sacrifice. So vivid and personal is Bernal Díaz's account that the reader feels as if she were there with him and his comrades. The *Historia verdadera* is unique in Latin American literature, and indeed it has no equal anywhere in American literature.

The Epic

The nature of the Iberian conquest of America provides us with a genre problem to consider. In Spanish America, the epic poem evokes grandeur. It reflects the awe-inspiring nature of the conquest, the clash of great civilizations, the ebb and flow of battles, and opponents of equal bravery and valor. And it deals with events of a certain scale and magnitude. The epic was the logical literary form for the conquering Europeans to turn to as they sought to capture the full extent of what had happened. And Latin American literature can boast one truly great one.

Published in three parts (in 1569, 1578, and 1589), *La Araucana* is the first epic poem about America. It is the model against which all other American epics must be measured. But it is also one of the great epic poems of the entire Renaissance period. Written in *octavas reales,* Ercilla y Zúñiga's masterpiece stands out for many reasons. "Fué la primera obra en que el poeta aparece como actor de la epopeya que describe; por lo tanto, fué la primera obra que confirió dignidad épica a acontecimientos todavía en curso; fué la primera obra que inmortalizó con una epopeya la fundación de un país moderno; fué la primera obra en que el autor, cogido en medio de un conflicto entre ideales de verdad e ideales de poesía, se lamenta de la pobreza del tema indio y de la monotonía del tema guerrero y nos revela el íntimo proceso de su creación artística" (Anderson Imbert and Florit 78–79; It was the first work in which the poet appears as a participant in the epic action he describes; it was, therefore, the first work that conferred epic dignity on events in progress; it was the first work that immortalized the founding of a modern nation with an epic; it was the first work in which the author, caught up in a conflict between the ideals of truth and the ideals of poetry, laments the poverty of the Indian theme and the monotony of the warrior theme and reveals to us the intimate process of artistic creation).

Composed of 37 cantos, 2,645 stanzas, and 21,160 lines, *La Araucana* can rightly lay just claim to being the first poem of true distinction to spring from the Americas (Englekirk et al., *Anthology* 44). Thematically, what most sets *La Araucana* apart is its author's admiration for the valor of the Spaniards' indomitable foe, the Araucanian Indians. Ercilla also recognized the legitimacy of their cause, for they were defending their homeland against foreign invaders. In this *La Araucana* speaks for all Native American peoples. A loyal Spanish soldier, Ercilla nevertheless castigates the Spanish for their arrogance and cupidity. In singing the praises of the "sincera bondad . . . de la sencilla gente de estas tierras" (the sincere goodness . . . of the simple people of these lands), where "la maldad, el robo y la injusticia" (wrongdoing, theft, and injustice) have not yet penetrated, the poet takes his countrymen to task for planting there the standard of greed "con más seguridad que en otra parte" (more securely than in any other place) (Englekirk et al., *Anthology* 55).

Like Bernal Díaz, Ercilla was a participant in the fighting he describes so elegantly. A long speech by Colocolo, one of the brave Araucanian chiefs, so impressed Voltaire that in his *Essai sur la poésie épique* (original version 1728) he compares it with the words of Nestor in book 1 of *The Iliad,* concluding that Ercilla's lines are superior to those of Homer! In his dedication to King Felipe II of Spain, Ercilla mentions that parts of *La Araucana* were written in the field, between battles, and that finding himself short of paper, he composed some lines on pieces of leather or even strips of tree bark. The best parts of the poem do have that sense of immediacy. Although uneven at times, and occasionally falling prey to needless digressions, *La Araucana* stands as a sixteenth-century masterpiece of American literature.

In Brazil the epic is quite different. Although it does, in all its manifestations, deal with the formation of a modern nation-state, the Brazilian epic lacks the grandeur and magnitude that animate *La Araucana.* The Luso-Brazilians did not have to deal with such powerful indigenous empires as the Aztec, the Mayan, and the Incan. The scale of the conflict between the conquerors and the people to be conquered is more limited, its ferocity tends to be reduced, and the several epics written about it are more self-consciously a matter of nation building. They are less martial and more political in nature, and with one exception (Basílio da Gama's *O Uraguai*), they are concerned less with war and more with creating Brazil as a separate and distinctive nation-state. Bento Teixeira's *Prosopopéia* (1601) is an example. In Teixeira's poem, the Brazilian landscape looms large, while the role of the epic hero, here presented as the quintessential American, is given to a particular Brazilian and, by extension, to Brazil itself.

Dealing with the settlement of the important northeastern state of Pernambuco by Jorge and Duarte Coelho, the *Prosopopéia* is an example of epic poetry writ small. Compared with *La Araucana,* the great Spanish

American epic poem, *Prosopopéia* seems overwrought, artificial, and at times even trite. On the other hand, it fosters a sense of nationalism, a sense of Brazil being its own entity with its own identity, that we do not find in Ercilla's work. Still, as epic poems, *La Araucana* and *Prosopopéia* are separated by a vast gulf.

Largely because of its greater military conflict, da Gama's *O Uraguai* fits the standard definition of an epic poem better than *Prosopopéia* does. The poem's opening lines create a sobering and intensely cinematic view of the costs of war:

> Fumam ainda nas desertas praias
> Lagos de sangue tépidos, e impuros,
> Em que ondeiam cadáveres despidos,
> Pasto de corvos. Dura inda nos vales
> O rouco som da irada artilharia.
> . . . .
> Aí tantas custas, ambição de império!
>
> (Moisés, *A literatura brasileira* 104–5)

> (Still fuming on the now deserted beach
> Are pools of blood, tepid and impure,
> In which bob dead bodies, naked, their clothing torn away,
> Food for the crows. Continuing on in the vales is
> The hoarse sound of angry artillery.
> . . . .
> Oh, so many costs, the ambition of empire!)

But like *Prosopopéia*, *O Uraguai* shines most brightly when it sings the praises of Brazil, its verdant landscape and its future potential as a nation. There is one exception, however: In a decisive battlefield scene the brave Indian leader, Cacambo, dies at the hands of the Portuguese commander, Gomes Freire de Andrade. Shot by a pistol at close range, he is dispatched by the superior technology of the Europeans but also by their quest for empire, their thirst for conquest. The Portuguese soldier, "o ilustre Andrade" (the illustrious Andrade), who is one of the poem's two heroes (the other being Cacambo), takes the hand of his valiant adversary to comfort him in his final moments. But this act of kindness is rejected. His chest suffering a gaping and fatal wound:

> o índio, um pouco pensativo, o braço
> E a mão retira; e, suspirando, disse:
> Gentes de Europa, nunca vos trouxera

O mar e o vento a nós. Ah! não debalde
Estendeu entre nós a natureza
Todo esse plano espaço imenso de águas.

(The Indian, now pensive, his arm
And hand he withdraws; sighing, he says
Men of Europe, would that the seas and
The winds never brought you to us! Oh,
Would it have not been in vain that Nature
This immense plane of water
Placed between us!)

From the perspective of the Native American peoples who resisted the European conquest, this line is poignant, as it speaks for all of indigenous America.

In addition to *Prosopopéia* and *O Uraguai*, Brazilian epics also include Santa Rita Durão's *Caramuru* (1781) and Gonçalves de Magalhães's *A Confederação dos Tamoios* (1874), an Indianist epic from the Romantic period centering on the theme of freedom. Caramuru, the name the Indians give to Diogo Correia, whom the poem celebrates, marries into the anthropophagous Tupinambá, who find him washed up on the beach after a shipwreck. As he is in bad shape, he is not eaten. He recovers, mixes with the tribe, learns their language and their ways, and eventually marries a chief's daughter, Paraguassu. Accompanied by his royal bride, Correia travels to France,[6] where she is baptized. Returning to Brazil, Paraguaçu, now going by her Christian name, Catherine, renounces her standing as princess and ruler of her people. This decision prefigures Alencar's later novel, *Iracema*. In *Caramuru*, the founding of Bahia serves as the foundation of Brazil itself. No violent struggle is required. Durão's poem also played a significant role in the writing and reception of the canonical Uruguayan novel of the same name (see Burgueño).

Another inter-American comparison presents itself here. As we have seen, the Spanish conquest of the New World differs not only from that of the Portuguese but from that of the English as well. Contending that Sahagún's accounts of Nahua culture were more humane and sympathetic than those of Bradford and the Puritans, Spitta and Zamora argue that even the reporting of the later-appearing Englishman Sir Walter Raleigh "betrays the more abstract and idealized nature of writing in the Protestant tradition" (198). If we assume, as Merquior believes, that the Luso-Brazilian tradition was less idealistic and more practical than the Spanish, then what would we say about how colonial Brazil compares to colonial New England? Would they be at opposite ends of the spectrum? It would seem so.

Then too, we would do well to consider what the historian J. H. Parry says about Spain and Portugal in the New World: "The deliberate, self-conscious purpose which was so characteristic of the imperialism of the Spaniards, and so conspicuously lacking in that of the Portuguese, and later that of the British, reflected the immense influence and importance of the Spanish legal profession" (2; see also Henríquez-Ureña 17–19). In the same context, we have Parkes's observation that while "the Hispanic colonies were settled mainly by impoverished members of the lower nobility and by adventurers from the lower classes, . . . most of the early immigrants to the United States came from the petty bourgeoisie in the English cities or from the yeoman farmers," with a few more seeking "to put into practice novel religious or political ideas" (5).

"The Portuguese," writes Freyre, "in addition to being less ardent in their orthodoxy than the Spaniards and less narrow than the English in their color prejudices and Christian morality, encountered in America not a people already formed into an empire with an established and vigorous system of moral and material culture—with palaces, human sacrifices to the gods, monuments, bridges, irrigation and mining works—but, on the contrary, one of the most backward populations on the continent" (81). Parry's assessment of early Spanish America and Brazil echoes that of Freyre, who, comparing the two, concludes with this thought: "As for the mechanism of colonial administration, marked by feudal tendencies in the beginning, it [colonial Brazil] was lacking in the severity displayed by the Spaniards; it was slack and weak, leaving the colonies and in many respects the proprietors to their own free will" (42).

This would lead to exactly what the Portuguese Crown did not want: the birth of an early and strong sense of Brazilian identity and nationalism. But Portugal was already committed to nurturing, and then to defending, its overseas empire, which, thanks to the spice trade, had become an extremely lucrative proposition for the Lusitanians. Brazil, not so much, although the red dye that could be extracted from certain trees was making money for the Portuguese in the European textile industry. For largely economic reasons, then, while the metropole was preoccupied with its East Asian holdings, colonial Brazil was allowed to develop on its own much more than colonial Spanish America was. The receptivity of Brazilian ports to global traffic, and the circulation of new ideas that accompanied it, only accelerated this process. An awareness of being different, of no longer being Portuguese but of becoming a strange, new thing called "Brazilian," characterized Brazilian culture, thought, and writing almost from the very beginning. This same process, a kind of early nationalism known as *brasilidade* in Brazil, would take longer to develop in the more tightly controlled Spanish America.

After 1492, however, as Spain labored to establish its several footholds in the Americas, North and South, the problem of its labor force quickly emerged. Who would do the work necessary to the creation of new societies? Who would grow the crops, who would tend the animals, who would build the buildings? At first, the Indians served this purpose, becoming very quickly the economic backbone of New Spain. Wherever Indian labor proved unavailable or in short supply, Black Africans began to be imported as slaves. This was especially true in the Caribbean region and in Brazil, where the Indian population was much less than in most of Spanish America. African slaves arrived in Cuba around 1512 and in Brazil in 1538 (Burns, *Latin America* 20). In North America, the domain of God's chosen people, slaves would enter the marketplace to be bought and sold in 1619.

But while Spain officially recognized interracial marriages between Spaniards and Native Americans as early as 1501, the Portuguese, always more malleable on these questions, actively encouraged sexual congress between the Portuguese colonizers, Native American women, and, a bit later, African women. The result, as many commentators have noted, was the almost immediate creation of a new and deeply mixed race of people, the Brazilians, and, to a lesser degree, the Spanish American mestizos (Ribeiro 320–22). Emblematic of Brazil's role in this is that in 1803 the city of Salvador da Bahia, in northeastern Brazil, could boast of a population of about one hundred thousand. Of that number, 70 percent or more were either Black or of mixed race (Burns, *Latin America* 22). A few years later, in 1818, only approximately 1 million of Brazil's 3.5 million inhabitants could be classified, and "very liberally" so, as white, while more than a half million were mulatto and a full 2 million were Black (Burns, *History of Brazil* 55). It is for good reason that the great Brazilian writer of the time, Father Antônio Vieira, could speak of Brazil as having "the body of America and the soul of Africa" (Burns, *History of Brazil* 55). Much the same happened in Spanish America, in Bolivia, Mexico, and Cuba, for example, but there the process was slower and more complicated and had more restrictions. In terms of its approach to this issue, Brazil was unique among American nations for the ease with which it, its church, and its social system embraced racial and cultural assimilation. This singular attitude would produce a national literature remarkable for the diversity and originality of its many voices.

Beyond those of its many First Peoples, America has an abundance of discovery texts and origin stories. In 1497, sailing for the English Crown under the name John Cabot, an Italian navigator whose given name was Giovanni Caboto reached the Grand Banks and explored Canada's eastern shore. He claimed it all for England, thus giving that nation its claim to America. No settlement ensued, however. Disappointed by what Cabot found and consumed by European affairs, the English were deterred and would not return to the Americas until 1607 and the founding of Jamestown, Virginia.

In 1534, the Frenchman Jacques Cartier explored the Saint Lawrence Seaway and claimed it, and the lands surrounding it, for France. Although the number of settlers was never great, settlement followed immediately. Thanks to Cartier and others, especially Samuel de Champlain, Canada was indigenous and French before it became English.[7] Similarly, the United States was indigenous and Spanish (and French!) long before it was English.

As we survey the literature of discovery and conquest that relates to Latin America, however, one fact stands out: in early Brazilian letters there are no figures like Hernán Cortés, Bernal Díaz del Castillo, or Alonso de Ercilla y Zúñiga. Neither are there texts like the five *Cartas de relación*,[8] the *Historia verdadera de la conquista de la Nueva España*, or *La Araucana*. At the same time, we can see, as Pagden does, that there is no Bernal Díaz in either English or French America, just as there is no Garcilaso de la Vega (66). This absence of a certain kind of text suggests that something very different was going on with respect to the conquest and settlement of Brazil. And that, indeed, is an accurate assessment. Without great native cultures to defeat in battle, as was the case in Spanish America, Brazilian colonial literature does not possess the same sense of heroic struggle, on both sides, that we see, and feel, so strongly in early Spanish American letters. Brazil has no equivalent to Castillo's extraordinary account of the battle for Mexico. The Portuguese encountered no great civilization they would have to bring down. Instead of narratives and poems about armed conflict, the writers of early Brazil produced a plethora of texts of a geographic, sociological, and administrative nature. In contrast to Spanish America, which was forged in wars waged to destroy the cultures of indigenous people, Brazil, which certainly did some of this, was formed in large measure by bureaucratic fiat. As Herring puts it, "Colonial Brazil was a land apart and quite unlike colonial Spanish America" (239).

The two great "discovery" documents of Latin American literature, Colón's *Carta de descubrimiento* and Caminha's *Carta de achamento*, reflect the different worldviews of their respective authors but also the very different historical experiences that produced their authors. The Spain of 1492 and the Portugal of 1500 were far from the same, and understanding this difference is crucial to understanding what transpired in colonial Spanish America and Brazil. Although both had profit and domination in mind, Spain and Portugal came to the New World with different plans and expectations. The letters of Colón and Caminha make these differences manifest, and this is why they differ so markedly, in both style and tone but also in the sense of self-awareness they project. In contrast to Colón, who was lost in a world of amazement, exaggeration, and projection, Caminha and the Portuguese were more cognizant of what they were doing and why. They had experience dealing with "the other," and they understood the value of flexibility. Their new American possession would immediately become a cog in their global commercial system. Colonial Brazil was thus plugged into the international community of nations in ways Spanish America was not. This would, from the beginning, have an effect on its literature.

4 The Flowering of Colonial Latin American Letters

Spanish America, 1600–1750, and Brazil, 1601–1768

COLONIAL LITERATURE in Spanish America and Brazil can boast some brilliant authors and texts. Indeed, Anderson Imbert and Florit argue that Spanish America produced "dos genios literarios" from this period, "el renacentista Inca Garcilaso de la Vega y la barroca Sor Juana Inés de la Cruz" (89). In all genres, except for prose fiction, which did not yet exist in the Americas, first-rate work was emerging everywhere in Latin America (see E. Fitz, "Colonial Literature in the Americas"). Although fiction writing per se was not yet being practiced, it had a vital antecedent in the form of the *crónica,* which was flourishing. A prime example is Juan Rodríguez Freile's *El carnero* (1636–38), which, in very creative fashion, blurs the border between reportage and invention. Lively and colorful, and judged by some to be scandalous, *El carnero* synthesizes the genres of fiction and nonfiction. But we must not get ahead of ourselves. At the time of its conquest of America, Spain had a rich European national literature, and Spanish America would draw upon it. Spain's Golden Age had begun earlier, in the sixteenth century, and its creative energies left their mark in colonial Spanish America. Yet Brazil did not want for an impressive literary heritage to draw upon. Portugal had its own great writers, traditions, themes, and forms. And these would of course be critical to Brazil's intellectual and literary formation.

It is also important to remember that for all their differences, Spain and Portugal have long shared what we might think of as a peculiarly Iberian sensibility, one relating to Europe but also to Africa and, especially in the case of the Portuguese, the Orient. And they have long interacted. Though rarely less than fraught, relations between the two European nations have a long history. In the early modern period, from 1580 to 1640, in what was known as the period of captivity, Spain controlled Portugal. This fact had repercussions in the New World. When one examines their histories, literary and otherwise, it does appear, argues Jonathan Wade, that Portugal, the smaller, less powerful of the two, has felt itself compelled to learn the ways of Spain and enter into its mainstream. This is especially apparent in the realm of letters. A great many of Portugal's most talented writers—Gil Vicente, Ángela de Azevedo, and Manuel de Sousa, among others—worked in both Portuguese and Spanish. Today, the steadily growing field known as comparative Iberian studies is working to integrate the rich national literatures of Spain and Portugal. Led by discerning young scholars like Wade, who are trained in both these great Iberian traditions, this exciting new project is already yielding fruit (see Wade).

But perhaps even more important to colonial Brazil was what we can term the political tradition it got from the Portuguese, whose ideas about social, political, and economic organization, dealing with people not like themselves, and matters of church and state differed from those of the Spanish. The moment when Pedro Álvares Cabral and the Portuguese dropped anchor off the coast of southeastern Brazil in April 1500, Brazil became an American player in a vast global enterprise. It was international at the moment of its inception. As K. David Jackson writes, "One of the most crucial distinctions in forming a sense of Brazil is its oceanic origin and history, as for centuries it was part of the world of Portuguese expansion that extended eastward to Africa, Goa, Malacca, Macao, and Japan" ("Introduction" 8). Far from being shut off from the world, as was more the case with Spanish America, Brazil came into being as part of a number of social, political, and economic systems that spanned the world. This interaction with the rest of the world would have tremendous consequences for Brazil's history, culture, and literature. "Brazil," as Putnam puts it, writing in the mid-twentieth century, "possesses a culture that is perhaps the least provincial, the most cosmopolitan and urbane of any in Latin America" (15). And even in 1500 this was the case.

But even so, the development of Brazilian literature was fraught with challenges. There was a productive intelligentsia, but there was no book-buying public. Illiteracy was rampant. Brazil did not even have its own printing presses until 1808, roughly three hundred years after Spanish America had begun to benefit from theirs. This meant that regardless of their quality or originality, fewer literary texts were published in Brazil than in Spanish America. Yet colonial Brazilian literature prospered. If, relative to Spanish America, its quantity was lower, its quality was high.

Spread over two continents, Spanish America, moreover, encompassed a vast amount of American geography, with each region developing its own distinctive culture. And stumbling upon fabulously wealthy Native

American cultures, whose wealth the Spanish took, Spanish America could quickly boast of two moneyed and sophisticated viceroyalties, one centered in Lima (in the heart of the recently conquered Inca Empire) and the other in Mexico (in the heart of the recently conquered Aztec Empire). Both these centers of social, political, and economic power produced a steady stream of poetry, prose, and drama. It was Mexico, in fact, that produced the peerless seventeenth-century poet, essayist, dramatist Sor Juana Inés de la Cruz.

Brazil, which, unlike Spanish America, had no colonial printing presses and no early universities, was at a disadvantage. Still, it did manage to do two crucial things: thanks to its widespread cultivation of the *ufanista* theme, it was able to nurture a very early sense of national identity *(brasilidade)* and unity; and it was also able to produce literary texts of real distinction. And while there was no Sor Juana in colonial Brazil, there was Gregório de Matos.

But first things first. Although it remains a moot point, Brazilian scholars still recognize the Jesuit father José de Anchieta as the founder of Brazilian literature. His case is a strong one. As Afrânio Peixoto has contended in his monumental *Panorama da literatura brasileira,* Anchieta, although born in the Canary Islands, was happy to live in Brazil and to write about it as a Brazilian and for other Brazilians. Then too, in addition to his didactic concerns, Anchieta was a very creative writer, one who, in the best Brazilian manner, knew how to synthesize different cultures, languages, and topics. To this day, there remains wide consensus in Brazil that it was the Jesuits, such as Anchieta and his brethren, who established Brazilian culture and literature. As if indicative of his desire for inclusion, Anchieta famously wrote his sermons and religious skits not merely in Portuguese but also in Spanish, Latin, and a variety of native languages as well, notably Tupi.

The Jesuits perceived literature in positive, productive terms and as a way of writing that could be useful to their mission. For scholars, the Jesuits "conceived of literature along Horatian lines *(docere cum delectare)* as a means of action on souls, more for proselytizing and instruction than for its pure aesthetic value" (A. Coutinho 91). And they found in the genre of theater the vehicle they needed. Hence it was that drama became "the baroque genre best suited to Ignatian intuitions" (91).

Almost immediately, in 1492 and in 1500, the Spanish and the Portuguese began to mix with the native peoples they came upon. Although this would have been unthinkable for the English Puritans a hundred years later, for the Iberians, given their long experience in dealing with people who were different, it was nothing. But it was especially inconsequential to the Portuguese, who, even more than the Spanish, were quite relaxed in these matters. And, of course, the Spanish ran into what were likely pre-Columbian America's three most sophisticated, most powerful, and, in the cases of the Aztecs and Incas at least, most warlike cultures, so their experience with indigenous America was quite different from that of the Portuguese, who encountered no such native civilizations. What is indisputable, though, is that with the Spanish and the Portuguese, biological and cultural mixing began immediately.

This close relationship between the Iberians and the indigenous peoples of the Americas, and with America itself, is consistent with what Sacan Bercovitch says about the motivations behind the early English settlers in North America. For Bercovitch, "the Puritan vision was transatlantic," linking Europe, and especially England, with Protestant New England, "rather than American," which was very much the case with the Spanish and Portuguese (37). The Portuguese vision, on the other hand, was distinctly global, thanks to that nation's already worldwide trading network. In contrast to what the Puritans would do in their corner of America, the earlier newcomers—the Spanish, the Portuguese, and the French— "brought utopian dreams to the New World, but in doing so they claimed the land . . . as European Christians, by virtue of" what they believed was "the superiority of Christian European culture" (39). For the Spanish, but most especially for the more flexible Portuguese, this meant a very diverse and fluid cultural mix. The Spanish, the Portuguese, and the French "justified their invasion of America through European concepts of progress" (39).

"The Puritans," by way of contrast, "denied the very fact of invasion by interpreting the newness of the New World as progress and then identifying themselves as the people peculiarly destined to bring that interpretation to life. They [the Protestant Puritans] were not claiming America by conquest . . . ; they were reclaiming what," in their reading of the Bible, "by promise belonged to them, as the Israelites had once reclaimed Canaan" (Bercovitch 39). From its inception, Puritan America was a theocracy, not a democracy. In the United States, the notion of "American exceptionalism" is thus deeply rooted in a sense of religious superiority.[1] When, in the early seventeenth century, the Puritans "crossed the ocean to settle in the New World, they brought with them ideas that would evolve into 'manifest destiny,' which held that the United States was a land that had been bestowed by God on Anglo-Saxon white people" (Dickerson 12). Others need not apply. As a result, the whole idea of being an

"American" here in the United States has "always been about exclusion" (12). Because they considered themselves God's chosen people, the Puritans could take this position; the Spanish and the Portuguese could not and did not. Their vision of America, far from egalitarian but less rigidly segregated, was thus fundamentally distinct from that of the Puritans.

Race, Culture, and Integration

Writing in 1961, the historian Hubert Herring observed that "more than half the population of Latin America is of mixed ancestry"; Brazil and the nations of Spanish America had formed "a new kind of people," one that the Mexican intellectual José Vasconcelos would term the *raza cósmica* (92, 93; see also 187). Having labored on his project since 1957, Herring was well aware of the building racial turmoil in the United States. This must have led him, in his book's second (1961) edition, to compare Black and Native Americans' experience in Latin America and in the United States. Contending that "Spain's record of dealing with the Negro was more humane than that of England, Holland, and France," Herring also argues that resistance to accepting "the Negro as a full partner in the creation of the New World of America" was greater, and more intransigent, in the United States than it was in either Spanish America or Brazil (89).

Perceptively, Herring goes further, making the important distinction between Portuguese-speaking Brazil and its neighbors in Spanish America. Even in its earliest days, he writes, colonial Brazil "was able to absorb a considerable number of English, French, Florentines, Genoans, Germans, Jews, and Spaniards. Theoretically, there were high barriers against the Negro, but actually Brazil shared Portugal's easy acceptance of men of all colors, a lesson acquired from long association with the Moslems" (237). In reality, Black men and women, and people with Black or Indian blood, could and did move up the social ladder to occupy positions of power. Money, as the old Brazilian adage goes, lightens. "It is therefore impossible," Herring continues, "to compare a Brazilian's and an Alabaman's figures on race: the Brazilian counts as Negroes those who are economically Negro; the Alabaman judges by blood" (237).

Incensed, seemingly, by the discrepancy between Brazil and the United States on matters of race and racial mixing, Herring then acidly concludes: "The English formula was liquidation; the Portuguese, assimilation. The Englishman, in the name of his God, shot his Indians; the Portuguese, with a slight nod to his God, slept with his Indians. . . . The English, out of a sense of sin, refused to recognize the offspring of such irregular alliances.

The Portuguese, in warm affection, took pride in their brown children, often trained them, and now and then sent them to school in Portugal" (239). In colonial Brazil, racial fluidity was the norm, more so even than in Spanish America.[2] The Puritans regarded the aboriginal Americans they encountered with suspicion, and as the devil's own children. When they understandably "resisted the Puritan advance, many New Englanders advocated exterminating them" (Parkes 71). The Puritans also believed that "the American wilderness" was full of "evil forces" and that it was "the devil's own territory," and so the people who lived there had to be eliminated as quickly as possible and their land taken (Parkes 207). This was God's will, and they were carrying it out. So much for the Christian doctrine of "Love thy neighbor."

But the Portuguese were not the Spanish. There were major differences. "The Portuguese colonizer of Brazil," Freyre avers, "in certain respects . . . resembles the Englishman, in others the Spaniard. A Spaniard without the warlike flame or the dramatic orthodoxy of the conquistador of Mexico and Peru; an Englishman without the harsh lineaments of the Puritans. The compromiser type." "With no absolute ideals, with no unyielding prejudices," he writes, the Portuguese colonizer had a "greater social plasticity" than "any other European colonizer" (185).

As the Mexican poet, diplomat, and intellectual Octavio Paz puts it, "It is quite clear that the reason the Spaniards did not exterminate the Indians was that they needed their labor for the cultivation of the vast haciendas and the exploitation of the mines. The Indians were goods that should not be wasted" (102). But for all that they were exploited, the Indians were part of the Spanish American social order. And in 1519 a Christianized Taino by the name of Enriquillo led what might have been the first Native American revolt in the Americas against Spanish authorities. Nevertheless, this "possibility of belonging to a living order, even if it was at the bottom of the social pyramid, was cruelly denied to the Indians by the Protestants of New England. It is often forgotten that to belong to the Catholic faith meant that one found a place in the cosmos. . . . The difference between colonial Mexico and the English colonies was immense. New Spain committed many horrors, but at least it did not commit the gravest of all: that of denying a place, even at the foot of the social scale, to the people who composed it. There were classes, castes and slaves, but there were no pariahs, no persons lacking a fixed social condition and a legal, moral and religious status" (Paz 102–3). The Spanish did not view the Native Americans they encountered, as the Puritans did those they encountered, as the progeny of the devil. Neither did the Portuguese, whose relationship with the native peoples they came across was even more fluid.

After the promulgation of the New Laws in 1542, which finally settled the passionately debated question about the official status of the Indians (who were, in essence, wards of the state), the Spanish, like the Portuguese (who were not bound by these laws), came to regard their indigenous people as men and women more or less like themselves. In Latin America the groups were able to mingle socially, and to a degree that was not the case with the Puritans. In the case of the Spanish, what is most notable here is that perhaps for the first time in human history, the rights of a conquered people are being seriously debated by the monarchs of the conquerors.

In 1601, Bento Teixeira Pinto, possibly a Portuguese Jew, composed Brazil's first epic poem, the *Prosopopéia*. The poem's authorship is not surprising since the Jews had been active in Portugal's intellectual, commercial, and political life since being expelled from Spain in 1492, and their role in building Brazil and its literature was not insignificant. Possibly born in Portugal, and thought by many to be a *cristão-novo* come to Brazil to seek his fortune, as many did, Bento Teixeira hoped with his poem to celebrate what he took to be the founding of his adopted country, Brazil.

If *Prosopopéia* fails to inspire as a stirring epic, it does have its moments, especially when it focuses on Brazil's many natural beauties. And by focusing on Brazil's still inchoate though fast coalescing sense of national identity, it does seek to cast it as a glorious new American nation, one not merely comparable to the fabled nations of Greece and Rome but superior to them! It is for this reason that today we can read this short, otherwise undistinguished epic and recognize in it that early spark of Brazilian national spirit that we know as *brasilidade* (Putnam 53). Still closely managed by Spain, Spanish America did not show such a literary flicker of independence until considerably later.

In 1618, another Brazilian writer, also likely a *cristão-novo*, took a major step toward Brazilian independence. In his *Diálogos das grandezas do Brasil*, Ambrósio Fernandes Brandão gave us a very readable text that sharply distinguished between the virtues of Brazil, still a colony, and what he laid out as the vices and failures of Portugal, the European mother country. In advancing his case, which is made, as per the title, in the form of a colloquy between a fictitious version of the author himself, Brandônio, and another character, Alviano, who finds Brazil to be the "terra . . . mais ruim do mundo," a vile place where hunger and want run rampant (Moisés, *A literatura brasileira* 57). In the course of the six dialogues that make up the book Brandão makes three main points: one, that the fecundity of Brazil as a source of food production cannot be minimized (and that the problem of hunger is one of distribution, and therefore a political problem, not one of production) (58); two, that Brazil is much more important to the Portuguese Crown than even India, the seat of its lucrative spice trade (58–59); and three, that the Portuguese in Brazil are consumed by greed and selfishness and care nothing about "o bem geral" (59; the common good). Only the Brazilians, Brandão suggests, care about Brazil.

This incipient sense of Brazilian nationalism and a concomitant desire to throw off Portuguese rule got a big boost when, in the early 1640s, Brazilians from a variety of social groups were forced by circumstances to band together in order to expel first the invading French and then the Dutch. In early 1645 a small unit of Portuguese soldiers was greatly bolstered by large numbers of *mazombos* (white people born in Brazil), Blacks, mulattos, and Indian troops. Some say that women too volunteered in the cause. Working together, they won decisive victories. The Portuguese, who had made peace with the Netherlands in Europe and who were concerned with strengthening their newly won freedom from Spain,[3] were reluctant to expend much in the way of men and resources to assist the Brazilians in expelling the Dutch from Brazil. This task thus fell, in the main, to the Brazilians themselves. And in 1650 they succeeded; the Dutch were driven out of Brazil (see Burns, *History of Brazil* 60–63).

For the comparative Latin Americanist, it makes sense to read *Prosopopéia* in the light of a similar text, *La grandeza mexicana,* published three years later, in 1604. While both works are celebratory in their tone, *Prosopopéia* lauds Jorge de Albuquerque Coelho and the founding of Brazil, the nation, whereas *La grandeza mexicana* sings the virtues and beauties of Mexico City, the viceregal capital. Balbuena's poem, written in tercets and in the Italian mode, comes off as less pedestrian than Bento Teixeira's effort, which is rarely praised for its nimbleness or freshness. One exception to this critical reaction, however, involves Bento Teixeira's lovely description of the reef just off the coast of northeastern Brazil. Here, *Prosopopéia* comes to life. What both works share at the dawn of the seventeenth century is a genuine enthusiasm for their respective cultures and New World civilizations. Brazil and Spanish America have produced flourishing nations and rich, complex literatures. American literature exists.

Early Spanish American and Brazilian literature begins to take shape under the star of the Baroque. Intellectually and aesthetically, Latin

American letters are a product of it (see Rabassa, "Survival and Revival"). And yet its full creative brilliance was not immediately apprehended, even by experts. As González Echevarría avers, "The crucial role the Baroque played in the cultural and artistic history of Latin America has been a gradual discovery," one that has involved a profound reevaluation of its importance ("Colonial Lyric" 204; see also 204–7). But this common Iberian origin must not blind us to the telling differences between the Spanish American Baroque and the Brazilian.

According to Afrânio Coutinho, the "literature of colonial Brazil is baroque literature. . . . Literature was born in Brazil under the sign of the baroque, from the baroque hand of the Jesuits. It was to the plastic genius of the baroque that was owed the implantation of the long process of interbreeding which was the principal characteristic of Brazilian culture" (97). These and other qualities make Brazilian Baroque writing very different from the Puritan literature of the early United States but also substantially distinct from the Spanish American Baroque, which was also strong. Throughout Latin America, the influence of Góngora, especially, was deep and wide. There is no Puritan Góngora. While Puritan literature may well lack the sweep, the scope, and the grandeur we associate with great ideas and brilliant writing, the early literature of Spanish America and Brazil do not. Not only is there no Góngora in Puritan America, there is no Sor Juana Inés de la Cruz or Gregório de Matos, either. For the inter-Americanist, this difference is fundamental.

At the same time, it is worth remembering that the Puritans prized literacy, for, in order for a person to parse the scriptures and thus have the word of God be revealed to her, she had to be able to read; "illiteracy," which was more widespread in Latin America, "was a tool of Satan" (Foerster et al. 1:11). This too would play a role in the development of literature in Puritan America and in Latin America. And Spanish America, we must remember, was even in the 1500s a clutch of culturally distinct regions, eventually to become nations, united by a single language and religion but stressed by a variety of social, political, and economic conflicts. Although its borders were then somewhat different than they are today, Brazil was always a single nation, in concept and in fact, and this too makes it different from Spanish America.

For González Echevarría, the major writers of the Spanish American Colonial Baroque were "Juan de Espinosa Medrano, the *Lunarejo,* Juan del Valle y Caviedes, Carlos de Sigüenza y Góngora, and Sor Juana Inés, all motivated by the passion to know," as well as "Juan del Valle y Caviedes, the major satirist of the period, and an important poet himself"

("Colonial Lyric" 215). While the sixteenth-century Spanish and Portuguese valued creative writing and held it in esteem, the Puritans did not. For them, such writing was dangerous and could lead one astray. As a result, colonial US America "produced no great works" of literary art and in this respect "was inferior not only to Europe, but also to the Spanish colonies of Mexico and Peru," to say nothing of Brazil (Parkes 59).

Different from the beginning, with the lushness and worldliness of the Iberian Baroque contrasting with the Puritan plain style, views of poetry here in the Americas have changed through time. In the colonial United States, Edward Taylor, and his "wilderness Baroque," makes for the best comparison with Sor Juana; although Anne Bradstreet is often offered up (see Aldridge), the better yoking is Taylor. In all of colonial America, Sor Juana, it must be said, admits of no peers. From Canada we have Marie de l'Incarnation, who in the early years of the seventeenth century wrote about her vision of God and the secular world in a prose "ripe with passion" (New 50; see also Urbas 1–2). While the Puritans viewed poetry with some suspicion, this form of creative writing was in full bloom when the Spanish and the Portuguese first set foot in America. And since that time, the poetry of Spanish America and Brazil has seemed a little odd to US readers. "To a North American reader," Tapscott believes, "the status of poems in Latin America can seem paradoxical. The poems seem more lyrically effusive but more publically important than our poems, richer with metaphors and their connective energy, and yet at the same time more publically responsible and revered, more attended to" (1).

Why, a comparative Latin Americanist might well ask, include references to early US writing in a discussion of colonial literature in Spanish America and Brazil? The answer is simple: Because both Spain and Portugal were concerned about England and its interests, as a competitor and as a threat to them in their part of the New World. Another, more concrete reason is that US leaders like Samuel Sewell and Cotton Mather, functioning as influential Puritan preachers, despised the Spanish and their Catholicism. One has to suspect that had the Portuguese acquired the wealth that Spanish America had afforded the Spanish, Sewell and Mather would have thought ill of them too.

In both Spanish America and Brazil (though less so in Brazil, according to Freyre), and as in Puritan New England, church and state were closely tied. And, again as in Puritan America, Catholicism touched every aspect of human life, especially in Spanish America, where the religious fervor of the Reconquista was still strong. In the still nascent United States the unholy marriage between money making and religion took place very early. In

1624, in fact, another Puritan leader, Edward Winslow, would state, with pride and approval, that Plymouth Colony had already become a place where "religion and profit could jump together" (quoted in Pagden 36). John Cotton's attempt to reconcile intense Puritan religiosity with the world of business, the pursuit of wealth, and rampant materialism would make it increasingly difficult for the Puritans to maintain "the great dream of a holy commonwealth" (Foerster et al. 1:8).

Drama

Although reviled in Puritan America, the theater flourished in early Spanish America and Brazil. Owing most likely to the particular vitality of this literary form back in Spain, there arose very quickly in colonial Spanish America a strong and flourishing public theater, one replete with "its own buildings, acting companies, and paying audiences" (Henríquez-Ureña 45). But Portugal too had its own vibrant theater tradition, and so it should be no surprise that as a literary genre theater existed in colonial Brazil as well. In the early years, Jesuit fathers, like Anchieta and Nóbrega, routinely made use of dramatic forms, including *autos,* to assist in the conversion of Indians to Catholicism. By the eighteenth century the theater had come to serve a political purpose in that it could present new ideas to a Brazilian public that, still mostly illiterate and lacking an established press, otherwise would not have had access to them. And, of course, a public theater also provided an occasion for people to discuss and debate these new ways of thinking.

One key difference is that in Spanish America the dramatic tradition goes back much further than anything we are aware of in Brazil's indigenous past. While Anchieta learned Tupí and cultivated it in the teaching and edification of his Indian charges, we do not know whether their ancestors possessed, as did the ancient Aztecs, Mayas, and Incas, a rich and varied history of ritual, song, and dance. It seems all but inconceivable to think that they did not, but we simply do not know as much about them as we do about these three other brilliant Native American traditions. This is why even today we cannot point with confidence to Brazilian parallels with productions like the seemingly uncontaminated *Rabinal Achí* or even the likely hybridized *Ollantay.* And while we know that Tupí culture has exerted an enormous influence on modern Brazilian culture, we remain frustrated by not being able to peer deeper into Brazil's indigenous past.

Satire

With respect to early American satire, the extant texts suggest that this kind of writing was both sharper and more vitriolic in Spanish America and Brazil than it was in Puritan America, where, by comparison, it tended to be more tepid and restrained, more intellectually suggestive than viscerally aggressive. In Puritan New England, there are no voices like those of Brazil's Gregório de Matos and Peru's Juan del Valle y Caviedes. While the Puritans "did not particularly nurture satire," Scheick writes, it was more cultivated in the southern US colonies (86). Ebenezer Cooke's *The Sot-Weed Factor* (1708) lampoons those English settlers in Maryland who allowed themselves to be gulled by the promotional materials designed to paint the New World as a paradise, a land of plenty where one could get rich easily and quickly. Cooke's narrator gives us a text that, though less scabrous than the poems of Caviedes, is nevertheless "replete with sexual nuance, misogynous portraits of women," and depictions of local inhabitants as "dangerous, animal-like predators" (Scheick 87). While Caviedes directs his ire at doctors, they demonstrate the same kind of predatory conduct that Cooke japes at. The political criticism inherent in Cooke's poem, however, brings to mind the satirical poetry of Matos, who also targeted not merely certain people in his colonial society but how it was structured and why it operated as it did. Can we conclude from this that satirical writers in colonial Spanish America and Brazil were freer to criticize their peers, leaders, and institutions than were writers in New England? Matos, we know, suffered for his lampooning of powerful people, yet his voice is the brightest light of colonial Brazilian letters. Among early American satirists, he and Caviedes stand out for the ferocity of their writing.

As comparative Latin Americanists and as comparative Americanists in general, I believe we can say this: Sor Juana Inés de la Cruz stands alone as the most brilliant writer in all of colonial America, North and South. But Gregório de Matos, I contend, is second only to her. For González Echevarría, Sor Juana Inés de la Cruz (1648–1695) "is the major poet of the Colonial Baroque, the last major figure of the Spanish Golden Age, and one of the classics of Spanish language literature" ("Colonial Lyric" 220–21; see also 207, 217–30). By any standard, Sor Juana stands as our first great American writer.

A comparison of her sonnet "Este que ves, engaño colorido" with the Matos sonnet "Discreta e formosíssima Maria" is an interesting exercise. Both writers, the Mexican and the Brazilian, were working under the influence of the eminent Spanish poet Luis de Góngora and his sonnet "Mientras por competir con tu cabello,"[4] so it is not surprising that the sonnets of Sor Juana and Matos have much in common. All three poems deal with the same defining themes of the Iberian Baroque: the instability of the world; the deceptiveness of material reality; and the destructive yet inexorable passing of time, the latter so powerfully evoked in the last line of each of these three poems.

In their opening stanza, Góngora and Matos set up a tension between life and the corrosive effect the passing of time has on it. Sor Juana, gazing at the portrait made of her, directs her comments to the fact that not even art can check or stay the flow of time.

In his second stanza, Góngora intensifies this theme and, with his use of *mientras,* which appears four times in the stanza, emphasizes the paradoxical situation inherent in all life, how the passing of the years increases beauty and the fullness of life even as it slowly snuffs it out, as in the life cycle of a flower, which is invoked as a symbol *of* life and beauty. As we can see in his parallel use of *enquanto,* for example, Matos follows the Spanish bard more closely here than does Sor Juana, who continues to work her comparison of life and art but also touches on how easily the senses are duped.

In the third stanza, both Góngora and Matos avail themselves of the verb *gozar,* while Sor Juana, eschewing it, begins to build a powerful block of verse that sets the reader up for her poem's concluding line. All three poets make use of the withered flower to focus attention on the destructive effects of time's fugacity. Of the three, however, it is Matos who actually mentions "o tempo" and who most emphatically shows us how it crushes us, flower-like, beneath its heavy tread. Although arresting, this image may be the most dramatic in the three poems.

The famous final line of Góngora's sonnet, so somber and yet so beautiful, enjoys marvelous re-creations in the hands of both Sor Juana and Matos.

> Góngora: "en tierra, en humo, en polvo, en sombra, en nada."
> Sor Juana: "es cadaver, es polvo, es sombra, es nada."
> Matos: "Em terra, em cinza, em pó, em sombra, em nada."

As we can see, Matos follows Góngora's use of the preposition *en* with the equivalent Portuguese form, *em.* And, again mimicking his master, Matos utilizes five nouns—*terra, cinza, pó, sombra,* and *nada.* It is also worth noting that all three poets elect to end the poem with the same potent yet mysterious and melodious word, *nada.* And although Sor Juana makes a deletion, all three poets make the final line show the degenerative progression of life and beauty to death and nothingness.

Sor Juana, continuing to show her originality and talent, moves away a bit from Góngora. Instead of using the same preposition, *en,* the Mexican poet continues to employ a verb, *es,* from *ser,* a decision she had already made and put into action in the preceding stanza. The result is that each of the last six lines of Sor Juana's sonnet begins with *es.* The effect of this slight alteration is very powerful. The reader is irresistibly driven from the poem's open words, "Este que ves" (referring to the portrait that inspires this poem), to its final six lines, which, like hammer blows, are delivered one after another. The effect is extraordinary. Even more than the reader of the Góngora original, Sor Juana's reader is left stunned. So much so that one is tempted to say that we have here that rare case in which the poem that imitates is actually superior to the poem imitated. Not everyone will agree with this response, of course, but the power of Sor Juana's slightly shorter and more concentrated closing cannot be denied.

Several other poems by Sor Juana and Matos also reward comparative analysis, including "Rosa divina" and "Debuxo singular," "Al que ingrate me deja" and "Ofendi-vos, meu Deus," and "Hombres necios" and "Aos vícios." While "Aos vícios" is a far cry from "Hombres necios," which has no counterpart anywhere in colonial American literature, it does showcase Matos's very substantial social consciousness. To be sure, Sor Juana is not lacking in this category; "Hombres necios" centers on the prevailing double standard and how it poisons relations between men and women and therefore within society generally. This we do not find in Matos, who can be hard on nonprivileged women and women of color, who are often the focus of his most graphic poems (Haberly, "Colonial Brazilian Literature" 58).

All in all, Matos, labeled by Moisés as Brazil's "primeiro grande poeta," appears here to hew more closely to Góngora than Sor Juana does, though he does not lack for originality either (*A literatura brasileira* 50). From a comparative perspective, we can see that while Matos is good, and at times very good, he is not as consistently outstanding as Sor Juana. The gold medal for colonial Latin American poetry goes to Sor Juana Inés de la Cruz, the silver to Gregório de Matos.

Given the reigning poetics of the time, one might reasonably ask, Should we regard the Brazilian as a practitioner of *culteranismo* or of *conceptismo?*[5] For Merquior, the answer is clear: Matos is a *culteranista,* more so than Sor Juana, whom he finds to be an inspired *conceptista* (364). Merquior also opines that within the confines of colonial Latin

American verse (and, one can think, in all the Americas) the multivoiced Brazilian "remains unrivalled" in terms of his "satirical and erotic pieces," the latter, sometimes regarded as pornographic, not becoming widely disseminated until the late 1960s (364).

As a satirist in Latin American literature, Matos is often thought of in the same context as the Peruvian Juan del Valle y Caviedes. Taken together, the two most certainly do stand alone in the Americas. No one else even comes close to their levels of vitriol. For Lúcia Costigan, Matos and Caviedes rank as "the two most notable satirists of the seventeenth century in the New World" (87). They certainly have no equal in Puritan America, where satire was of a more staid nature. Both writers cultivated a variety of forms and themes, both sought to expose the abuses and hypocrisies of colonial society, and both came from privileged families. Doctors especially caught the ire of Caviedes, while Matos comes across as a more equal-opportunity satirist. For Haberly, Matos's satirical verse especially reflects a profound disillusionment with how colonial Brazil had developed, how, in his estimation, it had failed to fulfill the *ufanista* promises and how it had become a culture that rewarded corruption, greed, venality, and sham ("Colonial Brazilian Literature" 58–59).

Comparative Latin Americanists, however, might regard Matos as more of a turning-point writer for Brazilian literature than Caviedes was for Spanish American letters. More than the Peruvian, who did integrate some Quechua words into his poems, Matos, embracing in his private life both indigenous and African culture, packed his compositions with Tupí, African, and new, uniquely Brazilian words. We can, in fact, consider Matos an early cultivator of Brazilian rather than Portuguese as his language of identity. He is an early example of cultural fusion and miscegenation in Brazil, and he changed Brazilian literature's line of development. This partially explains his appeal to the musicians of Brazil's Tropicália movement in the 1960s and 1970s. Yet Caviedes too was aware of his identity as an American writer struggling to find his place in a changing social order (see Lasarte). From our perspective today, we most prize Juan del Valle y Caviedes and Gregório de Matos for their withering, sometimes grotesque satirical pieces.

Oratory, Religion, and Politics

In colonial Latin America, oratory, religion, and politics were not kept separate; they were part and parcel of one another. And it is Brazil's politically astute Antônio Vieira who is renowned as colonial Latin America's

greatest orator. In Spanish America, Bartolomé de las Casas is often compared to him. And rightly so, though there are differences. Vieira, a Jesuit,
was, in addition to his work in Brazil, something of a troubleshooter
for the Portuguese Crown. He was sent on several sensitive diplomatic
missions and was a counselor to King João IV. He even served as confes-
sor to Queen Christina of Sweden. Las Casas, a Dominican, was less an
international negotiator for the Spanish Crown but more of a passionate
advocate for the Native Americans, who were being abused and exploited
as little more than slaves on the great *encomiendas,* or land tracts, in
colonial Spanish America. In contrast to Vieira, Las Casas traveled to and
from the royal court in Madrid, where he argued his case for better, more
just treatment of the Indians, contending that they were rational men and
women, that they could and should be converted to Christianity, and most
radical of all, that they deserved to be paid for the work they did. Still, the
comparison of Vieira and Las Casas is valid and merits study.

Except for the obvious fact that we have no recordings of people
orating to others, preaching would provide a fascinating genre for inter-
Americanists to explore. Instead, all we have are texts that they read
from or that allowed them to improvise. These same texts do, however,
reveal what matters and issues preachers like Las Casas, Vieira, and, in
Puritan America, Cotton and Increase Mather were concerned with. And
this in itself gives us valuable insights into the similarities and differences
between colonial Spanish America and Brazil and between Latin America
and the US part of North America. If Puritan America was primarily
religious in nature, then Spanish America, more, I would say, than Portuguese America, was legalistic (see Cardenas Bunsen 793–97, 807–11; see
also González Echevarría, *Myth and Archive*). Along these same lines, it
is interesting to note that the oratory of Spanish America and Brazil does
not feature the kind of fire-and-brimstone preaching we associate with
Puritan culture. Perhaps because it was Catholic, there is no equivalent
in colonial Latin America for Jonathan Edwards's "Sinners in the Hands
of an Angry God."

In colonial Spanish America, the figure of Inca Garcilaso de la Vega
looms large. The child of an Incan princess and a Spanish captain, Inca
Garcilaso paid homage to both traditions. Proud of both, he stinted on
neither. Two of his works in particular, *La Florida del Inca* (1605) and the
Comentarios reales (1609–17), have established themselves as landmarks
of Spanish American literature. Interestingly, and especially so for a culture so receptive from the very beginning to racial and cultural mixing,
there is no Inca Garcilaso in colonial Brazil; there is no corresponding

figure. And there is certainly not one in Puritan New England, where such comingling was discouraged. Even today, there are few uglier and more dismissive words than *half-breed*, which is what Inca Garcilaso, in all his grandeur, would have been to Protestant readers in New England.

"As Sérgio Buarque de Holanda has shown in his classic study, *Visão do Paraíso* (1959)," writes Merquior, "the Portuguese mind proved far less utopian than the Spanish one. Perhaps because of absence of large pools of native Amerindian labor, the geographical dispersal of colonists in an economy based on sugar, or the much later arrival of crown and church personnel, the masters of Brazil climbed down from the lofty dreams of high-minded Spanish *conquistadores*. At any rate, in Portuguese America the vision of El Dorado tended to be restrained," as evidenced in its key founding texts (Merquior 364).

How do these two Iberian "visions" compare with that of Puritan New England about 1620 and 1630, and what would become the southern colonies, beginning in 1607? To answer this question, we have to look at the kind of society the English wanted to implant in the New World. Three dates—1607, 1610, and 1620—are of critical importance: 1607 was the year of the founding of Jamestown, Virginia, marking the beginning of the English presence in the Americas, Spain and Portugal having been here for more than one hundred years by then and boasting long-established colonies with rich literary traditions; 1610 brought the separatist Pilgrims, who felt the Anglican Church could not be "purified" or redeemed and had to be separated from; and 1620 brought the less radical Puritans, who believed that perhaps the church could be rid of what they took to be its failings. Other Puritans, less extreme in their beliefs, would settle in Canada (Sutherland 61–65).

When, in the cold of November 1620, the radical Separatists arrived on their leaky ship, the *Mayflower,* not in warm Virginia, as they had planned, but in cold, snowy Massachusetts, they knew something had gone awry. Aside from the bitter wintry weather, for which they were not prepared, they now also had a serious legal problem, since their charter pertained only to Virginia. They had no legal status in Massachusetts. The forty-one people aboard the good ship thus decided to do here in the New World what they had done back in the Old World when they determined to separate from the Church: they would form a new "civil body politick." Their covenant, which would be known as the Mayflower Compact, was both civil and religious. But as has been pointed out, "These Pilgrims had not left Europe to found a democracy or to establish a free state. They merely sought a refuge for their own religious society, and they were determined to keep all who differed with them out of their new Jerusalem" (Foerster et al. 1:6–7). The principle of segregation was thus firmly established in Puritan New England in ways it was not in Spanish America and Brazil.

The intentions of the English settlers were both similar to and different from the intentions of the Spanish, arriving some one hundred years earlier, in 1492, and of the Portuguese, arriving in the Americas eight years later, in 1500. The Iberians had not come to the New World to build democracies, but neither had the Puritans or the Separatists. More like the Spanish in that they were driven by an intense mixture of religious zeal and political frustration, these early English settlers operated a closed system, one that considered itself threatened by outside influences. The two religions involved, Protestantism and Catholicism, would, in the Americas, replay the clash between the Protestant Reformation in Europe and the Catholic Counter-Reformation, led by Spain. But it is important to remember that from its origins, Protestantism "was a protest against the worldliness of the Roman Catholic church" and that the Catholic religion was, for the Protestant Puritans, "the Antichrist" (Bercovitch 35, 36). From 1607 on, this English animus toward Catholicism and, by extension, all of Latin America would adversely affect inter-American relations.

As always, the place of Portugal in these affairs was fluid. Small in size and in military might, but strong and rapidly getting stronger in terms of global commercial power, Portugal sought always to fend off Spain and to position itself in such a way as to gain maximum profit, in India and East Asia and then in Brazil. But as the Portuguese would eventually discover, it was difficult to hold such a vast commercial empire together. And they had bet, logically but incorrectly as it turns out, on maintaining control over their lucrative Asian possessions. They were not able to do so. Dutch and then English incursions could not be checked, and by the time the Portuguese sought to mitigate their losses in the East by turning their attention to Brazil, it was too late. Brazil was too far down the road of independence from Portugal to be stopped now.

In considering Brazilian literature, in which this growing sense of being different than Portugal can be clearly seen, against that of the United States, Putnam, one of the first in the United States to do so, concluded that whereas the literary production of colonial New England "remained parochial, the Brazilian . . . was far less narrow in outlook" (22). To understand what Putnam means, one has only to check two dates, 1601, when the erudite and secular Brazilian epic *Prosopopéia* appeared, and 1607, when Captain John Smith, an Elizabethan adventurer, was trying, at what would become Jamestown, Virginia, to establish the first English foothold in the Americas. When the newly arrived English were struggling to survive their first year in the New World, the Brazilians, like the Spanish Americans, had created rich, flourishing, and intellectually challenging national literatures. We would do well to remember, in thinking comparatively about American colonial literature, that "while the New England Pilgrims were still feeding their souls with Biblical inspiration Peru had splendid universities where scholars vied in fame with the most distinguished names of the old continent" (Putnam 42).

In 1608, one year after the English established the Jamestown Colony in Virginia, Samuel de Champlain founded Québec. Champlain and the French allied themselves with two powerful Native American peoples, the Algonquin and the Huron, but in doing so the French also made themselves the enemies of an even more powerful Native American nation, the Iroquois, who occupied much of what is today New York State. The 1985 Brian Moore novel, *Black Robe,*[6] was directly "influenced by" the work of the US historian Francis Parkman, who, in turn, had relied heavily on the *Jesuit Relations* and the functioning of the Iroquois Confederation in his own work (New 205). It appears that the early French explorers, the *coureurs de bois,* who dealt with the Native Americans they encountered as more or less equals, enjoyed much better relations with them than did the other early Europeans. Parkes, attempting a comparative and inter-American perspective, allows that while Puritan America produced no leaders like the intrepid Cortés, neither did it beget "the great French explorers of the St. Lawrence and the Mississippi" (36). Instead, "the expansion [of the English colonies] was a spontaneous movement of private citizens" into the western lands, where "they encountered wandering tribes of Indians, with whom they fought an unceasing warfare" (36).

Colonial Canada gives us one of the most useful and at times most compelling texts of this period. The *Jesuit Relations,* covering the years from 1611 to 1768, is the name given to a series of reports about Jesuit and French activities in the New World, including, perhaps most memorably, their relations with the Native Americans they came across. "The *Relations,*" writes New, "were the prime source for Francis Parkman's . . . seven-volume history, *France and England in North America* (1865–1892), an heroic and Protestant version of the times which in turn was to dominate English-language thinking about *L'ancien régime* for years to come" (47; see also Urbas 2 and Demos xi–xii).

Although referencing only relations between Puritan America and Spanish America in the mid- to late 1600s, Chevigny and Laguardia, building on pioneering work done by Stanley T. Williams, write that the Puritans had an "anxious interest in the reported opulence of Mexico City," that Samuel Sewall militated in favor of "'bombing of Santo Domingo, the Havana, Porto Rico, and Mexico itself' with a Spanish Bible," and that Cotton Mather decided "in 1699 to study Spanish in order to prepare such text to aid the evangelization of Latin America and the creation of a Puritan continent" (x–xi; Sewall quoted in S. Williams 17–18). Of the differences in play between the Protestant and Catholic approaches to the status of the indigenous Americans, Putnam avers that while the Portuguese Jesuits made "a most strenuous effort to convert the natives," our Puritan "forefathers, with the exception of a John Eliot, a Roger Williams, and a few others, did very little in this direction" (143). Pagden concurs, writing that "the British colonists . . . , Protestants whose religious beliefs might be broadly described as Calvinist, . . . had little real interest in converting Native Americans" (36; see also 37, 77–80, 150–51).

But this Puritan anxiety about Catholicism was not limited to Spanish America. It flowed to the north as well. John Demos expands upon this Protestant concern about Catholics in the New World by exploring relations between the nations of the Iroquois Confederation, the French who were exploring and trading for fur pelts in the area, and the English Puritans in New England. In Demos's view, the problem for the Puritans in the 1600s was how to deal with these two other groups, neither of which garnered their approval. Noting the existence of the "praying towns" that had been set up to evangelize the Native American peoples of the region, the acclaimed historian goes on to conclude that these "had borne distressingly meager fruit" (4, 41, also 4–5, 41, 57–60).

Faced with this dismal result, there was a growing concern among the Puritan leaders that their efforts to bring the "savages" into the light of Protestantism were actually having the opposite effect, especially on female captives, who may have been finding that they gained more rights, respect, and political power as women in the Iroquois Confederation, which some have described as, to a surprising degree, a matriarchy (Demos 165–66). "Instead of [the Puritans'] civilizing the wilderness (and its savage inhabitants), the wilderness might change, might *uncivilize them*." This, they would come to fear, was "an appalling prospect, a nightmare to resist and suppress by every means possible" (Demos 4). But the worst possible scenario was that some Puritan captives, and most pointedly the female Puritan captives, "would come to prefer *Indian* ways" and "refuse subsequent chances for repatriation" (4). Were the women of "Iroquoia" more respected, imbued with more rights, and entrusted with greater decision-making responsibilities than the Puritan women of "Euro-American 'colonial' society" (Demos 166, 165–66)? If not, Demos concludes, "how, then, to explain the large number of captive women who chose to remain with their captors," a number "larger by far than the number of similarly choosing men?" (166). Assuming that Demos is correct, how would such numbers, and such decisions, compare to those of Spanish and Portuguese women made captives by Latin American native peoples? In considering early America from a comparative perspective, it seems incontrovertible that one essential difference has to do with how the Native Americans were regarded by the Protestants and the Catholics.

As we consider the influence exerted by Spain, Portugal, France, and England on their American colonies, and as we seek to measure its relative effect here in the New World on their New World extensions, it is useful to review the thesis advanced by Isaac Woodbridge Riley. Riley argued that in the case of the United States, the last European power to arrive in America, its literature and culture would have evolved in less provincial ways if its main European influence had been Germany and not England. For one thing, this situation might well have spurred a greater interest in the study of the languages of other countries, along with their cultures, literatures, and histories. In terms of its applicability to the rest of colonial America, this is an interesting argument to consider. In the literary context, it highlights the abundant differences between the less than enthusiastic Puritan view of literary activity and the view of the lush and worldly Iberian Baroque, which was, as we have seen, thriving throughout Spanish and Portuguese America. In later years, the difference Riley speaks of emerged as the prevalence of French intellectual and artistic influence in Latin America versus the close and steady force of English influence in the United States. While the "special relationship" that has for so long bound England and the United States together has produced many admirable outcomes, an enthusiasm for cosmopolitanism and the study of "the other" is not one of them. The United States has from the beginning tended to be interested in itself only, in its own story. This is the downside of the myth of US "exceptionalism." To believe in it too zealously can lead to a crippling parochialism. Given the Puritan origins of the United States, a desire to maintain faith in US "exceptionalism" is understandable, and the rise of the United States is a truly remarkable story, but for it to continue to focus primarily on itself becomes, in a changing world, disadvantageous.

Latin American literature, on the other hand, has always been more cosmopolitan than the literature of the United States. From the very beginning, as we have seen, Brazilians knew they were part of a great, global trading system, one that required them to know more about other people, languages, and cultures. Later, in 1966, when Julio Cortázar's *Rayuela* (1963) appeared in Gregory Rabassa's exemplary English translation as *Hopscotch,* readers and critics in the United States were flabbergasted at how sophisticated, intellectual, and worldly it was. Nevertheless, of our two great Latin American literary traditions, the Spanish American and the Brazilian, scholars who know both traditions well tend to agree that it is Brazilian literature that has most easily and productively mixed with the rest of the world, even as, like its sister American cultures, it has labored to create itself. In the intensely and ever more globalized world of the twenty-first century, the people of the United States need to learn more about their other American neighbors and the world. Comparative American literary study can help achieve that worthy end.

As one considers taking such an approach to hemispheric, or American, literature, an important theoretical question, one having to do with foundational principles, presents itself. As González Echevarría has argued in his book *Myth and Archive* (1998) and elsewhere, the "Spanish Empire was ruled by the letter of the law, as was the Portuguese, but with lesser severity" (introduction 16). If, as comparative Latin Americanists, we accept this position, then the question before us becomes this: Did the English Pilgrims and Puritans who founded what would become the United States rule by law or by their particular view of the Protestant religion? And to what extent does González Echevarría's thesis apply to the early formation of the United States?

To help maintain our perspective in the comparative inter-American project, we would do well to remember that six years earlier, in 1601, Bento Teixeira's Brazilian epic, *Prosopopéia,* appeared, followed three years later by Bernardo de Balbuena's Mexican epic, *La grandeza mexicana,* which González Echevarría, perhaps thinking only of Spanish America, deems "the first significant American poem" ("Colonial Lyric" 204). In considering the importance of *Prosopopéia* and *La grandeza mexicana* to the development of Latin American literature, and to the history of American literature in general, it is also important to remember that Jamestown was not founded until 1607, and Québec not until 1608.

Even before its borders were formally set, Brazil was a single geopolitical entity united by a single language, Portuguese,[7] and by an external threat—Spain and Spanish America. It was also less tightly controlled by the European mother country, Portugal, which in 1500 was more interested in its economic and political ties with the Orient than in its colony in Brazil. One can understand how under such circumstances a more cohesive and coherent national literature might flourish in Brazil before it did in the more geographically disperse Spanish America. And it did. *Brasilidade* and *ufanismo* were early unifying themes that begin to separate the colony, Brazil, from European rule. Already in 1618, Brandão's *Dialogos* could be read as a full-throated expression of *ufanismo brasileiro*. As the texts themselves show, a sense of national unity came earlier to colonial Brazil than to Spanish America, which, again, was not a single nation but a conglomeration of different Spanish-speaking regions and cultures.

Colonial Brazilian letters offer two great lights. One, Gregório de Matos, the "Boca do Inferno" (Devil's mouthpiece), stands out for the variety of his work and for its daring. We prize him chiefly for his satirical poems. The other, Father Antônio Vieira, was a Jesuit priest born in Portugal who came to Brazil as a child and would identify with his adopted country for the rest of his life. In his "Sermon of Saint Anthony to the Fish," given on June 13, 1654, to what must have been a quite surprised audience, the defender of Brazil's native peoples addresses not one but two groups, the fish in the sea and the colonists, whom he had been officially banned from speaking to. Vieira preferred the fish, who ate one another out of honest hunger, to the colonists, who ate one another, metaphorically speaking, not out of need but out of greed, an acceptance of exploitation as natural, and hypocrisy. As he inquires of his two audiences, but especially his pseudo-Christian one, the one that denounces the Indians as "savages": "Do you think that only Tapuia Indians eat each other?" (33). Think again, he then admonishes them. "There is a much larger slaughterhouse here and white men eat each other much more" (33). He is talking about the social, political, and economic system that allows the planter class to abuse the Native Americans—and to debase themselves as they do so.

Vieira knew he was challenging the political and economic might of colonial Brazil. His defense of the Native Americans was a direct threat to the powerful large landowners. Very shortly after this sermon, he traveled to Portugal to propose to the king that sovereignty, over their own lives and lands, be returned to Brazil's autochthonous people. This was a radical proposal, and the colonists, who used the Indians as a cheap labor supply, would oppose it vehemently and with violence. Indeed, as Bosi points out, the entire seventeenth century in Brazil was marked by conflict between the colonists, who wanted to exploit the natives, and the Jesuits, who sought to protect them from this exploitation (52). What Vieira was doing was dangerous. He would be under threat of harm from the planters, but the Crown's power in its faraway colony would also be put in peril. Still, he persevered. Vieira's situation was complex in part because his defense of the Indians sometimes led him, as it did Las Casas, to become an apologist for Black slavery (Monteiro 11, citing the work of Bosi).

For Monteiro and Bosi, Vieira was "a tortured author," a man of the cloth who abhorred the abuse of both the Indians and the Black African slaves but who also understood that while the colonists, whose economic power hung in the balance, might accept his defense of one group, they would never accept his defense of both (Monteiro 11). Initially, Vieira chose to champion the Indians. According to the prevailing views of the time, the Black men and women brought to the Americas had been sold by their rulers in Africa and, unlike the Native Americans, who were naturally free, could therefore exist "legitimately" as slaves in the New World (Rodríguez Monegal, *Borzoi Anthology* 1:130). The power of the market indeed. In time, Vieira recanted and launched an ardent defense of both the Indians and the Black African slaves. An extraordinary figure in colonial Latin America, and in all of colonial America, Vieira deserves more attention outside of Brazil than he has so far gotten. As Vincent Barletta puts it, "We are due for a renewed appreciation of Vieira's complex but still relevant place within the broader debate regarding the legal rights of the indigenous populations of Brazil and the Americas as a whole" (18).

Excluding for a moment the myriad clashes between native America and the invading Europeans, the disagreement between Sor Juana and Antônio Vieira emerges as the first inter-American conflict. In the realm of US-based critical studies involving the Americas, Barrenechea believes that George W. Umphrey's 1943 study of how Spanish American literature compares to that of the United States may be the first (*America Unbound* 191n5; see also Shouldice). Brazil is not considered. The flap had to do with Sor Juana's response to an argument advanced by Vieira's "Maundy Thursday Sermon," which he had delivered decades earlier in 1645.[8] Known today as her "Carta atenagórica" (1690), that is, an epistle written in the manner of Athena, Sor Juana's critique of a position taken by a man who was her superior in the church hierarchy drew the attention of another of Sor Juana's superiors, the powerful bishop of Puebla, who responded to Sor Juana under the pen name "Sor Filomena." His condemnation of Sor Juana's refutation of Vieira's argument then led her to respond to him in her justly famous "Respuesta de la poetisa a la ilustre Sor Filomena" (1691), arguably the most powerful argument we have in all of colonial America in favor of intellectual freedom.

At issue was a point of Christian theology: what was the ultimate proof of God's love of humankind? Vieira had taken a position on this question in his 1645 sermon, and more than forty years later Sor Juana had the temerity—and the audacity—to disagree, albeit with respect, with the learned and widely venerated Jesuit leader. As nuns were not supposed to do this sort of thing, Sor Juana's lucid critique set off a firestorm in the colonial Spanish American church. She was reprimanded for her affront to church decorum and severely censured. Surely hurt and even angered by what she must have taken as an act of betrayal by her friend and supporter, the bishop of Puebla, Sor Juana then penned, in three months, her brilliant "Respuesta a Sor Filotea," which, while also refuting the charges brought against her, was a ringing defense of free thought and the right of women to gain an education. It is largely for this astonishing essay (given its time and place) that we think even today of Sor Juana as America's first feminist (see Schons; also Merrim). After sending her "Respuesta" along, Sor Juana abandoned theological debate forever. Four years later, in 1695, she would die, helping the people of Mexico City as they struggled with a plague.

The Brazilian scholar Alfredo Bosi, taking an inter-American perspective, argues that in essence the colonization of the Americas was a fusion of religious zeal and economic greed. "Together with the sword and the blunderbuss," he writes, "came the cross and the Bible. The Iberian, English, and French colonies were populated by men who practiced either a popular and still medieval Catholicism or its counter-reformist version, or a puritanical Protestantism in revolt against Anglican hegemony. Monotheism brought them together as Christians opposed to 'indigenous paganism,' though they were divided into active or passive contemporaries of the Inquisition, the Reformation, or the Counter-Reformation, and by the religious wars fought during the sixteenth and seventeenth centuries" (20).

Although initially at least it could not, as Spanish American writers would, draw upon a flourishing indigenous culture for strength and vitality, early Brazilian writers could tap the energy of the steady flow of foreign ideas that circulated there more freely than in Spanish America. This point should not be minimized or overlooked; it may well help explain the surprisingly international spirit, or consciousness, that informs so much colonial Brazilian writing. More tightly sealed off from the rest of the sixteenth-century world, Spanish America, which, it is true, did produce Latin America's greatest writer and intellectual, Sor Juana Inés de la Cruz, struggled to nurture this same sense, albeit inchoate, of cosmopolitanism, of being a player in the global game and the global circulation of knowledge.

In Latin America, the early years of the seventeenth century saw tremendous progress in literary production. They also saw events that, taken together, illustrate the changing state of affairs, culturally and politically, in North and South America. In 1601 the Brazilian writer Bento Teixeira published his epic poem *Prosopopéia*. Three years later, in 1604, the Mexican poet Bernardo de Balbuena brought out the still impressive *La grandeza mexicana*. The United States did not yet exist; in fact, Jamestown would not be settled until 1607. The French would settle Québec in 1608. Except for the various Native American traditions, the literatures of Spanish America and Brazil are therefore the oldest American literatures. And they were blooming. Poetry was leading the way, though the theater, which for both the Spanish and the Portuguese played such a key role in the conversion of the indigenous peoples, was also strong. Anchieta is the prototypical example. In only a few years, some extraordinarily talented Latin American writers, notable among whom are Sor Juana Inés de la Cruz, Gregório de Matos, Antônio Vieira, Ambrósio Fernandes Brandão, El Inca Garcilaso de la Vega, and Juan del Valle y Caviedes, would light up the American scene. At this point in American history Latin American literature was thriving in both Spanish America and Brazil. Finally, and to maintain a bit of perspective, it is worth remembering that Matos, who has been dubbed America's first "bohemian," was a contemporary of both Cotton and Increase Mather, neither of whom would have approved of either the Brazilian's attitude or his work (Putnam 68, citing José Veríssimo; for Matos and the Mathers, see Bates).

5 The Enlightenment and Independence

Spanish America, 1730–1832, and Brazil, 1769–1836

DURING THE 1700s, it is possible to argue, Brazilian literature moved ahead of Spanish American as a coherent national literature. The texts that bear this out are there, as is the requisite sense of identity. Several factors explain this: Brazil was a unique American nation. It was united by its language, Portuguese, and not Spanish; it had a different, more open relationship to the rest of the world; and by the eighteenth-century it saw its future in its own terms. Its literature, simultaneously Brazilian, American, and global, reflects all of this. Long experienced at survival in a hemispheric environment that viewed them as different, if not with outright hostility, Brazil's artists, thinkers, and political leaders have maintained their independence from Spanish-speaking America while cultivating generally cordial relations with it. This situation has a parallel with French-speaking Québec, which, at the end of the French and Indian War later in the century, will find itself surrounded by English-speaking Canada and in danger of being swallowed up by it. Much the same can be said of Canada in its entirety and its relationship to the United States. Survivance in the Americas is thus a concept not limited to French Canada (see Atwood). In addition to foreign texts, Brazilian writers of the eighteenth century were also reading Brazilian writers of the sixteenth and seventeenth centuries, and this produced a sense of homogeneity in Brazilian literature. We can see a national literature in the process of formation.

In the eighteenth century, the American political context was changing fast, and with it inter-American relations. Issues of influence and reception were developing that hitherto had not been seen. Latin Americans watched carefully the political drama that was gaining momentum in the United States and would come to a head in the US war for independence. Earlier, with the defeat of the Spanish Armada, in 1588, the power of the Spanish Empire had begun to erode. As a consequence of this, Spain's ability to control the destiny of its distant American colonies begins to decline as well. Growing sclerotic, the old Spanish Empire was weakening and increasingly unable to control its vast New World possessions. People in Spanish America were chafing at Spanish control. Its growing creole class was particularly restive.

The US experience with England only spurred this process on in Spanish America. As the original thirteen colonies of British North America grew increasingly militant about their status and identity, they would rise up in revolt and in 1776 win their war of independence. An English colony became the United States of America. The meaning of this momentous event was not lost on the Latin Americans. Indeed, the social, political, and economic repercussions of US independence were felt throughout Spanish America and Brazil. The winds of change were blowing hard in the Americas.

In 1789, a Brazilian delegation was dispatched to Paris to discuss with the US plenipotentiary there, Thomas Jefferson, how the United States might respond if Brazil were to overthrow its monarchy and replace it with a democratic form of government. Jefferson responded that while the United States would be sympathetic to the Brazilian cause, it was not in a position to formally recognize and support such an effort. Disappointed, the Brazilians returned home. But inspired by events in the United States, revolutionary sentiment was still strong in Brazil. In 1789, with the ill-fated Inconfidência Mineira, it experienced its first attempt at independence. The rebellion, with a group of poets playing a prominent part, was put down and its participants punished. But the seeds of independence had been sown.

Throughout this period of time, the old question of racial injustice in the Americas continues to fester. The Haitian slave revolt of 1791, which has to be thought of as the direct New World consequence of the French Revolution, was the spark that brought the question to a head. The social, political, and economic repercussions of the events in Haiti reverberated throughout the Americas. On New Year's Day, 1804, Haiti became an independent nation, the second in the Americas and the first in Latin America. Its history-making story would later be told by a variety of American writers, including Cuba's Alejo Carpentier. Seeking the support of the Haitian government, Simón Bolívar met with its president, Alexandre Pétion, and the two struck a deal. Haiti would help supply Bolívar's forces on one condition: that Spanish America free all slaves within its jurisdiction. Bolívar agreed. With two exceptions, Puerto Rico and Cuba, where the global demand for cheap sugar kept this loathsome institution in place, slavery was officially abolished in Spanish America between 1821 and 1854, long before it was abolished in the United States. Parkes, discussing slavery in the United States, postulates that "the strange and sinister phenomenon of race prejudice had already established deep roots in American society for reasons which are somewhat obscure" (56). Interestingly, Parkes seeks to drive this point home by contrasting the racial history of the United States with that not of Spanish America but of Brazil. He does this by saying, correctly, that Brazil was an American nation where "Negro slavery was established over a longer period than in the United States" and, incorrectly, that in Brazil the issue of slavery "never became important" (56–57). But while Parkes is wrong about this, his comment does serve to remind us that as an institution slavery was different in Brazil—different from what it was in the United States but also different from what it was in Spanish America (see Castilho).

The eighteenth century in Spanish America has long been unusually complicated, difficult to assess, and all but impossible to summarize. A period of extraordinary transformation, it encompassed unprecedented change for Spanish American literature and culture. Rife with conflicting forces and momentous events, it presents a challenge to the literary historian. "For many readers," writes Karen Stolley, "the eighteenth century represents not a bridge but an abyss between the Colonial Baroque and nineteenth-century Romanticism" (337; see also Bush). Stolley's sage point is less applicable to the situation in Brazil. As Haberly sees it, "Two central problems confronted Brazil's writers in the eighteenth century: how to find stylistic and thematic approaches to local reality, for despite the rebirth of faith in the land and its potential, it was clearly impossible to return to the essentially Medieval traditions of both the Jesuits and the *ufanistas;* and how to construct a literary society and achieve personal success in a colony still crippled by an inferior educational system, by limited intellectual opportunities, and by Portugal's refusal to allow printing presses to operate in Brazil" ("Colonial Brazilian Literature" 60–61). On the other hand, as Merquior argues, "the Brazilian Arcadians," so important to eighteenth-century Brazil, constituted "the first significant group of conscious writers in the Americas" (365).

In terms of literary production, then, in the eighteenth century the paths of Spanish America and Brazil began to diverge. "The striking contrast as concerns the colonies," writes Merquior, "was that, while extraordinary texts in verse and prose—Vieira's sermons or Sor Juana's *Primero sueño,* for example—were created in Iberian America under the star of the Baroque, as soon as baroque models gave way to Neoclassicism the literary landscape of Spanish America became relatively barren, whereas the mining towns of Brazil produced a first-rate poetical harvest—the Arcadian lyricism of the late eighteenth century" (365). These Arcadians developed, in Monteiro's words, "a coherently neoclassical literature in which bucolic and idyllic motifs, taken from classical tradition and filtered through a Renaissance or Petrarchan sensibility, are incorporated into the local landscape," thus imparting to it a uniquely "'Brazilian' tone" ("Editor's Notes" 101). For most critics, the principal Arcadian poets were Tomás Antônio Gonzaga (the great love poet of the group), Manuel Inácio da Silva Alvarenga, Cláudio Manuel da Costa, Alvarenga Peixoto, and José Basílio da Gama, whose lyric poem O *Uraguai* (1769) was the antecedent for Brazilian Romanticism. In a more inter-American context, we have the example of Frei José de Santa Rita Durão, whose foundational epic, *Caramuru* (1781), antedates the myth of John Smith, John Rolfe, and Pocahontas in the United States (see Moisés, *A literatura brasileira* 73–113). Because of their fear of miscegenation, stories of this sort were, however, "unimaginable for most English settlers in America" (Pagden 150). In Brazil they were commonplace.

Several of the Brazilian Arcadian poets—Manuel Inácio da Silva Alvarenga, José da Natividade Saldanha, and Domingos Caldas Barbosa—were men of color. Of these, Caldas Barbosa broke definitively with Arcadian forms and unapologetically embraced "Indianisms and Africanisms" in a way that presaged "the independent literature which Brazilian poets and novelists would create in the nineteenth century" (Haberly, "Colonial Brazilian Literature" 68). Black writing now helped define the heart of Brazilian literature, enriching and defining it.

We can see that by 1850 Brazil, conscious of its own heterogeneity, had become not only a cohesive and unified nation but "an intense amalgamation of Indians, Africans, and Europeans" and on a scale unlike anything else in the Americas (González Echevarría, Pupo-Walker, and Haberly 3). And all were contributing to a new and vital American literature, one that looked both inward and outward. "By the end of the eighteenth century literary creation in Brazil had surpassed Portuguese letters in quality and content. With a renewed sense of assurance, Brazilian authors looked to French, English, and German models as incentives for renovation" (4). A product of the national and the international, Brazilian literature was coming into its own.

From the perspective afforded us today, it appears that the Enlightenment was longer lived and of greater impact in the United States than in Latin America, where its orderly, progressive, and salubrious temper struggled to make its presence felt—not for lack of leaders who knew the value of Enlightenment thinking and who endorsed it but for lack of the social, political, and economic systems that would allow it to take root and flower. The legacy of Latin America's largely medieval origins was now holding it back. Put another way, we can see that the reason for this different reception of the Enlightenment's hopeful message would seem to have been the different political situations in the United States and Latin America, and most particularly Spanish America, which in the power vacuum created by the departure of the Spanish fell prey to a kind of Balkanization. This was not the case with Brazil, which, though still a constitutional monarchy (albeit a relatively progressive one), was more stable. And under the enlightened and proscience leadership of Dom Pedro, it was moving forward, and in an orderly fashion.

Literarily, this was an advantageous situation, and in fact Brazil was evolving in a similarly cohesive and coherent fashion. Merquior contends that in the eighteenth century Brazilian literature surpassed that of Spanish America. The most often cited Arcadians were the love poet Tomás Antônio Gonzaga, the lyrically charged epicist José Basílio da Gama, and the voice of Black and indigenous Brazil, Manuel Inácio da Silva Alvarenga. Merquior argues that "with Metastasio instead of Góngora for a paradigm, these poets not only surpassed their Portuguese predecessors and contemporaries, but also had no peer in Mexico or Lima" (365). Their work, moreover, "planted the roots" of a uniquely Brazilian literature in an organized, integrated, and "systematic sense" (365). In a more hemispheric sense, it is also Merquior who argues that "the Brazilian Arcadians were the first significant group of conscious writers in the Americas" (365).

In Spanish America, still under repressive Spanish control and, in the arts, reduced to producing servile imitations of the Spanish masters, the eighteenth century has traditionally been regarded as the century everyone wants to forget. As Torres-Ríoseco puts it, referring to Spanish American letters, the "sterile eighteenth century . . . is best passed over as quickly as possible" (42–43). Today, however, scholars see it in more positive terms. Yet even as they do, the contrast between the output of literature in eighteenth-century Spanish America and Brazil is evident. Seen in the context of hemispheric American literature, while more and more literary texts of quality were being produced in the United States in the 1700s, there was still a dearth of "what could be called artistically distinguished" works (Foerster et al. 1:182). Not so in Latin America, where more high-caliber literary works emanated, especially from politically stable Brazil.

By 1787 the United States had won its war for independence and was seeking to determine what kind of American nation it wanted to be. The reasoned and balanced approach to life promoted by Enlightenment thought was of great benefit to the people of the United States in the postrevolutionary period. And it was enthusiastically embraced. England became the principal foreign influence on US cultural activity, though German thought was gaining force as well.

One distinguishing development in the United States of the Neoclassical age was its ardent embrace of commerce as a defining characteristic of US culture. During the 1700s, as the nation spread further and further west, agricultural, business, and industrial output increased exponentially. Its population was growing, as was its need for new markets. The United States was rapidly becoming known as a business-oriented civilization, a fact the Latin Americans (and Canadians) of the period noted with some consternation. They feared that this turn to business, and to the aggressive and acquisitive mores that governed the world of business, as opposed to those that governed democracy, would eventually have dire consequences. As history shows us, they were right to be concerned. In 1803, when President Jefferson negotiated the Louisiana Purchase, the United States more than doubled in size. Five years later, in 1808, John Adams would remark, not incorrectly, that in the ostensibly classless (though nevertheless slaveholding) United States "we have one material that constitutes aristocracy, and that material is wealth" (Foerster et al. 1:176).

In 1763, England emerged victorious in the French and Indian War, and New France went to the victors. This meant that most of Canada was under British control. With fewer than seventy thousand *habitants,* the French had no chance of holding their New World territory against an overwhelming number of English settlers.

While the conditions were right for the postrevolutionary United States to benefit from the lessons of the Enlightenment, in Spanish America the situation was more difficult. Strife and division prevailed among the many newly independent Spanish American states, which, long under a heavy Spanish yoke, had never had a chance to develop the various institutions needed for democracy to flower. Andrés Bello had to know that his Neoclassical exhortations, though badly needed, would not fall on the same fertile ground as in the unified and growing United States. Some sort of hemispheric comity had to be achieved by America's Spanish-speaking nations. Splintered and at odds with itself, Spanish America had to come together. Possessed of a common heritage, it had to unify itself, if not in the political fashion envisioned by Bolívar then culturally. Bringing this herculean task to fruition would be Bello's contribution to Spanish American literature.

At the conclusion of the wars for independence, and at the very moment when the enthusiasm of the still slave-owning United States for Spanish America and for its independence and with respect to an enhanced inter-American sisterhood was cooling, Bello composed two poems that would call for a new kind of Spanish American unity. Both would rely on classical models, as would much of the Neoclassical poetry in the United States, and both would call upon the youth of Spanish America to drop their grievances with one another and begin to pull together in the creation of a brighter and more equitable future. This was Bello's vision of what the American future should be.

The first poem, "La alocución a la poesía" (1823), calls for the classical muse of poetry to abandon old Europe and put down roots in America. Considered by many to be a declaration of Spanish American intellectual emancipation, the poem calls upon young Americans to understand more fully their potential, their worth, and their common future. The second poem, "La agricultura de la zona tórrida" (1826), urges the newly liberated Spanish Americans to value more their food-producing capacity, to celebrate rural life, and (à la Virgil and book 2 of the *Georgics*) to eschew the vices, falsities, and machinations of the city. At times Bello can seem like a Spanish American Emerson, albeit a more exalted one. In later sections of the poem, the Venezuelan author advises Spanish Americans to reject petty, partisan bickering in favor of hemispheric comity. Subtitled "Silva Americana," "La agricultura de la zona tórrida," described by Andrew Bush as "the acme of the Enlightenment in Latin American verse," exhibits a clear debt to Virgil, Horace, Lucretius, and other classical writers as well as standing alone as a paean to America and all it represented (388; also 389). Bello had intended to publish the two poems together as part of a greater epic poem to be titled *América,* but it was never realized.

The poem proclaims, "Salve, fecunda zona,/que al sol enamorado circumscribes/el vago curso, y cuanto ser se anima/en cada vario clima,/ acariciada de su luz, concibes!" (Englekirk et al., *Anthology* 119; Hail, fecund zone,/that dost circumscribe the enamored sun's/vague course and dost conceive every being/that stirs in every varied clime/caressed by its light! [translated by Donald Walsh, in Rodríguez Monegal, *Borzoi*

Anthology 1:201]). Enumerating the abundant delicious edible flora that exist in the New World, and emphasizing its lushness and life-sustaining power, Bello's poem appeals to Anáhuac feliz, the Aztec name for the fertile and, Bello tells us, happy valley of Mexico, but also to the still living forces of such pre-Columbian leaders as "Atahualpa y Motezuma" ("Silva a la agricultura de la zona tórrida," in Englekirk et al., *Anthology* 120, 123).

Crucially, however, given his intention of uniting all of Spanish America, Bello, like Olmedo and many other Spanish American writers, links indigenous America to a broader notion of America itself. Writing of how "la innata mansedumbre" that sleeps "en el pecho americano" (Englekirk et al., *Anthology* 124; innate gentleness . . . in the American breast [Rodríguez Monegal, *Borzoi Anthology* 1:203]) must be awakened so that together the Americas can lead the hemisphere and the world forward in peace and harmony—with one another and with Nature itself, Bello ends with one final plea to the young nations of America to rise above the rest and gift liberty with a permanent dwelling place in the New World:

Oh, jóvenes naciones, que ceñida
alzáis sobre el atónito occidente
de tempranos laureles la cabeza!

(Englekirk et al., *Anthology* 124)

(Oh, young nations, who raise
above the astonished occident
your heads girt with early laurels!)

(Rodríguez Monegal, *Borzoi Anthology* 1:203)

After urging his fellow Americans to honor the timeless values of the agricultural world, hard work, the production of food, and peace, and to reject the snares and deceptions of the city as they build their new civilization, Bello calls on the Americas to erect a new civilization, one based on freedom, restraint, and the rule of law.

Así tendrán en vos perpetuamente
La libertad morada,
Y freno la ambición, y la ley templo.

(Englekirk et al., *Anthology* 124)

(Thus liberty will have in you
A perpetual dwelling,
Ambition a restraint, and law a temple.)

(Rodríguez Monegal, *Borzoi Anthology* 1:203)

Today we remember another celebrated Neoclassical writer, José Joaquín Olmedo, of Ecuador, known chiefly for his ringing ode *La victoria de Junín: Canto a Bolívar* (1825), which, as heroic poetry in the classical mode, still stands unsurpassed. Written to celebrate the first of the two 1824 battles in which the Spanish were defeated, sealing the victory for the Spanish Americans in their long struggle for independence, *La victoria de Junín* begins with the poet invoking Pindar and compares the events of the conflict to those celebrated by the great Greek poet. Taken together, the battles of Junín and Ayacucho, both fought in Peru, thus represent for Spanish Americans what the battle of Yorktown represents for the people of the United States.

La victoria de Junín's fame in Spanish America has not been without a degree of controversy, however. The main issue has to do with Olmedo's decision to inject into the poem the shade of the long-dead Incan emperor Huaina-Cápac, who before Pizarro's invasion was the last Inca to rule the Incan Empire intact. Bolívar himself objected to this addition, arguing not incorrectly that Olmedo's long speeches were both verbose and muddled, both of which would have been uncharacteristic of Incan emperors, who prized clarity and concision. Also there was the inconvenient fact that at the more famous of the two decisive battles, the one at Ayacucho, the Spanish American forces were led not by Bolívar but by Sucre. This meant that Olmedo, who wanted to honor Bolívar, had to find a way of doing so without seeming to make him less important than Sucre. The result was not entirely successful. Even so, *La victoria de Junín* is, on balance, a stirring example of the militaristic Spanish American epic poem. And one that anticipates, in spirit, tone, and style if not in form (which was resolutely classical), the coming Romantic revolution.

The opening stanza of the poem, "El trueno horrendo, que en fragor revienta/y sordo retumbando se dilata," is "a direct imitation of the Fifth Ode of Book III of Horace: *'Coelo tonantem credidimus Iovem Regnare.'*" (Torres-Ríoseco 50–51). The rolling, rumbling Spanish r's in the opening lines are onomatopoetic in their imitation of the sounds of thunder and thunderous artillery. And while they cannot be perfectly reproduced in English, the Donald Walsh English translation does suggest the same effect: "The horrendous thunder that crashing bursts/and swells in muffled rumbles /throughout the flaming globe/announces to god that He reigns in Heaven" (Rodríguez Monegal, *Borzoi Anthology* 1:198).

The great mountain chain of the Andes, the spine of America, will never be cowed. They endure, and Bolívar, their hero, will emerge victorious in this struggle and lead South America into the light of freedom: "Los Andes," enormous, imposing, and standing guard forever over their "bases de oro," a reference to the gold mines so coveted by the Spanish, mock the tyrannical Spanish forces who are about to be defeated. At the end of the day, the silent, eternal crags know that

> Los Andes . . . sentados sobre bases de oro,
> . . . .
> dirán del mundo
> Venció Bolívar: el Perú fue libre;
> y en trunfal pompa Libertad sagrada
> en el templo del Sol fue colocada
>
> (Englekirk et al., *Anthology* 112–13)

> (The Andes . . . resting upon golden bases,
> . . . .
> thus speak:
> Bolívar conquered: Peru was free;
> and in triumphal pomp sacred Liberty
> was placed within the Temple of the Sun)
>
> (Rodríguez Monegal, *Borzoi Anthology* 1:199)

Although it does have its awkward moments,[1] Olmedo's invocation of the ancient Incan leader does allow him to validate the South American independence movement by appealing to its brilliant indigenous past. And this ploy is a key component of Latin American Romanticism. While the use of the Native American motif is also present in US Romanticism, it is fair to say that it plays a more crucial and perhaps more realistic role in Spanish America and Brazil. Thus it is that Olmedo has the majestic Andes, the home of the Incan people, connect Spanish American independence to the Incan Temple of the Sun, the Sun God being the principal deity of the Incas.

It is Olmedo's intention to hail Bolívar for his liberation of Spanish America, and he succeeds in doing this:

> Será tuya, Bolívar, esta gloria;
> tuya romper el yugo de los reyes,
> y a su despecho entronizar las leyes.
>
> (Englekirk et al., *Anthology* 116)

> (Yours it is, Bolívar, this glory;
> yours to have thrown off the yoke of kings,
> and in their place to have enthroned the law.)

But politically astute, Olmedo also sings of Latin America's sister American nation, the United States, which, for a variety of reasons, some admirable, some not, was supportive of Spanish American independence:

> el pueblo primogénito dichoso
> de libertad, que sobre todos tanto
> por su poder y gloria se enaltece,
> como entre sus estrellas
> la estrella de Virginia resplandece,
> nos da el ósculo santo
> de Amistad fraternal.

(Englekirk et al., Anthology 117)

> (The glorious first-born and free American nation
> that above all others is exalted
> as much for its power and glory as for its stars
> the star of Virginia[2] is yet resplendent
> imparts to us the sainted buss
> of fraternal friendship.)

We can see that by the late 1820s, then, Spanish America, having won its independence from Spain, would now have to make a reality the dream of unity and cooperation that its leaders, such as Bolívar, had envisioned. This would prove even more challenging than throwing off the Spanish yoke had been. Spain had left Spanish America without the requisite social, political, and economic institutions to sustain functioning democracies. A political vacuum resulted, and into it stepped a long list of tyrants, strongmen, and *caudillos,* none of whom were interested in the kind of grand vision endorsed by Bolívar and others. As a result, Spanish America was plunged into a period of chaos, internal strife, and oppression. The light of democratic self-rule, which had driven the revolution against Spain, had grown dim.

The United States did not have to face the same problem. After defeating England in the Revolutionary War, the country entered the 1800s with a sure sense of national identity and a desire to expand westward. Only Native Americans would stand in its way, and they would be displaced and dispatched whenever it was deemed necessary, or convenient, to do so. Only a few voices objected to how it would be done. Expansion and prosperity were the orders of the day, and a still vague but growing belief in white nationalism guided thinking about how the newly born United States would define itself.

Vis-à-vis its hemispheric neighbors, the position of the United States at this time was complex. On the one hand, it was genuinely enthusiastic about other American nations following its lead and seeking independence and freedom from foreign rule. But on the other, many in the United States, which was rapidly becoming a business-oriented culture, saw Latin America more and more as a market to be exploited and a source of raw materials for US industrialization. The Brazilians and the Spanish Americans were aware of what the United States was doing, as it grew economically and expanded to the west, and of its newly dominant motivations, which were rapidly becoming more commercial than democratic. And it was this latter trend that worried them.

The Brazilians, who had not had to fight a long and bloody war for independence, were in a better position to deal with the United States. And they knew it. This knowledge, plus the relative stability of their society, allowed the Brazilians to negotiate a different role for themselves, one in which they would present themselves as what they truly were, a different American people and a different American nation. But they also wanted to be recognized by the United States as the leader of Latin America, its voice in Washington. For the Brazilians, this turned out to be a solid and effective strategy, remnants of which are still in effect today. Like their literature, Brazilian politics were distinctly international in nature.

For the comparative Latin Americanist, the eighteenth century is interesting for both literary and political reasons. In terms of its literature, we see Spanish America enmeshed in a felt need to imitate already exhausted Spanish models. This was the primary problem. Close Spanish domination over its American colonies all but required such an approach to creative writing, and it was stultifying. To be successful, one must appease one's critical establishment, not challenge it. But there were also signs of change, of a desire to innovate and seek greater authenticity. Texts like Sigüenza y Góngora's *Infortunios de Alonzo Ramírez* (1690), Alonso Carrió de la Vandera's *Lazarillo de ciegos caminantes* (1773), and those by Fray Servando Teresa de Mier all point in this direction. Nevertheless, breaking new ground, literarily speaking, was difficult in eighteenth-century Spanish America. The authorities of even a declining regime could still hurt one. Centuries of tight Spanish control had made literary innovation a daunting and sometimes dangerous prospect.

In Brazil, which was more loosely governed by Lisbon, the situation was different. There, we see more originality of expression and steady progress toward a cohesive and identifiable national literature, one that was increasingly both national and international in nature. Grafting classical forms onto intensely Brazilian themes and realities, the poets of the Escola Mineira were instrumental in this process. In Spanish America, the *crio-llos,* sensing Spain's ebbing power and influence over its colonies, were seeking more control over their lives and their societies (see Landers). Brazil saw its first stab at independence in 1789 with the Inconfidência Mineira, an inspired but ill-starred revolt led by its writers and intellectuals. Although its political leaders were restive and wanted the kind of democratic self-rule they saw in the United States, Brazil avoided the kind of internecine warfare that would tear Spanish America apart. In both Brazil and Spanish America, the examples of the United States and France and their respective revolutions loomed large. Eighteenth-century Latin America was thirsting for autonomy, in politics and in literary production. But while Brazil surged ahead, Spanish America faced particularly difficult political and literary challenges.

6   The Nineteenth Century

WITH THE arrival of the nineteenth century, inter-American relations really begin to heat up. Although we often associate the 1800s with burgeoning nationhood, in 1815 there were only two independent nations in the Americas, the United States and Haiti. Canada would have to wait until 1867 and Confederation to achieve independence. Indeed, in the case of Canada, "there was no Canadian *nation*" before 1867, when the Confederation Poets, Sir Charles G. D. Roberts, Bliss Carman ("a distant relation of Ralph Waldo Emerson"), Archibald Lampman, Duncan Campbell Scott, and Isabella Valancy, would seek to give it a national identity (New 25; see also Frye 826). Spanish America was on the verge of becoming independent, but it would have to fight a continent-wide war with Spain to gain it. Only then would Spanish American ports be open to world commerce and to the new ideas that would move it forward as a cluster of would-be democratic nations. Brazil, a constitutional monarchy, would gain its independence without bloodshed in 1822. Its diplomatic dance would involve parlaying its status as a separate new American republic, as a powerful Latin American nation, and as a possible ally to the United States into a unique hemispheric status.

Looking on from its still parlous position to the north, the United States began to view Latin America in much more serious, if complicated, terms. President Monroe and Secretary of State John Adams, however, were not interested in forming a vast, Pan-American union, not even with the United States at its head (Morison 412). But political realities were changing fast in the Americas. By late 1822 nearly all of the New World states were independent, and most were staunch believers in the idea of America being governed by a series of republics. But by 1823 a new, more hemispheric and more comprehensive concept of America began to emerge from the United States. "America, North and South," a then retired Thomas Jefferson would write, "has a set of interests distinct from those of Europe, and particularly her own" (quoted in Morison 413). With this change in position on the part of the United States, the stage was set for the declaration of the Monroe Doctrine, which took place on December 2, 1823. The United States was now officially in the inter-American game.

In Spanish America, literary independence went hand in hand with political independence. The one cannot be properly appreciated without the other. Just as new nations had to be created, so too did new national literatures. Doing so in a way that maintained a commonly held sense of hemispheric unity would be Bello's heroic task.

But the problem—political fragmentation—was daunting. The splintered landscape of Spanish America's postindependence period was also reflected in its cultural landscape. Spain had not prepared its American colonies to accommodate independence. The now separate nations of Spanish America knew very little about one another. The cultural differences between places like Mexico City, Tegucigalpa, Cuzco, and Buenos Aires were huge. In some cases, rivalries and animosities existed. Systems of communication, commerce, and exchange were sparse, uncertain, and poorly developed. Even roads connecting the newly independent Spanish American nations were few in number and poorly maintained. A desire for freedom and a common language aside, Spanish America possessed little sense of unity or commonality of purpose. A European import, Romanticism, would serve the nations of the Americas well. A constitutional monarchy, Brazil was an exception to this rule. It enjoyed a unity, both geographic and political, that its Spanish-speaking neighbors did not have. Yet, it too would benefit from the new thinking that Romanticism offered.

When, as Latin Americanists, we speak of this close connection between Romanticism, political independence, and cultural autonomy, we must remember that by 1830 this meant independence not only from Spain, as the United States had won its independence from England some fifty years earlier, but also from the local tyrants and *caudillos* who rushed into the political void created by the departure of the Spanish. The vision of a great union, or confederation, of the newly liberated Spanish American states simply could not be realized. Ironically, a hard-won independence prevented Spanish American political leaders from being able to work together in the formation of a new, more democratic alliance. Old grievances, real and perceived, made cooperation difficult. The dream of unity died, thwarted by the rise of such strongmen as Juan Manuel de Rosas.

Brazil's transition to political independence, achieved in 1822, was different. Never as tightly controlled by Portugal, which had from the beginning been more interested in its wealth-producing East Asian possessions than in its American colony, as Spanish America was by Spain, Brazil had slowly but steadily grown apart from its European progenitor. When Napoleon invaded the Iberian Peninsula in 1808, the royal family fled to Brazil, which, with their arrival, effectively became the center of the Portuguese-speaking world. And when Brazil officially became a kingdom in 1815, a "turn of events" that "has no equivalent in the history of Spanish America," the die was cast (González Echevarría, Pupo-Walker, and Haberly 3). Brazil was on the road to independence, and no blood would have to be spilled in finally attaining it; only the signing of a paper. In the Americas, only Canada would enjoy a similar experience.

Again in contrast to Spanish America, Brazil did not fall into internecine strife after independence. Because of this, it would not require a Bello to call for unity. Instead, it began to strengthen its already considerable internal ties and to develop as a progressively run constitutional monarchy. In this respect too Brazil differed from its Spanish-speaking American neighbors, all of which struggled, because of an almost total lack of preparation, to become functioning democracies. Toward the end of the century, Brazil would transition once again, this time converting itself, again bloodlessly, into a republic.

Latin America's struggle for political independence did not go unnoticed in the United States, which only a few years earlier had won its independence from England. The entire period from 1775 to 1825 can with reason be termed the age of revolution in America, North and South. As Caitlin Fitz has shown, in fact, many political leaders in the postrevolutionary United States followed events in Spanish America and Brazil with keen interest. Babies, as well as towns and counties, were being named in honor of Venezuela's Simón Bolívar, heralded as the George Washington of South America. Latin American independence was overwhelmingly regarded as a good thing, and in keeping with the founding norms and values of the United States itself. But there were complications. Religion was one, racially mixed societies was another, and of course the questions of slavery and Bolívar's abolition of it in Spanish America were always in the background.

Although by this period Puritanism's old fires of anti-Catholicism were largely banked, they were still there, as was the more toxic problem of racial prejudice. So while there was, in the United States of the early 1800s, an ardent desire to see a free and independent Latin America, and especially one that could be developed as a market for the products of US farms, plantations, and businesses, there was also a gnawing fear of becoming tainted by dealing with supposedly mongrelized and inferior people. Still, slavery could always be justified as long as it turned a profit. And as Caitlin Fitz shows, by 1826 slave-holding US southerners had decided that US support for Latin America had to end. In their thinking, Latin America, which was moving more and more Blacks and mulattos into positions of power, had become too radical and too Black. In large part, the doctrine of Manifest Destiny, an unstable admixture of religion and politics, was concocted in the United States in order to do two things: save Latin Americans from their subhuman and misguided condition and, in the process, transform them into more enlightened citizens and reliable consumers of US-produced goods and services.

Brazilian literature, in contrast to that of its more fraught Spanish American neighbors, followed the same path of smooth, organized development as its government. A relatively stable political history allowed Brazilian literature to evolve in a coherent, self-aware fashion. This would produce a national literary tradition upon which each new generation of writers could draw, while also responding to a constantly growing influx of new ideas from abroad. One of these was the idea of political liberty, which, in the case of Brazil, would follow, and not precede, political independence. Beginning with their *ufanista* enthusiasm and their burgeoning sense of *brasilidade*, Brazilian writers had early on nurtured a sense of national identity, of being Brazilian. By the time independence came in 1822, the Brazilians already knew who they were and what made their culture, and their literature, unique.

In Spanish America, held at first on a very short leash by Spain and then, after its wars for revolution, plagued by factionalism and division, it took writers longer to achieve this sense of national unity. Although he had called for it, Bello would be frustrated. Indeed, for the Chilean writer José Donoso a literarily unified Spanish America would not come to pass in a cohesive, continental sense until the mid-twentieth century (10). Up until then, writers, artists, and thinkers in Uruguay and Argentina knew little or nothing about what their counterparts in Colombia or Venezuela were doing, and those in the Caribbean and Central America had little contact with events in Mexico or Chile or Peru. What we think of today as Latin America was, in the early nineteenth century, a chessboard, a clutch of very different nations loosely connected by language, religion, and history. Because of this lack of unity, Spanish America was not, and indeed is not today, a single nation but an amalgam of quite distinctive nations and cultures; its long struggle for identity would have to be both individual and collective. We would have Mexican, Nicaraguan, Puerto Rican, Chilean, Colombian, or Argentinian literature, but especially here in the United States we would also speak of them as somehow constituting what we regard as Spanish American literature. The dangers of incorrect generalizations and mischaracterizations are many.

Brazil did not have this problem. In truth, from its colonial era on it was different. And it must always be understood this way. Although part of what we think of as Latin America, it is not, historically speaking, the same as the Latin America we imagine we know here in the United States. Its Portuguese heritage was different, and as we have seen, even colonial Brazil was receptive to foreign influences. It was much more difficult for Spanish America to benefit from this, restricted as it was by Spanish authorities who were deeply suspicious of what they viewed as contaminating forces from the outside. This position hurt the development of early Spanish American letters.

For the inter-Americanist, it is always interesting to compare and contrast the English heritage that the early Puritans and Separatists brought to their part of the New World with those brought by the Spanish and the Portuguese to theirs. Differences abound, as of course do similarities. From colonial Canada, for example, we have the figure of Henry Alline, who preached a more temperate version of Puritanism. The American experience, as played out by different groups in different parts of the hemisphere, varied dramatically. But it is, in truth, our collective American experience, and never forgetting our vast indigenous heritage, it belongs to all of us. This is why inter-American literature, with all its sundry tensions and interconnections, is so fascinating to study.

Yet by the third decade of the nineteenth century both Spanish America and Brazil would embrace the new ideas and forms of Romanticism. For Spanish America, the date most often cited is 1832, with *Elvira,* by the Argentine Esteban Echeverría, while in Brazil it is 1836, with *Suspiros poéticos e saudades,* by Gonçalves de Magalhães. Predictably, however, they would embrace Romanticism in different ways. For the Brazilians, the first stirrings of *Romantismo* had more to do with the Indian than with politics, as was the case in Spanish America. As Brazilian Romanticism reaches its end, however, it veered into the political sphere, while Spanish American Romanticism took up the importance of the Indian and such regional types as the *gaucho* (see Merquior 366–67). The *gaucho*'s presence in Latin American literature is more a function of Spanish America than of Brazil, whose own *gaúcho* tradition differs from its Spanish American counterpart. This is a project an enterprising Latin American comparatist could do much with. In Spanish America, however, the prototypical *gaucho* text is José Hernández's 1872 epic *Martín Fierro,* which endows this Argentine type with mythical status. Hugely popular in its time, *Martín Fierro* failed, curiously enough, to achieve its author's primary purpose, which was to achieve justice for the *gaucho,* a figure Hernández felt had been wrongly persecuted. On the other hand, the poem, notable for its authentic portrayal of *gaucho* life and its use of the *gaucho*'s language, transformed the *gaucho* into an immortal symbol of Argentine identity. Brazilian literature has no corresponding text. The question is, why?

While the main similarities between Romanticism in Spanish American and in Brazilian literature are clear—political independence, national identity, and the Indian, for example—it is worth asking what the essential differences are. One, as Merquior has pointed out, is that they begin and end in opposite places; another is that Brazilian *Romantismo* evolved into three very distinctive periods, each marked strongly by European, and especially French, trends; and third, the political aspect of Brazilian Romanticism relates less to issues of political independence (which it already had) and its chaotic aftermath (as in Spanish America) and more to the burning questions of abolition (achieved in 1888) and the formation of the republic, formally established the next year, in 1889.

To celebrate the peaceful formation of the Brazilian Republic, no less a figure than Walt Whitman penned a congratulatory poem. Entitled "Welcome, Brazilian Brother!," the poem expresses a sense of kinship between the two American countries, both of which Whitman paints as paragons of democratic self-rule. Singing the praises of Brazil's new status as another free American state, the US poet gushes that the United States extends to its giant southern neighbor "a loving Hand—a Smile from the North—A Sunny Instant Hail" (Lynn 13). "Ours, Ours, the Present Throe, the Democratic Aim," he burbles on, exuding an unmistakable ethos of hemispheric leadership and comradeship (quoted in Lynn 13). If this reading of Whitman's paean to Brazil is accurate, it underscores both Brazil's intention of becoming indispensable to the United States and the latter's embrace of this strategy.

While Spanish America gained its political independence between 1810 and 1825, Brazil remained a monarchy until 1889. Slavery, abolished in Spanish America (with the exception of Cuba), continued in Brazil until 1888, the year before it became a republic. In contrast to Spanish

America, where printing presses appeared early, Brazil did not allow them until the nineteenth century. This was an odd posture for the Portuguese Crown to take, since during the colonial period the Crown had been much freer about allowing its ports to be open to global traffic and ideas and much less strict than the Spanish about allowing novels to be read.

Castro Alves, "O Poeta dos Escravos" (The poet of the slaves) and the dominant figure in the third phase of Brazilian *Romantismo,* ranks as one of Brazil's greatest poets. A lyricist of exceptional talent as well as a socially committed writer, Alves was a prodigious talent. Some of the most powerful antislavery poetry in the Americas came from his pen. He did for the African slave what Dias and Alencar had done for the Brazilian Indian. "In a society based on slavery," writes Fábio Lucas, "Alves made the slave a hero" (80). Interestingly, he influenced abolitionists in New England as well (see Braga). In his still extraordinary poem "O navio negreiro," Alves used the slave ship as a metaphor for what was happening in Brazil itself. While all is calm and beautiful on the outside, it is grotesquely inhumane on the inside. Seen at a distance, even the slave ship, its white sails billowing in the wind, appears to be an object of beauty, a man-made thing in "doce harmonia" (sweet harmony) with the universe (Alves, *Major Abolitionist Poems* 10–11). But from close up and from the inside, it reveals itself to be a hellhole. The speaker of the poem compels us to look at and acknowledge the "quadro d'amarguras" (well of grief) before our eyes and to hear the screams of the slaves, who are crammed, inhumanely, into the ship's hold:

> Que funéreo cantar! . . . Que tétricas figuras! . . .
> Que cena infame e vil, meu Deus! meu Deus, que horror!
>
> (Listen to the death-songs, gaze into their deadened eyes! . . .
> This theater of evil . . . My God, My God, what horror!) (14–15)

The reader, not released from the agony of the slaves and the cruelty of their supposedly Christian masters, must endure more:

> Qual n'um sonho dantesco, as sombras vôam! . . .
> Gritos, ais, maldições, prreces resoam! . . .
> E ri-se Satanaz! . . .
>
> (As in a dream of Dante, the shades fly! . . .
> Screams, curses, prayers are lifted up! . . .
> And Satan laughs.) (16–17)

Then, invoking God himself, the poet demands justice:

> Senhor Deus dos desgraçados!
> Dizei-me vós, Senhor Deus!
> Se é mentira . . . se é verdade
> Tanto horror perante os céos?!

> (Lord God of the disgraced,
> Speak to me, Lord God!
> Is it a lie, is this your justice?!
> Can you allow such horror beneath your heavens?) (16–17)

But God does not respond, and the crime continues.

In "A Cachoeira de Paulo Afonso" (The Paulo Afonso Falls), Alves treats the two runaway slaves, Maria and Lucas, less as types than as complex characters. In Alves's hands, the slave comes alive as an individual rather than as a category apart or an abstraction. His protagonists are not wooden stereotypes. The reader responds to them sympathetically, but as human beings who risk everything to be free. This deep humanization of Maria and Lucas amounts to a singular achievement. It is also a major step forward in the portrayal of the Black experience in Latin American literature (see R. Jackson). In the Cuban antislavery novel, for example, the protagonist, usually male, is typically cast as the focus of a propagandistic narrative, one that serves the abolitionist cause but does not impress for its literary qualities. The shame of slavery is the focal point of these not infrequently melodramatic texts, and not their characters, as is the case in the Brazilian poem.

In this same context, it is worth noting that while Brazilian writers of color had already begun to assert themselves during the closing years of the eighteenth century, they would do so even more in the nineteenth. Three poets in particular stand out: Manuel Ignácio da Silva Alvarenga, whose *Glaura: Poemas eróticos* (1799) was widely hailed in both Portugal and Brazil; José da Natividade Saldanha, whose *Poesias oferecidas aos amantes do Brasil* (1822) show him to be an ardent republican; and Domingos Caldas Barbosa, who was acutely conscious of being a Black writer and whose prolific use of Indian and African words and phrases alongside traditional Neoclassical allusions made him one of Brazil's most powerful and most original voices of the time. In Brazil, Black writing has become not merely a reality but a core reality, an identifying characteristic of Brazilian literature.

Brazilian-Based Inter-Americanism

In the fifty-year period from 1876 (when one of the versions of *O guesa* appeared) to 1926 (when Ronald de Carvalho's *Toda a América* was published), Brazil produced a number of writers and thinkers with a distinctively hemispheric and inclusive approach to American literature. One of these was Mathias Carvalho, whose *Poemas americanos I: Riel* (1886) was discovered by two Canadian scholars, Jean Morisset and Alberto Braz. In the 1960s, Carvalho began to be promoted in Brazil by a number of Brazilian critics, including possibly the influential de Campos brothers, Haroldo and Augusto (see Morisset "La coquête du Nord-Ouest," *L'identité usurpée 1,* and "Louis Riel"; see also Perrone and Infante). Original to the point of being idiosyncratic, *Poemas americanos* features not only indigenous America, Brazil, the United States, and Spanish America but also Canada. It is an extraordinary piece of American writing. The "only known South American work on the subject, . . . Carvalho's poem is simultaneously a republican manifesto, an anti-English diatribe, and a paean to pan-American solidarity" (Braz, *False Traitor* 76; see also Braz, "Promised Land"). Carvalho, a Brazilian, casts the mixed-blood Canadian Louis Riel as both a national leader and "a New World liberator," an American liberator in the company of Benito Juarez of Mexico, the Brazilian Tiradentes, and "the U.S. abolitionist John Brown" (Braz, *False Traitor* 76, 77).

Carvalho's poem, featuring the still controversial Canadian Métis leader Riel, nevertheless is set against the backdrop of the US Civil War (1861–65). For the US slaves, over whose status the war is being fought, Canada initially represents freedom. It lives in the poem as a dream, a vision of a better future. But as the Brazilian poet reminds us, this cannot be, because in his view Canada itself is an oppressed state, one where freedom does not dwell. And the oppressor, England, is yet another Old World nation, one whose power over a sister American nation must be once again thrown off. For Carvalho, Canada must free itself from English rule, as the United States, Spanish America, and Brazil have already done. A hemisphere of free, self-governing, and cooperating nation states is Carvalho's grand vision for America.

Riel's inter-Americanism cuts both North and South. Like the Puritans, Riel came to believe, particularly after 1875 and a period of time spent in Washington, DC, that he and his people, "le peuple Métis," were "the new Israelites," and the "chosen people" (Braz, *False Traitor* 31, 30). Riel was convinced of this because for him "les sauvages de L'Amérique du Nord sont Juifs et du plus pur sang d'Abraham" (The savages of North America are Jews and of the purest blood of Abraham), a position not uncommonly held during the nineteenth century (31). And again like the Puritans, Riel believed that he and his people were destined by God to play a "providential role" in the Americas (30).

But like the Latin Americans, Riel also believed in the future of America as a mixed-race hemisphere, one blessed because of its "sang sauvage" (31). After experiencing a kind of spiritual epiphany in a Washington, DC, church, Riel envisioned the Métis, some of whom lived in Montana as well, as "a new people," a people of mixed blood who would one day rise up in the Americas and of whom he would be their New World prophet (30). This line of thought about the future of mixed-race people in the Americas puts Riel in the company of such like-minded American thinkers as José Vasconcelos, of Mexico, whose theory of a future *raza cósmica* posits exactly this, and both Gilberto Freyre and Darcy Ribeiro of Brazil. While Riel's vision of America's racial future is comparable to that of many in Spanish America and Brazil, his self-importance in it is less so.

Rodríguez Monegal argues that a unified, integrated, and continental Spanish American literature did not exist until the late nineteenth century, when the intercommunication that characterized *Modernismo* as a multi-voiced and continental movement demanded it. While the earlier political independence had set the several Spanish American republics moving in this direction, they would not achieve their goal of establishing a single, cohesive Spanish American literature until Rubén Darío and the group of writers from throughout Mexico and South America that surrounded him finally did so (for Rodríguez Monegal, Andrés Bello was the key figure in this early impetus toward a new and unified Spanish American literature, and the *modernistas* are its fruition [*Borzoi Anthology* 1:337]).

On this point, González Echevarría demurs, arguing that this "pro-cess" of literary consolidation had "begun at least forty years before" ("Brief History" 19). Bello, however, remains the key figure. A kind of Spanish American Franklin (though tending toward the intellectual rather than the practical), Andrés Bello stands as a pivotal figure in American literature during the first half of the nineteenth century. Merquior is of a similar mind. Comparing Brazil to Spanish America, he also finds that "in Brazil, the whole period stretching from 1800 to 1840 was dominated by publicists of neoclassical-cum-Enlightenment upbringing, the background also shared by the Minas Gerais poets and by Bello" (365). Can Brazil boast a Bello? I think not. But while there may not be a single figure like Bello, can we argue that through its earlier *brasilidade* movement and the work of the later Escola Mineira poets, Brazil developed a uniquely Brazilian literature before Spanish America did, indeed, that it *existed* by the eighteenth century and, more loosely, perhaps even earlier, in the colonial period? I think so.

Although the fact is not widely appreciated, science played an important role in the development of nineteenth-century Latin America. In the view of González Echevarría, the Brazilian Euclides da Cunha, author of *Os Sertões* (1902), "reflects Brazil's commitment to science in the nineteenth century, which for various reasons outstripped that of the rest of Latin America" ("Lost World Re-Discovered" 128). "From early on," González Echevarría continues, "Brazil established institutions for the promotion of scientific research and exploration" (129; see also Stepan 26–27). In contrast to Spanish America, which suffered wrenching and, in the end, isolating wars for independence, Brazil remained a constitutional monarchy until 1889. As a result, it benefitted educationally from the strong ties it maintained with several European cultures, including France, England, and Germany. Engineering, which da Cunha had studied, became central to the system of Brazilian higher education. It was no accident that French Positivism was more ardently embraced in Brazil than in any other Latin American nation. Only Mexico rivaled Brazil in this.

In Canadian letters from the first half of the nineteenth century, the work of two sisters, Susanna Moodie and Catharine Park Traill, stands out. Moodie's *Roughing It in the Bush,* published in 1852 but set in 1830s Canada, can be read as nonfiction or as "a coherent quasi-novel" (New 56; see also 69). In terms of outlook, New links Moodie to Harriet Beecher Stowe and Margaret Fuller (55). Although Frances Brooke ranks as "Canada's first novelist,"[1] the "first English-language novel by a native-born [Canadian] writer was a melodramatic account of shipwreck and seigneurial Quebec entitled *St. Ursula's Convent* (1824), Fredericton's Julia Catherine Beckwith" (New 57, 74). Forty-nine years later, "*Les anciens Canadiens* (1873), by Philippe Aubert de Gaspé *(pére),* . . . told the story of a French (Canadian) noble and a Scots noble, whose friendship is disrupted when they find themselves on opposite sides in the Seven Years War. . . . His short-lived son and namesake (1814–41) had written the first French-language Canadian novel, *L'influence d'un livre,*" several years earlier, in 1837 (New 75).

In the United States, the novel form began with William Hill Brown's tedious and melodramatic *Power of Sympathy* (1789) and Susannah Rowson's very popular *Charlotte Temple* (1790). In Brazil, where, as in French-Canada, the novel developed rather late, the honor of being the first novel is usually accorded to Macedo's *A moreninha* (The little brunette), which appeared in 1844. *Sab* (1841), by Gertrudis Gómez de Avellaneda, and *Francisco* (published in 1880 in New York), by Anselmo Suárez y Romero, "were the first anti-slavery novels in America, for they preceded Harriet Beecher Stowe's *Uncle Tom's Cabin* (1852)" (Benítez-Rojo 444). With its additional concern with "women's lack of freedom" and with the alienation its author must have felt at being a woman writer "in a misogynist society," *Sab* stands out for being unique among other Cuban abolitionist novels of the period (Schlau 495; see also Schulman 363). New World works that reflect on slavery, the status of women, class, and marriage as an institution include *Sab* (1841), *Uncle Tom's Cabin* (1852), Castro Alves's abolitionist poetry, Alencar's *Senhora* (1875), and Henry James's *Portrait of a Lady* (1881). For the US-based Americanist, James's novel makes for an interesting reading in the company of *Senhora, Sab, The Posthumous Memoirs of Brás Cubas* (1880), and *Les anciens Canadiens* (1863). An even more intriguing comparison, and one that merits more attention, would involve *The Posthumous Memoirs of Brás Cubas* and *Huckleberry Finn* (1885).

Scholars concerned with the James–Machado de Assis comparison, however, have long looked at their respective experiments with point of view. Whereas Machado probed the possible uses of the unreliable self-conscious narrator-protagonist, James is famous for his use, especially in *Portrait of a Lady,* of the third-person limited perspective. When, late in the novel, the reader moves from viewing Isabel Archer from the outside to viewing her from the inside, when we see things as she sees them, the effect is dramatic. This shift prepares the reader for the novel's uncertain conclusion, where, as with Machado, ambiguity reigns. While James's reader wonders whether she should regard Isabel's now fully perceived situation as optimistic or pessimistic, Machado's reader wonders whether she should laugh or cry—less because of Brás Cubas's situation (he, after all, was dead and could not care less) than because of the human condition. More importantly, Isabel, who has struggled mightily throughout the novel to be "free," finds herself returning to a loveless marriage as a captive (albeit one in a gilded cage). Machado's narrator-protagonist, the deceased Brás Cubas, sees himself as completely free—free enough, in fact, to reveal himself (inadvertently, one feels) to the reader for what he really is, an egotistical and uncaring elitist. If, for James, the tragedy (if it truly is a tragedy) of Isabel is that of an individual, whereas for Machado it is collective, having to do with the selfish nature of the human creature. A final though crucial difference between these two great American novels is that while Machado's bubbles with eroticism, both male and female, James's seems stunted, or repressed, in this regard. Given the changes he made in other editions concerning Isabel's burgeoning self-awareness at the end, it appears that James was not uninterested in the idea of her embracing new levels of sexual desire, which Machado does, easily and naturally, with his characters. Isabel and Virgília, Brás's married lover and a character who, if anything, is tougher, stronger, and even more selfish than he is, are polar opposites. It is with Virgília that the American woman reaches a hitherto unseen level of agency. As should be clear from even this cursory glance, a focus on the nineteenth-century American novel can make for a most interesting course (see E. Fitz, "First Inter-American Novels").

An Indianist novel that takes place during Pontiac's Rebellion and features both real Indians and Europeans pretending to be Indians, is *Wacousta* (1832), by Canada's Major John Richardson. Despite all its wooden dialogue, its melodrama, and its rather contrived plot, which involves the Old World as well as the New, *Wacousta* continues to capture the interest of readers (see New 77). For American readers bred on the Indianism of Longfellow, Cooper, Alencar, Mera, and Zorrilla, *Wacousta* offers a different take on the inherent conflict between the First Peoples and the Europeans. In this same vein, Canada also gives us Charles Mair's long verse-drama *Tecumseh* (1886), which, focusing on the War of 1812, celebrates the great Native American leader of the same name while also criticizing US American policy and cultural practices. *Tecumseh* is lauded as an exemplar of the man who sacrifices his own welfare for that of his people, while US Americans are savaged for their selfishness.

In 1823 the US president, James Monroe, laid out the Monroe Doctrine, which sought to curtail European intrusions into New World, or American, affairs. Alone among the Latin American nations, Brazil accepted the doctrine, seeing in it an opportunity to establish itself as the leader of Latin America and to secure a closer working relationship with the United States, an emerging power. Spanish America, fearing US interference in its own affairs, rejected it (see Herring; and Burns, *Latin America*). Already in the second decade of the nineteenth century, Brazil, looking to its future as an American power, was realigning its status with respect to both the United States and Spanish America. For the comparative Latin Americanist and the hemispheric Americanist, what we have here is more evidence of the dark side of inter-Americanism: imperialism, whose legacy haunts inter-American study even today.

In the United States, literature began to establish itself during the first few decades of the nineteenth century. Centered in New York, the writers of the Knickerbocker Group—Charles Brockden Brown, Washington Irving, James Fenimore Cooper, and William Cullen Bryant—made creative writing in the United States a viable professional activity. Two of them, Irving and Bryant, had an interest in Spanish-language literature, with Irving having written romantically about Moorish Spain and Bryant having popularized Heredia's "Niágara" by translating it to English. Spanish was beginning to gain a foothold in English America, as were Spanish America and Brazil (see E. Fitz, "Nineteenth Century").

In midcentury, Walt Whitman produced *The Leaves of Grass* (1855), a collection of poems destined to become influential throughout the Americas. For comparative Americanists, and for comparative Latin Americanists in particular, this landmark text was of particular importance. It called for a new, more inclusive sense of what America meant, something Latin American writers and artists had been cultivating for a long time. For Spanish Americans and Brazilians, Whitman's great work seemed to recognize their place in the Americas while also suggesting that the United States might now accept them as Americans too. And as equals. In Spanish America especially, it would influence a number of writers, most notably Neruda, but many others as well. Whitman's grandly affirmative vision of America was like catnip to them. If you were a citizen or a resident of the United States, you would of course read *The Leaves of Grass* as yours, a salute to your America and its democracy. Yet while Whitman unquestionably had the United States in mind when he wrote the poem, might he also have been thinking of the entire American hemisphere, a place where the many blades of grass (the many nations) might achieve a vast intercontinental democracy, a place where the democratic spirit not only lived but thrived? Latin Americans certainly did. In short, could an inter-Americanist read *Leaves of Grass* as a continuation of the old trope of the America as Utopia? It is tantalizing to think so. But is there, even in Whitman, a note of hegemony, of superiority, of dominance? A close reading of the poems suggests that there might be. Does Whitman extend to the rest of the Americas the same sense of equality and generosity of spirit he lavishes on the people and cultures of the United States?

Literary Trends in Latin America: Romanticism in Spanish America (1832–1888) and Brazil (1836–1881)

Romanticism in Spanish America is often subdivided into two movements, one running from about 1830 to 1860, the other from about 1860 to 1880 (Chang-Rodríguez and Filer 107). Anderson Imbert and Florit see it as dividing into two different groups as well, the first comprising texts written before 1850, the second, texts written after 1850 (217). Jorge Isaacs's *María*, the great exemplar of the Romantic novel in Spanish America, belongs to this second group, as it was published in 1867. Still regarded as "la mejor novela idílica de su tiempo," *María* was a "precursor of . . . twentieth-century negrista narrative" (Anderson Imbert and Florit 369; Kutzinski, "Afro-Hispanic American Literature" 184). Reading *María* through a comparative lens makes one think of Taunay's *Inocência* (1872), which in Brazil is regarded as a transition text between *Romantismo* and *Realismo*. Like *María, Inocência* is at least in part a love idyll; it features similarly lovely descriptions of Brazil's flora and fauna (of the *sertão*, however, rather than of Colombia's lush Cauca valley), and, though the circumstances are different, both María and Inocência die in the end. While Isaacs's novel casts María's death in the most exquisitely romantic terms, Taunay implies that Inocência's untimely demise is more a factor of rigid patriarchal thinking.

Brazilian Romanticism had a different historical development, one that traditionally is seen as subdividing into three very distinct phases: the first (1836–53) featured Indianism and the poetry of Gonçalves de Magalhães and Gonçalves Dias, the first Brazilian novel, and the theater of Martins Pena; the second (1853–70) was characterized by an ardent embrace of Byronism by Álvares de Azevedo and others in poetry and the work of Manuel Antônio de Almeida in prose fiction; and the final phase gained a special urgency with the abolitionist poetry of Castro Alves (see Moisés, *A literatura brasileira* 117; see also Lucas 70–71).

For Merquior, Brazilian Romanticism began with Indianism but ended with politics, whereas Spanish American Romanticism had exactly the opposite history, beginning in politics and ending with Indianism (366–67). In assessing Brazilian Romanticism, it is possible to think that its Indianism was more strategic, systematic, and influential, especially with regard to nation building, than it was anywhere else in the Americas. As Brotherston and Sá point out, "Recognition of the native palimpsest was there already before Independence and certainly was an ingredient in the Americanism that typified above all the literature of Brazil in the nineteenth century" (15).

In the context of comparative Latin American literary history, it is useful to examine Spanish American Romanticism in terms of its beginning, its middle, and its end. The traditional starting date for Romanticism in Spanish America is 1832, with *Elvira, la novia del Plata,* by Esteban

Echeverría. In Brazil, it is typically given as 1836, with the appearance of *Suspiros poéticos e saudades,* by the abovementioned Magalhães. A close reading of *Elvira* against *Suspiros poéticos* reveals several interesting things. Affective though also imitative and derivative, Echeverría's poem is a deliberate attempt to plant European Romanticism in Spanish American, and specifically Argentine, soil. Its author had spent the years 1825 to 1830 in Paris, studying not only the French Romantics but also the Germans Schiller (a major influence) and Herder as well as the English Romantics. Byron and Scott were especially influential. The result is a text that strikes the reader as being less Argentine, or Spanish American, than European. The reception of *Elvira* was underwhelming. Part of the problem was that Echeverría simply did not have a talent for poetry. Enrique Anderson Imbert summed this up rather succinctly when he wrote that "Echeverría no tenía ni vocación ni genio para la poesía" (226). Rodríguez Monegal would dismiss *Elvira* even more tartly, declaring it "a collection of bad romantic verse" (*Borzoi Anthology* 1:172). Echeverría would have more success a few years later with the narrative poem *La cautiva* (1837) and with his prose work, notably *El matadero* (1838?). Spanish American *Romanticismo* does not get off to a dazzling start.

Brazilian *Romantismo* would fare a bit better. Like the poems of *Elvira,* those of *Suspiros poéticos* announce a new kind of writing. Magalhães, like Echeverría, had studied in Paris and was steeped in the issues of the time. The difference between the verse of *Elvira* and that of the Brazilian is that while they are uneven, the poems of *Suspiros poéticos* do score some successes, notably "Napoleão em Waterloo." As a harbinger of Romanticism, the poetry of Magalhães tends, on balance, to be a little better than that of *Elvira,* which, though thematically powerful, lacks the technical skill that would make it good poetry.

The best poem in the collection, "Napoleão em Waterloo" recounts in grandiloquent and sonorous fashion the story of the battle and of Napoleon's defeat, but it does so in such a way that it makes the reader, and especially the Brazilian reader, feel the pain of liberty lost. Indeed, freedom from the rule of kings and queens is the poem's main subject, and so it is easy to see why it would appeal so powerfully to Brazilian readers. In Brazil as in Europe, there was a desire to throw off the yoke of monarchs and to embrace democratic self-rule. And while Brazil (a constitutional monarchy) would not require a Napoleon to free it, the value of the French leader's symbolism to the Brazilians was immense. The poem is quite successful in developing this symbolic value and in linking it to the Brazilian situation. "Napoleão em Waterloo" thus reveals itself, as do several of the other poems in *Suspiros poéticos,* to be more Brazilian than the poems of *Elvira,* in which Argentina at times seems more of an afterthought.

The Brazilian novel came into being during this first period of *Romantismo* with Manuel de Macedo's *A moreninha* in 1844. Several other narratives also vie for the honor of being Brazil's first novel. The one with the least viable case is the heavily allegorical narrative *História do predestinado peregrino e seu irmão precito* (1682), by the Jesuit Alexandre de Gusmão, which Tolman considers "the first of its kind in the Americas" (3). We also have Nuno Marques Pereira's moralistic *Peregrino da América* (1728), which, like many later Brazilian texts (e.g., *Grande sertão: Veredas*), employs a local, Brazilian setting to discuss universal questions, here the nature of humankind and humans' many weaknesses.

A much stronger and more interesting contender is Teresa Margarida da Silva e Orta's still didactic but less ponderous *As aventuras de Diófanes* (1752). Showing the progressive influence of Fénelon, this is a narrative that gains advocates every year, especially as a novel of ideas (see Daniel, "Brazilian Fiction from 1800 to 1855" 127). For modern readers, of special interest in Silva e Orta's text are its surprisingly progressive positions on the place of women in society (see Versiani 23–26). Excluding *A moreninha,* which has not been dislodged from its prestigious position in Brazilian literary history, the title most bandied about is Teixeira e Sousa's "lachrymosely sentimental" *O filho do pescador,* of 1843 (Putnam 139). *A moreninha* is considerably better and merits its somewhat shaky status as Brazil's first official novel. Full of lively dialogue and featuring at least one interesting character, the "little brunette" of the title, and soon to be a popular Brazilian type, the quick-witted and resourceful *moleque,* or slave boy, *A moreninha* has its moments. The chapter featuring a disquisition on hemorrhoids (Macedo was a physician) still gets one's attention, as does the much more significant case that runs through the entire text in favor of more and better education for women. The text references Mary Wollstonecraft's *Vindication of the Rights of Woman,* which was then circulating in Brazil thanks to a translation by the Brazilian writer Dionísia Gonçalves, better known as Nísia Floresta, the author of several "positivistic and abolitionist essays" but also of two influential novels, *Daciz, ou A jovem completa* and *A lágrima de um Caeté* (Daniel, "Brazilian Fiction from 1800 to 1855" 134–35).

Owing perhaps to its more tumultuous political history, Spanish American Romanticism appears more consistently *engagé* than that of Brazil, which, though also politically aware, especially toward the end, also shows more diversity of theme and development. The intense political impetus that drove the early years of Spanish American *Romanticismo* continued on into the middle years of its development. We see this same concern with justice and the same ringing objections to oppression in virtually all major Spanish American writers of the time, including such figures as Gabriel de la Concepción Valdés ("El Plácido"), Gertrudis Gómez de Avellaneda, José Eusebio Caro, Rafael Pombo (who translated Bryant and Longfellow), Olegario Victor Andrade (who evokes comparisons with Whitman and Longfellow, a major influence on him), and Juan Antonio Pérez Bonalde (who, like Caro and others, found himself a political exile in the United States and who, interested in the literature of the United States as were so many of his compatriots, translated Poe into Spanish). Prominent among this midway group is the prolific and multifaceted Domingo Faustino Sarmiento, whose masterwork, *Facundo, o civilización y barbarie* (1845), explains the several factors, social and historical as well as geographic, that led to the rise of one of Rosas's most brutal henchmen.

The middle period of Brazilian *Romantismo* offers something very different. The figure of Álvares de Azevedo is unique in Latin American Romanticism. A super-Romantic, in the mode of Byron and Musset, Azevedo was, for all his excesses, something of a child prodigy. For Fábio Lucas, he was Brazilian Romanticism's "most perfect writer of sonnets,"[2] and he was master at merging the morbid with the erotic (74). An assiduous cultivator of the tormented *I* associated with Romantic poetry of this sort, Azevedo does not appeal to everyone, least of all to those seeking a political aspect to the writing. Arguing that for the Spanish American Romantics literature was "a form of public service," Henríquez-Ureña contends that "only in Brazil do we find, toward the middle of the century, an epidemic of *mal du siècle*" individualism (127, 128). In a rare moment of pique, the esteemed Dominican critic further contends that what he describes as the "infection" of Azevedo by Byron's later, self-centered poetry (not his earlier, political poetry) spread to other Brazilian writers, including Laurindo Rabelo, Junqueira Freire, and Fagundes Varela (128). For Moisés, Azevedo was Brazil's "poeta 'maldito,' cultivando as flores do tédio, no mesmo clima rarefeito de Baudelaire . . . numa fluência expressiva de base sensual" (*A literatura brasileira* 164–65; *poète maudit,* cultivating the flowers of tedium, in the same rarefied atmosphere as Baudelaire . . . in the expressive fluency of a sensual base).

During this second stage of Brazilian *Romantismo,* the novel began a time of dramatic improvement. Five titles stand out: José de Alencar's two Indianist novels, *O Guarani* (1857) and *Iracema* (1865), Manuel Antônio de Almeida's *Memórias de um sargento de milícias* (*Memoirs of a Militia Sargeant;* serialized 1852–53, book 1854–55), Maria Firmina dos Reis's *Úrsula* (1859), and Bernardo Guimarães's *A escrava Isaura* (1875). For many a Brazilian abolitionist novel, *A escrava Isaura* has often been compared to Harriet Beecher Stowe's *Uncle Tom's Cabin* (1852). Haberly sees it differently, however, and questions whether it is really an abolitionist novel at all. For Haberly, *A escrava Isaura* is less an abolitionist novel than it is "an utterly unrealistic Indianist novel in which the Noble Savage . . . happens to have African genes" ("Brazilian Novel" 146). But whether *A escrava Isaura* actually spurred on the cause of abolition in Brazil, as Stowe's novel did in the United States, it does offer up a serious condemnation of slavery. A reflection of its time, and of all those stylistic qualities that make Romantic prose fiction what it is, Guimarães's narrative does give the reader a surprisingly realistic portrayal of *sertão* and the people who live there. Stylistically, it can at times plod, but thematically *A escrava Isaura* brings to the surface a number of deeply American issues, including questions of race, class, gender, and sexual identity, that startle the reader. In this context, a more interesting comparison with a US text pairs it with Nella Larsen's *Passing* (1929), a novel in which Brazil is invoked as a place having more relaxed attitudes about race and sexuality. Like the main female characters in *Passing,* Isaura is light skinned and able to "pass" in white society, though she, like Larsen's creations, has reservations about doing so. While these are never explored as deeply by Guimarães, they are there, as is the question of sexual desire, both male and female. Allowing for differences of time and place, and for the fact that *Passing* is a superior piece of work, there are several points of comparison with *A escrava Isaura.*

Also an abolitionist novel, and one that is only now getting the attention it deserves, is Reis's *Úrsula.* "In Brazil," writes Cristina Pinto-Bailey, "Reis is one of the very first female novelists," and while her singular 1859 narrative "is not the first novel by a Black Brazilian writer, it is the work that truly initiates an Afro-Brazilian literature." *Úrsula,* moreover, can claim a place of honor in the pantheon of American literature as well. It appeared in the same year as Harriet Wilson's *Our Nig: Sketches from the Life of a Free Black,* which has long been regarded, along with Hannah Craft's *The Bondwoman's Narrative,* as one of the first two novels written in English by an African American woman (Pinto-Bailey xii–xiii).

Another Latin American text, this time from Cuba and Spanish America, that merits comparative study with both *A escrava Isaura* and *Passing* is Cirilo Villaverde's *Cecília Valdés* (1839). Here too we have the light-skinned mulatto woman who "passes" in white society. The plot, involving seduction, betrayal, and death, is both Romantic and conventional in nature. Villaverde condemns the inherent racism and injustice of a society that judges people by the color of their skin and not by their qualities as human beings. *Cecília Valdés,* appearing twenty years earlier than its Brazilian counterpart, would appear to offer several interesting points of comparison with Reis's *Úrsula,* as well as with *A escrava Isaura.*

In the latter years of Latin American Romanticism, we see the Spanish Americans turning to their indigenous past for inspiration, while the Brazilians, moving closer to the establishment of their long-anticipated republic, were embracing political themes, especially abolition, with a new passion. In the Americas, Romanticism involved a great many cases of reception and influence. Cooper, Whitman, and Poe were important for Latin Americans, while writers and political leaders like Heredia, Bolívar, Miranda, and Sarmiento were influential in the United States. The main sources for US Romanticism were England and, to a lesser degree, Germany; in Latin America the primary fount was France. In English Canada especially, the desire to create a unified Canada began in earnest after Confederation in 1867. It was in this politically charged context, the creation of a Canadian nation, that the Confederation Poets made their most important contributions. "Politically," notes Tapscott, "Romanticism [in Latin America] lost its early Pan-American grandeur. The early Romantics' optimism about the United States as a potential political ally and as a model of the virtues of enlightened utilitarianism faded in the glare of realpolitik" (223).

Linking Indianism, which had been a staple of the nationalist cause and a potent force in Brazil, to inter-Americanism, Machado de Assis in 1873 published one of his most important critical essays, "The Instinct of Nationality." In this study, which was published not in Rio de Janeiro, as it easily could have been, but in New York City, Machado takes up two separate but interrelated topics, nationalism in literary expression and how the features that guide and define it might be applicable as well to the greater human condition. The first, easier question, how a writer of nationalistic literature presents her homeland, allows Machado to consider

Brazilian literature in a wider, global context. The editor and publisher of the journal in which Machado's piece would appear, O *Mundo Novo* (The New World), was dedicated to promoting closer relations between the United States and Brazil and, more generally, to promoting Brazil's place in the Americas. This was an opportunity to expand awareness of Brazilian literature, and Machado would not pass it up.

The second, less obvious topic Machado discusses, then, is how Brazilian writers might take their rightful place in the pantheon of American literature. His own collection of poems, *Americanas,* appearing two years later, in 1875, was Indianist in nature and shows his understanding of how fundamental Native American culture was to the hemispheric American and human experience. After commenting on the excellence of other Indianist texts, including Longfellow's *Song of Hiawatha* (1855) and *Os Timbiras* (The Timbiras) (1857), the latter an epic poem by Gonçalves Dias built, quite inventively, around Brazilian Indian culture, Machado avers that instead of only pursuing examples of *cor local* (local color) and other such narrowly and exclusively nationalistic motifs, we should also be cultivating the many themes, forms, and issues that bind us together, here in the Americas and, by extension, globally as well (*Obra Completa* 3:804). In this 1873 essay, published in a New York City–based journal, which the journal's publisher, José Carlos Rodrigues, wanted to translate into English and disseminate more widely to his English-speaking audience, Machado calls for American writers to explore topics that are both national and international in significance (Brune 61–62). Machado wanted Brazilian writers "to look beyond the specific" and the narrowly nationalistic "to find inspiration in shared experiences of the Americas" (63). Although it exists here in inchoate form, Machado's vision clearly reflects a comparative and systematically inter-American perspective. Imbued with both a national and an international perspective, and interested "in defining American writing," he eschews isolation and embraces comparatism, first in the Americas and then more broadly internationally (K. Jackson, *Machado de Assis* 12). Taking this position in 1873, Machado prefigured the two driving forces, nationalism and internationalism, behind the advent of Brazilian *Modernismo,* which flowered some fifty-five years later.

An outstanding Spanish American text from this late nineteenth century is Juan Zorrilla de San Martín's *Tabaré* (1886). More lyrical than heroic and more elegiac than epic, *Tabaré* is based on real events, the struggle that took place in colonial Uruguay between the fierce and proud Charrúas and the conquering Spanish. Rather than martial in nature,

however, *Tabaré* is haunted by the ghosts of a past lost forever to the win-
ners. There is a sadness to it that makes the Latin American comparatist
think of Alencar's Indianist novel, or *poème en prose*, *Iracema*, though
without the affirming nod to the future that marks the Brazilian text. The
protagonist of *Tabaré*, moreover, is a mestizo, the product of the two
heritages, the indigenous and the Christian, that will fight to the death
for control of this corner of America. However, as he is the offspring of
a Charrúa chief and a white woman, "una cautiva Española," the common trope of the rape of America by the European conqueror is reversed
(Anderson Imbert and Florit 394).

Iracema can be regarded as a pivotal text for other reasons as well,
including its function as a force in Brazilian nation building. In his triadic
comparative study of Washington Irving, the Mexican writer Justo Sierra,
and the Brazilian Alencar and how these different American writers make
use of the legend, Haberly concludes that this particular form, the legend,
was of particular importance to American nations seeking to create themselves. "During the course of the nineteenth century," he writes, "writers
throughout the Americas faced a common task: to re-create or create a
national past, and to use that past as a means to understand the present" ("Form and Function" 42). The raw material for this very American
project was, precisely, Americans' Amerindian heritage. Other Indianist
narratives include Eligio Ancona's *La cruz y la espada* (1866), set in Mexico's Yucatán Peninsula; Juan León de Mera's *Cumandá* (1871), which
may have been influenced by both Chateaubriand and James Fenimore
Cooper; and Manuel de Jesús Galván's *Enriquillo* (1882), which takes
place in the time of Bartolomé de las Casas, who has a role in the novel.

The essay too was assiduously cultivated during this period. A confirmed Romantic but also a pragmatic realist, Ecuador's Juan Montalvo
was also possessed of an inter-American vision. In his celebrated *Siete
tratados* (Seven treatises), of 1882, Montalvo makes his famous and perceptive comparison of Washington and Bolívar. He finds both leaders
committed to the independence of their respective American peoples, and
he concludes that both were successful in winning it. Further, he finds that
both Washington and Bolívar had a grand vision for their nations and
for America. The differences, Montalvo observes, are, however, telling:
While Washington was surrounded by leaders like Franklin, Jefferson,
and Madison, Bolívar had to deal with quarrelsome (albeit able) subordi-
nates, men out for personal gain and not committed to independence. As
a result, Washington and his cohorts were able to form a great republic,

while Bolívar's vision of a great, unified America soon fell apart, largely because the various people who would compose it had not benefitted from the many social, political, and economic institutions that would have made a confederation of self-governing democracies possible. Spanish America had the desire for democratic self-government and the talent to make it work, but it lacked the necessary internal systems, education, a sense of unity, a belief in civic responsibility, transportation, and so forth, to do so. The idea was good, but the preparation was not.

By midcentury, Latin Americanists were very much aware of the acquisitive interest their neighbor to the north was showing in them. And it was causing them concern. In the 1850s, for example, a prominent US American, Matthew Fontaine Maury, was keenly interested in taking control of the vast Amazon region in order to secure a steady rubber supply for a rapidly expanding United States and its growing industries. An "ardent advocate of slavery," Maury believed that if the slaveholding South were to lose a seemingly inevitable civil war, an outcome he judged to be likely, southern sympathizers might flee the United States, settle in Brazil, and simply "annex the Amazon basin" (Mann, *1493* 260). The entire Amazon basin, he argued, should be preemptively turned into "the biggest U.S. slave state" (261). Many thousands of defeated southerners did decamp to Brazil after the Civil War, and though most returned almost immediately to the United States, some stayed and tried to set up a new slave-owning society in the middle of the Amazon rainforest. Even today, their descendants celebrate, in Brazilian Portuguese, what they regard as their southern US heritage. While Maury's scheme did not greatly inconvenience Brazil or its Spanish-speaking neighbors, later US forays into Latin America would have very different, more deleterious consequences.

Arguably the most unique American poet of the nineteenth century, and an early practitioner of inter-Americanism, the Brazilian Joaquim de Sousa Andrade was an inveterate traveler and a restless, freethinking intellectual. Known today in Brazil as Sousândrade, he had a vision of the Americas as a coherent whole but also as clusters of individual players on the global stage. He was an American original. Renowned principally as the author of two long poems, *O guesa errante: Poema americano* (1876) and *O guesa* (1888?), Sousândrade is proof that Latin Americans have long been interested not merely in the United States but in the Americas, in the concept of America as a collective, interconnected whole. An epic poem of thirteen cantos, four of which were never completed,

O guesa sings of the greater American experience, from pre-Columbian times to the final decades of the nineteenth century. The poem exudes not only "a fundamental Americanism" but an integrated, functioning globalism, yet one in which the vitality of the New World shines through (Perrone 107). But the genesis, the taproot, of our hemispheric Americanism is Latin America, Spanish America *and* Brazil. Deftly, but often with a roughness and energy that recalls Whitman, Sousândrade blends a formally disruptive structure with neologisms, mythology, and "a certain imagistic objectivity" into a paean to greater America and to its ancient past, its turbulent present, and its potentially glorious future (Lucas 82). But for all its reliance on myth and mythmaking, *O guesa* grounds itself in historical fact. Involving North, Central, and South America and native America, plus Europe, Africa, and Asia, and more than ten languages (including several indigenous ones), Sousândrade's sprawling poem unifies the Americas, while maintaining the links between the New World and the Old as nothing had before.

The title, written in Brazilian Portuguese but coming from the mythology of the Muisca people of present-day Colombia, refers to a wandering hero (the *guesa*) destined to be sacrificed one day. Sousândrade thus links a pre-Columbian myth related to ritual sacrifice to another kind of sacrifice, one linked to the rapaciousness of US Big Business and depicted in canto 10, known today as "The Inferno of Wall Street" (see Sousândrade). To tell its story, *O guesa* weaves together many disparate elements: indigenous America; the poet's home state of Maranhão (whose capital city Perrone identifies as "the Ithaca-like home or center of the world"); Brazil; the ancient Inca Empire; "the Americas as a whole"; and, finally, the world (Perrone 105). Read in its entirety, the poem implies more and more that the American experience is the prototype of the human experience and that as such, with all its struggle and strife, it is worthy of such an epic song, one the poet does not hesitate to speak of in the context of Homer. As the text of *O guesa* shows, its author echoes Whitman, the poet of democracy, while also presaging, as Augusto and Haroldo de Campos would argue later, in the 1960s, the Imagism of Ezra Pound (Infante 124–29).

If one reads only canto 10, where a newer kind of human sacrifice takes place in the confines of the New York Stock Exchange, one might well assume that Sousândrade was an enemy of the United States. But that was not the case. The Brazilian poet had no illusions about what Wall Street was or what was done in the Stock Exchange. As he writes in the second strophe:

(Xeques surgindo risonhos e disfarçdos em Railroad-*managers*,
    Stockjobbers, Pimpbrokers, etc., etc., apregoando:)
        Harlem! Erie! Central! Pennsylvania!
        = Milhão! cem milhões! mil milhões!!!
            —Young é Grant! Jackson,
            Atkinson!
        Vanderbilts, Jay Goulds, anões!

([Xeques appearing, laughing and disguised as Railroad-*managers*,
    Stockjobbers, Pimpbrokers, etc., etc., ballyhooing:]
        Harlem! Erie! Central! Pennsylvania!
        = Million! hundred million! ten digits!!!
            Young is Grant! Jackson,
            Atkinson!
        Vanderbilts, Jay Goulds are midgets!)

                                  (trans. Perrone 110)

As the engaged reader sees, the villains of the poem are the "Xeques," those high priests not just of ancient America but also of Wall Street, those people in any society who are always willing to sacrifice others to their ambitions and ritualistic beliefs. For as great as their potential for creating something better is, the Americas are not immune to this human failing. Canto 10 ends with Sousândrade merging an unquenchable thirst for money (Mammon), the judgmental rigidity of Puritanism, and a weakness for crass materialism. This blending points to the corruption of the highest principles (those that, in the beginning, inspired US democracy) by the lowest and most debasing. That it is a Latin American poet, and a Brazilian at that, who points this out about the United States, at the time in its post–Civil War period, is for inter-Americanists a salient fact.

At another point, the poet reminds his reader of the savagery that, horrifying to a Latin American, marks the racism of the United States: "Que dancem à eternal *Lynch Law!*" (Perrone 111; Let them dance th'eternal *Lynch Law!*). Just as Gilberto Freyre was aghast at the hangings and the mutilations that white, self-professed Christians inflicted upon Black Americans during the 1920s, so too is Sousândrade appalled in the nineteenth century about the same things. And yet his belief that America and the Americas could correct these errors, these human flaws, and erect if not truly Utopian societies then at least more just ones, was unshaken. That, for Sousândrade, was America's destiny.

Clearly, Sousândrade is critical of Wall Street and of all the human pain it causes in its endless pursuit of wealth. But he also knows there is more to the United States than this alone. "The democratic United States, eventually, offers much to be admired, even if forms of oppression, corruption, and colonialism merit satire and derision" (107). Already in the late nineteenth century it was a global force to be reckoned with, and that is why the poet could write of the United States, "E mais de ti, portanto, é que reclamo./De ti depende o mundo do futuro" (108; And so of thee I demand more./On thee depends the future of the world). Sousândrade excoriated US "savage capitalism" and all the harm it did, but he also prized the value of leaders like Washington and Lincoln. An astute interpreter of the United States, Sousândrade understood the violence and ugliness capitalism produced, but he also understood the good it could do if it were harnessed in ways more consistent with the founding principles of the United States. This was a position he shared with a great many other Latin American writers and intellectuals of the period.

Although *O guesa* began to take form as early as 1852, in the midst of the Romantic movement in Brazil, this astonishing and egregiously little-studied "Pan-American epic poem" was completed in New York City, where the author was then living, having relocated there in 1871 (Infante 121). In expanded and abridged forms the work was then published in both 1876 and 1877. "The final edition" of his poem, now bearing the title *O guesa*, "was registered in the British Museum in 1888 and published by the Moorfields Press in London at about the same time" (Infante 121). Fábio Lucas reminds us that one of the poem's many permutations was *O guesa errante: Poema americano* (82). The "mad genius of Maranhão, . . . Sousândrade conceived of Brazil as a continuous link to Latin American neighbors and as a potential site for republican life inspired by the United States" (Perrone 114, 116–17).

Although long overlooked by scholars, *O guesa* was not entirely dropped from critical scrutiny. And its author was known by some in Spanish America. As Fredrick Williams has pointed out, no less a figure than Ricardo Palma has identified *O guesa*, along with Ercilla's *La Araucana* and Zorrilla's *Tabaré*, as one of the three works that best achieve "an ideal Americanism" and "satisfy most completely the ideal of literary Americanism" (Perrone 113; F. Williams, "Wall Street Inferno" 15; Palma 129). Arguing that *O guesa* "provides a poetics of an unparalleled modernity and originality within Brazilian and Latin American literature," Augusto and Haroldo de Campos further assert that "Sousândrade's revolutionary style essentially pre-dates . . . the formal innovations that characterize Anglo-American modernism" (Infante 124).

Suddenly, with the Brazilian Sousândrade the concept of American literary history takes on an entirely new cast, one that is more comprehensive, more integrated, and more self-fertilizing than previously thought. Importantly, this nascent inter-Americanism begins with a Brazilian poet possessed of a pan-hemispheric vision. In this context, it is important to remember that the Brazilians have long had more of an interest in an inter-related America encompassing all the nations of the Americas, including the indigenous nations and cultures, than have the Spanish Americans. While the difference is neither vast nor absolute, it does exist. Martí's very influential "Nuestra América," for example, does not include Brazil in its discussion of "our America," but the American vision of several Brazilians, including Sousândrade, Mathias Carvalho, Ronald de Carvalho, and in more recent times Marcus Accioly and Regina Rheda, among others, includes Spanish America plus the rest of the Americas as well. It is distinctly comprehensive. While this does not say anything about the quality of the literature produced in Spanish America and Brazil (both cultures have produced texts of exceptional richness, complexity, and diversity), it does stand as a thematic, or conceptual, difference, one with, moreover, a historical basis. We can conclude, therefore, that while there is no Spanish American equivalent of the extraordinary Sousândrade, neither is there one in Canada, the United States, or the Caribbean. He is a one-of-a-kind American writer.

With the exceptions of the ultra-Romantic Álvares de Azevedo and the unique case of Sousândrade, "for much of the nineteenth century, Brazil's romantic poetry was not fundamentally different in form and function from that produced by Spanish America," though they did diverge in several "important ways," such as in the use of the Indian in the formation of a national ideal, the (for the Brazilian elite, fraught) question of miscegenation as a national characteristic, and the nonexistence of *gauchesca* literature, as the latter would become a staple of Spanish American culture (González Echevarría, Pupo-Walker, and Haberly 6). In 1823 Andrés Bello began a sequence of poems (beginning with "Alocución a la Poesía" in 1823 and then "A la agricultura de la Zona Tórrida" in 1826) exhorting Spanish Americans to cease their internecine conflicts and seek a new continental unity. In 1822 Brazil had gained its independence from Portugal; the dates 1822 and 1823 are thus crucial for the development of Latin American culture.

A critical text in Brazil's literary history, José de Alencar's *Iracema* celebrates *mestiçagem*. In Spanish America, it conjures up comparisons

with Cortés and Doña Marina, with *Cumandá,* by Juan León Mera, and
Tabaré, by Juan Zorrilla de San Martín. *Cumandá* especially bears some
plot similarities with *Iracema.* Given its topic, if not its thesis, *Iracema*
also brings to mind a host of other American works, including works by
such canonical Spanish Americans as Ricardo Palma, Asturias, and Paz.
From the United States, one sees potential comparisons with Cooper's
Last of the Mohicans (1826) and Helen Hunt Jackson's *Ramona* (1886),
as well as the many other texts dealing with this same topic.

Comparisons of Cooper and Alencar have long been popular. And
the reasons are clear. Alencar, however, explicitly denied this influence in
Como e porque sou romancista (How and why I am a novelist), a short
text written in 1873 but published by his son six years after his father's
death in 1883. Alencar writes here about his interest in the novel form and
how important it will be to Brazilian literature. He is also cognizant of the
novel's political significance, specifically its role in the creation of a national identity for Brazil. Aware of the comparisons being made between
his work and that of others, Alencar declares that while Chateaubriand
provided him with a model for how the theme of the Indian might be
developed, he was not influenced by either the Frenchman (whose work
he would improve upon) or Cooper, whose work he knew well but found
wanting. Alencar shows himself to be an astute critic of Cooper, whose
maritime tales are, the Brazilian writer believes, his best work. He praises
Cooper, in fact, as a gifted writer and a true poet of the sea.

Cooper and his work were well known in Latin America. As Wasserman says, "Cooper's Leather-stocking series was read most attentively and
fruitfully not in Europe but in other parts of the Americas, where a collection of Spanish colonies and the single Portuguese one were pupating
into nations and, like the United States, creating national literatures," and
Cooper, featuring "autochthonous subjects," showed them "that it could
be done" (*Exotic Nations* 186). For the inter-Americanist, consequently,
comparisons between Alencar and Cooper were inevitable, most notably
on the topic of miscegenation, which Alencar promoted as a defining feature of Brazilian nationality. This was not the case in the United States.
Cooper, though clearly titillated by the prospect of a sexual union between
his Noble Savage, Uncas, and Cora, the dark-haired but racially "tainted"
daughter of the British commander, Colonel Munro, does not allow the
budding romance to come to fruition; instead, he has Uncas and Cora die,
not even, moreover, to be united in the afterlife—but only after playing
with the theme of racial mixture for the entirety of the novel. This led
the US critic Leslie Fiedler to write that "even beyond death, the ferocity

of Cooper's dread of miscegenation will not yield" (205). The historian Anthony Pagden comes to much the same conclusion (see 37, 150–52). The early English colonists of America found the idea of mixing with the Native Americans, sexually or any other way, to be abhorrent.

At this point, we can see the theme of racial mixing emerging as a marker of profound difference between US literature and culture and that of Brazil. In Spanish America, the theme of miscegenation was more commonly cultivated than in the United States, where it remained a largely taboo subject, but one should not conclude from this that it was treated as in Brazil, for this was not the case. In Brazil, the question of cultural and biological mixing had by this time become commonplace, a widely accepted fact of life. In Spanish America much the same was true, though here the desirability of miscegenation appeared in more problematic fashion in not a few texts, some, like *Cumandá* and *Tabaré*, canonical in nature. Pagden points out that the "Spanish crown did nothing to encourage" sexual unions, even in marriage, between its colonizers and native women. "Racial integration in Spanish America, although it was to result in wholly new groups of peoples with distinctive cultures, and ultimately political aspirations of their own, played no part in the crown's conception of the empire" (150).

In *Tabaré*, for example, as in Faulkner, the past haunts the present. In the Americas, much of this guilt derives from the destruction of native peoples. This fact imparts to *Tabaré* a tragic quality that, though present, is more muted in Alencar's *Iracema*, whose title, its symbolism clear, is an anagram for *America*. The protagonist of the Uruguayan's poem is not an Indian woman of royal bloodlines but a blue-eyed mestizo, whose two heritages, Indian and white Christian, are not in harmony but in fatal conflict. The tragedy of Tabaré the character, the one who gives the poem its title, is that he is neither Indian nor white. In a racialized society he is without an identity. The other critical character is Blanca, the orphaned sister of the Spanish commander charged with extinguishing the Charrúa people. In love, but also in a relationship that cannot be countenanced, Tabaré and Blanca (the name, of course, being significant) are doomed, as is their love for each other. Tabaré eventually saves Blanca from being attacked by a Charrúa warrior. Upon returning Blanca to the Spanish post, Tabaré is killed with a sword thrust by her enraged brother, the Spanish officer who mistakenly assumes Tabaré to be his enemy. In Zorrilla de San Martín's poem, there is no merging of the races that points, symbolically, to an integrated future, as there is in Alencar's text. For the Charrúa, there is only extinction.

Published only a few years earlier, in 1871, Juan León Mera's novel *Cumandá* is based, as is *Iracema,* on a native legend, in this case a violent and bloody one. A family of white settlers is virtually wiped out by marauding Indians, with only the father and his young son, Carlos, escaping with their lives. The father, beset by grief and swearing to dedicate his life to peace, becomes a man of God who determines to spend the rest of his life converting the Indians. Also as in *Iracema,* in *Cumandá* a young Native American woman, Cumandá, is the protagonist. In the course of the novel, Cumandá, who becomes baptized, repeatedly saves the life of a young man named Carlos. Here we see a parallel in terms of what Iracema does for her man, the Portuguese conqueror, Martim. Cumandá and Carlos fall in love, but she must die, as prescribed by the traditions of her tribe, the Jíbaros of eastern Ecuador. It is at this point that the reader learns that she and Carlos are actually siblings, both being survivors of the original attack on their family. Cumandá, who had been carried away by the Indians as an infant, and Carlos are biologically white but culturally of different "races." Aside from the question of incest, culture here trumps blood. For Mera, a staunch supporter of García Moreno, the theocratic and dictatorial president of Ecuador, the specter of miscegenation was fraught with conflicts involving beliefs about religious and cultural superiority and the ongoing debate about whether people living in a state of nature could be virtuous or whether they must accept society's sanctions, mores, and requirements. For Mera, an ardent Catholic, it was the latter. Thus, Cumandá's situation is highly problematic. In contrast to Iracema's experience, which remains more true to the traditions of her people, Mera requires that Cumandá be baptized into the Catholic faith before she can seek to undertake acts of true goodness. This, the key difference, explains the *drama entre salvajes,* "drama among savages," which serves as the subtitle of Mera's narrative. Cumandá is not permitted to do what the unbaptized Iracema, an exemplary Noble Savage who is also female, does for Martim, a man she aggressively takes not in Christian marriage but in the nuptial rites of her tribe. There is in *Cumandá* a religious and political militancy and a violence that we do not find in *Iracema.* This reading squares with the more general sense we have of early Spanish America being more sternly ruled, religiously and administratively, than the more loosely run and more flexible Brazil, where even the Portuguese church viewed sexual and cultural liaisons between settlers and Native Americans as only mildly problematic.

In Spanish America, then, three Indianist texts stand out: Juan León Mera's novel Cumandá, Manuel de Jesús Galván's novel *Enriquillo,* and

Juan Zorrilla de San Martín's long narrative poem *Tabaré*. Of these, it is *Tabaré* that most invites a comparison with Gonçalves Dias's great Indian epic "I-Juca-Pirama" (1851), which in Tupi translates as "He who is going to die." Less epic than elegiac, *Tabaré* also differs from its Brazilian counterpart in that it deals more with the tragic relationship between the fierce Charrúa, the original inhabitants of today's Uruguay, and their extinction by the conquering Spanish. In this sense, *Tabaré* recalls Cooper's *Last of the Mohicans,* especially at the end, as the son, Chingatchgook, is slain and only the elderly father remains of the once noble tribe, now doomed, like the Charrúa, to oblivion.

Dias's "I-Juca-Pirama" is, according to Merquior, "simply the best poem, in the strong poematic sense, produced in Portuguese during the whole of the nineteenth century" (366). It may also be the best poem of its type in all the Americas. Dias, a highly regarded ethnologist and a man of mixed blood himself, was also the author of *Os Timbiras,* also a powerful and technically inventive poem. "I-Juca-Pirama" and *Os Timbiras* are driven by an authenticity that is less common than in either *Cumandá* or *Tabaré,* both highly regarded Indianist texts from Spanish America. Another Indian epic, *A Confederação dos Tamoios,* by Gonçalves de Magalhães, plumbed the theme of liberty, so important to the Romantics and here rooted in an indigenous Brazilian culture.

Taking a different tack, "I-Juca-Pirama" focuses entirely on two indigenous people, the Tupi and the Timbiras, who are sworn enemies. Composed of ten cantos, "I-Juca-Pirama" lyrically merges ethnographic accuracy with a celebration of the Brazilian Indian as a noble savage, a politically charged tactic that fed into Brazil's then burgeoning sense of national pride and identity. As Sadlier puts it, "If ever there was a work that reinforced the idea of the Amerindian as the quintessential noble savage and symí of Brazil, it was 'I-Juca-Pirama,' a story about a young Tupi warrior who is captured by the enemy Timbiras and asks to be released so he can care for his blind father. The story ends with the father returning his son to his captors so that the young man can die as a hero" (141). The powerful sense of cultural realism that the poem produces is crucial to its success. On this point, "I-Juca-Pirama" stands apart from Longfellow's *Song of Hiawatha,* which, appearing only four years after the Brazilian poem, takes a much more romantic and idealized view of Native American culture. Then too, Longfellow's native hero, Hiawatha, who suffers a rendering as the ideal bourgeois citizen, is required, in the final lines, to embrace Christianity and lead his people in accepting the ways of white civilization. Reading these two American Indianist texts

comparatively, one is also struck by how plodding and eventually monotonous the versification of the US poem is. Though powerfully rhythmic,
The Song of Hiawatha does not dance.

Dias, ranked by Moisés as the first authentically Brazilian poet, was
a gifted lyric poet, and his best lines sing with a music that accentu-
ates the grandeur of his topic (Moisés, *A literatura brasileira* 122). A
trained ethnographer and himself of mixed-blood heritage, Dias had two
years earlier been commissioned by Pedro II to "write a comparative
study" for the highly respected Instituto Histórico e Geográfico Brasileiro
"about the Indians of Brazil and of other American nations" (Sadlier 141).
An outcome of this 1849 study, "I-Juca-Pirama" celebrates the sense of
honor, bravery, and sacrifice that the author ascribes to "the nation's first
peoples, whose rich, proud heritage is conveyed by Dias's incorporation
of ethnographic detail and indigenous terms" (Sadlier 143).

José María Heredia, who spent the years 1823 to 1825 in exile in
the United States and whose powerful and moving poem "Niágara" was
quite successfully translated by William Cullen Bryant, was a full-fledged
romantic. The relationship between Heredia and Bryant was both interesting and productive, and it can be taken as an example of incipient
inter-Americanism, albeit of the kind that focuses only on the United
States and Spanish America. This makes it a bit dyadic. If, as it sometimes is in the United States, which tends to ignore Brazil when thinking
of Latin America and to think of Canada not at all, this methodology is
taken to be the norm, then the inter-American becomes more two-sided
than it should be. Still, the connection between the Cuban poet, unhappily
exiled in the United States, and Bryant, a major US poet, is a real one and
deserving of study. It is thanks largely to Bryant, as the English-language
translator of "Niágara," that Heredia gained some renown in the United
States of that era. The poem, an ode, opens with a note of grandeur mixed
with pain:

> Templad mi lira, dádmela, que siento
> en mi alma estremecida y agitada
> arder la inspiración. Oh! Cuánto tiempo
> en tinieblas pasó, sin que mi frente
> brillase con su luz! . . . Niágara undoso,
> tu sublime terror solo podría
> tornarme el don divino, que ensañada
> me robó del dolor la mano impía.

> (Englekirk et al., *Anthology* 152)

Bryant's rendering opens thusly:

> My lyre! Give me my lyre! My bosom finds
> The glow of inspiration. Oh, how long
> Have I been left in darkness, since this light
> Last visited my brow! Niagara!
> Thou with thy rushing waters dost restore
> The heavenly gift that sorrow took away.
>
> (Rodríguez Monegal, *Borzoi Anthology* 1:205)

After pondering, sadly, the swaying palms and fragrant flowers of his native land, Heredia grows indignant at the ambitions and lies of the vain, unworthy men who drove him away:

> Omnipotente Dios! En otros climas
> vi monstrous execrables,
> blasfemando tu nombre sacrosanto,
> sembrar error y fanatismo impío
>
> (Englekirk et al., *Anthology* 153)

Bryant, synthesizing here several points and reordering others, nevertheless brings through Heredia's main points:

> God of all truth! in other lands I've seen
> Lying philosophers, blaspheming men,
> Questioners of thy mysteries, that draw
> Their fellows deep into impiety.
>
> (Rodríguez Monegal, *Borzoi Anthology* 1:206)

It is because of this pain, the poet then tells us, that he seeks, and finds, succor in the wild majesty of Niagara's rushing waters. As if speaking to God and to Nature at the same time,[3] Heredia writes:

> Por eso te buscó mi débil mente
> En la sublime soledad.
>
> (Englekirk et al., *Anthology* 153)

> (And therefore doth my spirit seek thy face
> In earth's majestic solitudes.)
>
> (Rodríguez Monegal, *Borzoi Anthology* 1:206)

The Novel

In Latin America, as in French Canada, the novel form was a late bloomer. As a particular kind of literature, until the second half of the nineteenth century it had finished behind poetry, both lyric and epic, in terms of development. Excessive imitation of existing European forms was one problem, and with it came a second problem, lack of originality. While this overly imitative approach to novel writing could be accommodated in terms of theme and even style, it was deadly in terms of form.

There is, moreover, a difference between the evolution of the Spanish American novel and that of the novel of Brazil, which made extraordinary advances in the second half of the nineteenth century. As D. P. Gallagher sees it, "With the exception of the Brazilian novelist Machado de Assis (1839–1908)," Spanish American writers who cultivated longer narrative forms in the 1800s "were usually too immature and too derivative to merit the serious consideration of anyone not specifically interested in the Latin American context as such" (1). As a result, "the Latin American novel . . . took longer to mature" (82). Brazil, however, was once again the exception, in Latin America but also in the Americas, a point made in 1976 by Jon M. Tolman. "Within the context of the Americas," Tolman writes, "the Brazilian novel is remarkable for its sustained excellence," which he attributes to "the exceptional social stability of Brazil" (1).

Everywhere in the Americas, as in Europe, the novel was regarded with disdain, as not being worthy of serious artistic attention. Nevertheless, the novel's origins in the Americas are quite interesting, with Canada and Brazil leading the way (E. Fitz, "First Inter-American Novels"). From eighteenth-century Canada we have Frances Brooke, who, as New writes, in 1769 published "*The History of Emily Montague,* the first novel written in Canada, an epistolary tale of politics and romance that combines a shrewd eye for life in the English garrison in Quebec in the 1760s with a conventional sense of what constituted culture and civilization. Satire interweaves with sentimental stereotypes" (57). And, as already noted, Silva e Orta and Brazil gave us *As aventuras de Diófanes* in 1752.

As a genre, the novel, suspected of bearing heretical ideas, was formally banned from Spanish America, and while novels did circulate, they did so under severe penalty of law. To be caught reading or writing one was a serious offense. The vacuum created by the banning of novels in Spanish America was filled by colorful and inventive *crónicas* and histories. Two of the most interesting of these were Carlos de Sigüenza y Góngora's *Los infortunios de Alonso Ramírez* and Alonso Carrió de la Vandera's *El Lazarillo de ciegos caminantes* (1775–76). In Brazil, novels were trafficked more easily, which was consistent with colonial Brazil's more relaxed attitudes about foreign influences. Although the question has never been definitively settled, and although there are several contenders for the honor, the title of first Spanish American novel usually goes to *El Periquillo Sarniento* (1816), José Joaquín Fernández de Lizardi's sprawling picaresque.

In Brazil, this honor is still regularly bestowed on Macedo's *A moreninha,* though, as in the case of Spanish America, there are several other possible texts. Given the later brilliance of the Brazilian novel, it is ironic that it did not appear until midway through the nineteenth century. Why was the Brazilian novel so late to appear? Mary Lou Daniel, building on the work of David Salles, speculates that its delay had to do with the dominance of poetry as the prestigious genre in Brazil, the "lingering" presence of neoclassicism, the "popularity of ecclesiastical and oratorical rhetoric, the immediate appeal of combative prose," and a general lack of editors and publishing houses interested in devoting time and resources to an as yet "unproven genre" ("Brazilian Fiction from 1800 to 1855" 127).

In comparison with its Spanish American counterpart, the Brazilian novel had a smoother evolution. "Mirroring the stability of Brazilian society," Rodríguez Monegal observes, "it developed more harmoniously and coherently than the Spanish American" (*Borzoi Anthology* 1:174). By the beginning of the nineteenth century, Brazilian writers were reading one another and thinking of themselves as being part of growing national traditions. But they were also drawing on a variety of global sources that were then disseminated nationally. This produced a novel that was simultaneously identifiably national in language, types, and theme and international in style and technique. This is discernibly the case with José de Alencar, often credited with pressing for an authentic Brazilian literature that, as in his own work, reflected these two trends, but it is also discernible in Manuel Antônio de Almeida (where the Brazilian *malandro* emerges), in the brilliantly innovative narratives of Machado de Assis, in the naturalistic dissections of Aluísio Azevedo, and in the impressionistic but dark world of Raul Pompéia. In studying the development of the Brazilian novel, one can see how every generation benefits from reading its predecessors and learning from them. As Tolman, making a comparison with the Spanish American novel, writes, "In contrast to the chaos of Latin America in the nineteenth century, Brazil maintained intact its socio-economic institutions. For this reason its literature undergoes an unbroken organic evolution from period to period, beginning in the eighteenth century. Succeeding generations could enrich themselves in a tradition even while rebelling against it" (1). The result was a coherence in the novel form that we do not see in a still splintered Spanish America. This explains how and why "the Brazilian novel of the nineteenth century solidly established a narrative tradition that in the course of its evolution in the next century would continue to produce some of the best Latin American writers" (Rodríguez Monegal, *Borzoi Anthology* 1:174).

The Brazilian novel became a powerfully original genre during the second half of the nineteenth century, surpassing the Spanish American novel, which still felt the need to imitate Spanish models. While several Brazilian novelists—Almeida and, later, Alencar, for example—scored major technical and thematic breakthroughs, it was Machado de Assis who would take the gold medal. "By 1900," González Echevarría, Pupo-Walker, and Haberly write, "Machado was already the finest Latin American novelist, though few knew his work outside Brazil" (5). For writers like Machado, Alencar, and Azevedo, importantly, "the social and economic roles of women and other marginal sectors of Brazilian society came into sharper focus" (5). For Machado in particular, women became major subjects for the depiction of the new Brazil that was struggling to come into being as the monarchy was being shucked off and the republic was being formed. A new form of government for Brazil would require new ideas about civil rights and citizenship, and women, as literary characters and as participants in the success of the new Brazil, would have to have a lot to say about this national transformation (see E. Fitz, *Machado de Assis and Female Characterization*). "By mid-century," as Merquior astutely points out, "there was no Brazilian *Facundo*—but then there was no *Iracema* (1865) in Spanish America" (367). And there was certainly no Machado de Assis, a point driven home by no less a figure than the Mexican novelist and intellectual Carlos Fuentes. Fuentes argues that Machado, a Brazilian, continued the grand tradition of Cervantes and *Don Quixote* more effectively and with more fidelity than Spanish American writers have done. "El milagro" of Machado de Assis, he writes, "se sostiene sobre una paradoja: Machado asume, en Brasil, la lección de Cervantes, la tradición de La Mancha que olvidaron, por más homenajes que cívica y escolarmente se rindiesen al *Quixote,* los novelistas hispanoamericanos" (9–10; the miracle . . . sustains itself as a paradox: Machado, in Brazil, learned the lesson of Cervantes, and the tradition of La Mancha, that the novelists of Spanish America, because of their felt need to pay civic and honorific obeisance to the *Quixote,* forgot). High praise, this. And deserved.

Realism and Naturalism in Spanish America (1854–1918)

Although in *El matadero* (1839?) Esteban Echeverría wrote what might easily be considered a realistic or even naturalisitic narrative, Spanish American literary historians more commonly take a somewhat different position on the arrival of Realism, a movement closely associated with narrative,[4] particularly the novel form. It is often felt that "Spanish American novelistic production from 1854 to 1918 was characterized by attempts to write more or less objectively about external reality" and to eschew the romantic emphasis on emotion and idealized states of being (Englekirk et al., *Outline* 90). The Spanish realists Pereda, Galdós, and Valera were especially influential here. Chile's Alberto Blest Gana is the author most often cited as initiating Realism in Spanish America.

But Blest Gana, who, in addition to Galdós, was well versed in Balzac and Stendhal, having studied them during his sojourn in France as a student of military engineering, was receptive to other influences as well. Indeed, his interest in analyzing the different social classes and their motivations may well have come from Balzac. His first novel, *La aritmética en el amor* (1860), reflects this keen interest in social types, customs, and interactions. This trend continues in *Martín Rivas* (1862), his most successful effort, and in *El ideal de una calavera* (1863). Both narratives, but especially the earlier *La aritmética en el amor,* recall Alencar's *Senhora* (1875) in that the institution of the arranged marriage is scrutinized. But *El ideal de una calavera* also brings to mind Alencar's novel because the theme of the arranged marriage, and the shameless social climbing and sexism that go with it, is expanded to consider whether true love between people can exist in a society that values only money and status. In Blest Gana's case, it is a young man who does the questioning, while in Alencar's arguably feminist narrative it is a young woman, the proud *senhora* of the title. Both authors, the Chilean and the Brazilian, reveal their concerns with questions of gender equity and justice in rigidly structured and deeply patriarchal societies. And both revel in contrasting the social values and mores of the New World with those of Europe. And both employ the American-in-Europe motif to structure their plots.

There is something else that needs to be noted here. Beginning with Alencar, significant changes were taking place in Brazilian literature regarding the status of women, as literary characters but also as citizens. Committed to establishing a distinctly Brazilian literature, Alencar devoted an entire series of novels to women, their representations in literature, their lives, and their positions in Brazilian society. Of these, his 1875 novel, *Senhora,* whose title one could translate as "mistress" or "master," was enjoying considerable influence outside Brazil. Its English translator, Catarina Feldman Edinger, has written of the novel's author that the Brazilian had a more progressive view of his female characters than did Cooper, Hawthorne, or Melville (introduction xi–xv; see also Edinger, "Hawthorne and Alencar"). As Edinger concludes, Aurélia, the protagonist of *Senhora,* is "a heroine very different from those found in American," meaning US, "works of the same period" and so represents a new chapter in the "literary production of . . . the Americas" (introduction xv; see also Edinger, "Machismo and Androgyny"). Very aware of Alencar's thematic and technical achievements, Machado de Assis would carry this trend to its apogee (E. Fitz, *Machado de Assis and Female Characterization*).

A later Blest Gana novel, *Los transplantados* (The transplanted ones), of 1904, takes up a theme well known to readers of Henry James, the penniless European aristocrat who takes advantage of a rich but innocent American woman. One key difference is that Blest Gana's Europeans are much less charming than those of James, and they are much more crassly materialistic, the seductive lure of materialism being a major target of the Chilean's ire. Another difference is that in *Los transplantados* the young woman in question, Mercedes Canalejas, commits suicide rather than accept what she rightly sees as her cynical sale to an impoverished European nobleman, a transaction that is designed to gain for her shallow family the patina of nobility.

On the question of the status of women, there is yet another Latin American connection with Henry James to be examined. James's female characters, long regarded as strong, even dominating creations in his fiction, call to mind some interesting comparisons with those of Brazil's Machado de Assis, a contemporary of James and a writer often compared to him (see Putnam 178, 183–84, 194; see also E. Fitz, *Rediscovering the New World* 95–120). In their views of women, important players with intelligence and agency if not yet the right to vote, both James and Machado were very American (see E. Fitz, *Machado de Assis and Female Characterization;* see also Parkes 274).

And yet, in reading James against Machado one becomes aware of key differences. For one thing, neither Isabel Archer (of *The Portrait of a Lady*) nor Milly Theale (of *The Wings of the Dove,* 1902), nor Maggie Verver (of *The Golden Bowl,* 1904) would have ever had the erotic dream that Sofia experienced in chapter 161 of Machado's *Quincas Borba* (1891, first translated as *Philosopher or Dog?*). Not even the coquettish

Daisy Miller, one feels, would have had, or been allowed to have, Sofia's dream. In short, none of the Jamesian females possesses the same enjoyment of her own body, her own pulchritude, as Sofia. And none of them would have enjoyed displaying it—and having her scheming husband, the capitalist Palha, ask her to show it off—as she does. The text makes clear, and on repeated occasions, that not only does Sofia, a more clear-eyed version of Emma Bovary, know what she is doing, she revels in it! Early in the novel,[5] the narrator tells us this about Sofia: "Let us do justice to our lady. Though at first she yielded to her husband's wishes [which involved having his wife dress in 'low cut gowns'] with indifference, so great was the admiration garnered . . . that finally she came to enjoy being shown, very much being shown, for the pleasure and provocation of others" (*Philosopher or Dog?* 46). Later, we learn this: "She took pleasure in contemplating herself, her opulent figure, her arms, bare from shoulder to wrist, her dreamy eyes. She was twenty-nine years old, and she thought she looked the same as she had at twenty-five. She was not mistaken, either. As she pulled in and fastened her corset, she lovingly adjusted her bosom, leaving a large expanse of her beautiful neck uncovered" (163). And there is nary a whiff of either guilt or sin. Sofia's characterization surges forth from pure female sexual pleasure. With none of the female characters in James's pantheons does this occur, not even with Maisie Farange (of *What Maisie Knew,* 1897), often taken to be James's attempt to write about a "fallen women."

While some have found the women of both James and Machado to be grasping, sly, or manipulative, a closer look reveals them to be more often than not clear-eyed, strong, and forward looking. This is especially so for Machado's female characters, who after 1880 tended to be notably progressive. In the novels, the clearest example of this tendency is Dona Fidélia of *Memorial de Aires* (*Counselor Ayres' Memorial*), of 1908.

Yet another of Machado's later works that advances this same theme, which we might think of as the newly emancipated woman and her role in the formation of the new democratic republic of Brazil, is *A lição de botânica* (A botany lesson). Much more than a romantic comedy, which it is often taken to be, this fast-moving and funny play features two things of note: one involves an ironic reversal, in which a man believes he is giving a lesson (in botany, science) to a young woman, the widowed Dona Helena, when it is she who ends up giving a lesson (on life, intellectual freedom, and the liberation of women) to him, while the other features the creation of a smart, strong-willed young woman who feels no compelling need to seek another conventional marriage with a new suitor and sees no reason why she cannot dictate the terms of her own life (see E. Fitz, "Writing Womanhood in the New Brazil").

More and more after 1880, Machado's fictional women see themselves as being less and less trapped in a patriarchal social, political, and economic structure. Fully aware of their situations, they want more, and they begin with their personal lives. Unlike James's Isabel Archer, who seems resigned to her fate, Machado's female characters, for the most part white and middle to upper-middle class, reject being confined to life in a gilded cage. And they take steps to prevent it from happening. We see this with Dona Fidélia, and we see it even more with Dona Helena. Having seen the emancipation of Brazil's Black slaves and, in the case of Dona Fidélia, having furthered the abolitionist cause, Machado's women now want emancipation for themselves. And no one epitomizes the need for this double emancipation than Fidélia. Perhaps most notable in this comparison with James is that Machado's female characters are more outspoken, more eroticized, and more geared to strengthening Brazil's newly formed republic by demanding rights equal to those of men. While, as per Machado's mature style, they are never explicit about this, the careful reader can easily discern it in their characterizations.

But as I tried to show in *Machado de Assis and Female Characterization*, Machado's interest in developing strong female characters was present, albeit in embryonic form, even in his early work. In the novel *Helena* (1876), even today a rather lightly regarded narrative from Machado's early phase, Machado's interest in creating determined, visionary female characters is obvious. In chapter 6, to cite the novel's most prominent example, the vivacious yet mysterious young woman of the title, Helena, is masterfully sketched out by means of an extended metaphor, her unexpected skills as a horsewoman. Encompassing nearly the entirety of the chapter, Helena's characterization is also drawn in the context of the needs of the new Brazil that is about to emerge with the formation of the Brazilian republic, a topic of considerable interest to Machado. As Sydney Chaloub points out, the carefully phrased and extensive attention given to the mare Moema allows Machado to use the proud and capable young Helena to dissect the "paternalist ideology" and the "structures of domination" that ruled in Brazil during the 1850s, when the action of the novel takes place (Chaloub 60, 57). For Chaloub, Helena operates inside this paternalist ideology and does so in order to pursue "her own goals" (60). But what are her goals? Are they limited to her own self-interest? Or could they be construed by an imaginative and engaged reader (the kind Machado wanted) as encompassing Brazil's political future? The two interpretations are not mutually exclusive; Helena's own goals could easily be those of a new and more democratic Brazil—more freedom, more equality, more opportunity for women, for example.

It does not require much effort for the reader to equate Helena's skill with her horse—the mare's name, Moema, alludes to a character cited in other works by Machado himself[6]—with what we are led to contemplate as her skill as a future political leader of a more progressive and egalitarian Brazil. Although she states it in semantically oblique, symbolic language, and although she speaks in an impish voice (one befitting her function here as an astute observer of her situation), what Helena wants is agency. And when the reader considers not only what she says but how this chapter is structured, it becomes easy to interpret her adroit utilization of Moema, the female horse, as a demonstration of how well she, as a woman, could lead the Brazilian nation, which, the reader feels, becomes equated with the mare. In the final decades of his long career, as a writer and as a commentator on the Brazilian scene, Machado's most memorable women show a political commitment to leadership and to justice and equality for all that, with the possible exception of Christina Light (of *The Princess Casamassima*, 1886), we do not see in James's female characters.

But Machado de Assis is not the only Latin American writer we can connect with US writers. The Argentine great, Jorge Luis Borges, taught Hawthorne, along with many others, in courses he gave at the University of Buenos Aires on the literature of the United States. Borges was keenly interested in Hawthorne, and during his career as a university professor he wrote a spate of critical essays on Hawthorne and a host of other US authors, including Whitman, Twain, Poe, Melville, Faulkner, and Eliot, among others. One of these essays, "Nathaniel Hawthorne," is of particular interest to inter-Americanists. Dating from 1949, this fascinating consideration of the US writer is not concerned with his obsession with sin and guilt, which Borges regarded as standard-issue Puritanism, but with Hawthorne's style, specifically his cultivation of symbols. The question Borges, who, perhaps having been influenced by the linguistics of Saussure,[7] had come to regard all language use as symbolic in nature, asks is basically this: Why, given Hawthorne's seminal importance to US literature, did the writing of the United States develop its "curious veneration" of Realism and realistic writing in general (*Other Inquisitions* 64)?

To use language is to use a set of symbols to discuss reality. By 1880 Machado understood this, and it would alter how he thought about language and reality and about how he wrote. In Spanish America, Borges came to the same realization in the 1930s with his *ficciones*, which are less innovative as subject matter than they are because of the new theory of language, structure, and meaning that drives them. Taken together, these two great writers, Machado and Borges, make late nineteenth- and all of twentieth-century Latin American narrative different, more language conscious. Rodríguez Monegal would explore this point from a slightly different perspective in his 1969 essay "The New Latin American Novelists."

As indicated, Borges posed his question about Hawthorne at the very time he himself was experimenting with his anti-realistic *ficciones* (fictions), the earliest examples of what would later be termed the *nueva narrativa hispanoamericana* and of the later-developing *realismo mágico,* or magical realism, associated with such Spanish American writers as Juan Rulfo, Julio Cortázar, and Gabriel García Márquez. Interested, perhaps, in a new approach to American literary history, one that would integrate North, Central, and South American writing, Borges knew perfectly well at this point that his own *ficciones* had more in common with Hawthorne's understanding of language than they did with those many adepts of conventional Realism who stud the narrative history of the United States (see E. Fitz, "Borges as Historian of American Literature"). What we can also say is that in terms of sheer stylistic precocity, the Stephen Crane of *The Red Badge of Courage* (1895) probably ranks as the greatest of the US realists, and Borges seems likely to have recognized this.[8] Nevertheless, we can conclude from Borges's tantalizing comments that it was Hawthorne who was influential and who was as important to the development of *la nueva narrativa hispanoamericana* as were Faulkner and Edgar Allan Poe, whose *Narrative of Arthur Gordon Pym* (1838) was of special interest to the Argentine scholar and writer (see Rodríguez Monegal, *Jorge Luis Borges* 247–49; for more on Borges's debt to Faulkner, see 372–73). Crane's concern with language was of a different sort, more mimetic than iconic.

For Pedro Henríquez-Ureña, the realistic novel began in Brazil "even earlier than in the neighboring Spanish-speaking countries" (148). In taking this position, Henríquez-Ureña is looking at *Memórias de um sargento de milícias,* by Manuel Antônio de Almeida, who here shows "himself already a follower of Balzac" (148). Appearing as it did in the midst of Brazilian Romanticism, Almeida's novel is often looked upon as something of an anomaly because it breaks with Romantic convention to offer a text that, frequently funny, is also quite realistic. Almeida's text has been judged by at least one critic to be, if not the first Brazilian novel, then "the first Brazilian novel of real literary importance" (Putnam 149). While this opinion could be said to be a bit harsh, it is not entirely without justification. Although still far from what Machado de Assis would do, or even from what Alencar would do, *Memórias de um sargento de milícias* does mark a real step forward for the Brazilian novel.

The Spanish American equivalent to Almeida's novel is Lizardi's *El Periquillo Sarniento,* which appeared some years earlier, in 1816. Both texts are picaresque in structure, both are strongly realistic, and both have humorous moments. In contrast to the upper-middle-class urban novels of Alencar and Machado de Assis, which Brazilian readers were accustomed to, Almeida's narrative focuses exclusively on the lower-class characters of a Rio de Janeiro from an earlier time, one that was, in the time of the author, already fast fading into the past. His characters are working men and women or men and women of even more marginal status. The more structured of the two, *Memórias de um sargento de milícias* is set in the final years of the monarchy in Brazil, during the Joanino period (1808–21),[9] and evinces a sense of nostalgia for those long-ago days. There is no nostalgia in *El Periquillo Sarniento.* Inspired by the ideas of the *Ilustración francesa* (French Enlightenment) and the *philosophes,* the vision of the past that it conjures up is entirely negative. What Mexico needs, Lizardi, a progressive, insists, is radical social, political, and economic reform. The past, associated with conservatism, corruption, incompetence, and ignorance, is an anchor holding it back. While Almeida looks back to a somewhat romanticized past for his inspiration, Lizardi looks forward to what he hopes will be a better future.

For the inter-Americanist, an interesting question emerges here. Why did Realism appear earlier in the United States, where it came into being around 1865, in the post–Civil War period, than it did in Spanish America and Brazil, where it did not materialize until around 1880, some fifteen years later? One seemingly plausible theory, advanced by Rodríguez Monegal, is that because Romanticism arrived in the Americas so late, it simply took longer for it to run its natural course (*Borzoi Anthology* 1:172–73). Another theory, perhaps even more plausible, is that Romanticism in Spanish America, tied as it was to political freedom, first from Spain and then (in the aftermath of the Spanish withdrawal) from the reign of local tyrants who had seized power, took longer to achieve its primary purpose—the ouster of the strongmen and the establishment of democratic self-government. We can also say that in both Spanish America and Brazil as in the United States, regionalism served as the bridge between Romanticism and Realism.

Naturalism in Latin America: Brazil (1881–1922)

It was on the basis of its scientific foundation that Naturalism differed from Realism, its literary cousin. In contrast to the realists, who prized objectivity, the naturalists, seeing life as a grand chemistry lab, believed that all human motivation and behavior could be explained by deeply primal biological imperatives, prominent among which was the sexual impulse. The influence of Zola, along with that of Dr. Claude Bernard and the brothers Goncourt, was paramount throughout the Americas, though nowhere was it embraced more ardently than in Latin America. Naturalism exerted a powerful influence in both Spanish America and Brazil, where it was a well-defined and prolific school. Perhaps because of the French model, which was parsed so carefully, Brazilian Naturalism showed an affinity for developing distinct literary schools. In addition to Naturalism, Brazilian literary history features other such schools, including Parnassianism and Symbolism, that follow the same French pattern. Naturalism and Zola were also strong in the United States, though it seems to have been tied more to issues of religion and sexual morality, Social Darwinism, and the determinism of Big Business (see Mitchell). Understanding how these issues relate to Canadian literature enriches our American experience of Naturalism even more (see New).

Was there something about Naturalism that made it particularly attractive to the *culturas americanas?* It would seem so. Perhaps the answer to this question is best summed up in Ezra Pound's dictum that we need to "make it new," to constantly rethink, reimagine, rebuild, and rewrite in hope of doing better. To seek "the new," typically equated with what was presumed to be "better," was the American quest. In Brazil, Naturalism appears to have had a special appeal for writers, intellectuals, and political leaders, who, as we have seen, were already in the early nineteenth century much more committed to science than their Spanish American cousins were (González Echevarría, "A Lost World Re-Discovered"). For the Brazilians, the scientific basis of Naturalism had profound appeal. It was science, in fact, that generated one of the most important turn-of-the-century American books, Euclides da Cunha's *Os Sertões*. Originally translated by Samuel Putnam, da Cunha's extraordinary narrative, which churns constantly over the then current but erroneous belief in racial superiority and inferiority, is often compared, on the basis of its scientific approach to explaining national identity, with Sarmiento's *Civilización y barbarie* (1845), though it also merits comparison with James Agee's *Let Us Now Praise Famous Men* (1941; see E. Fitz, "William Faulkner, James Agee, and Brazil").

Although widely cultivated, and producing several interesting novels, Naturalism in Spanish America did not coalesce to form the coherent school that distinguishes its life in Brazil. As a result, Spanish American Naturalism never became the force it was in Brazil. "There was," Merquior writes, "no Naturalist boom in Hispanic American letters, scarcely anything comparable to" the kind of writing that "overwhelmed Brazilian fiction after the publication of *O mulato* (1881), by Aluísio Azevedo. Nor was there as effective an instance of *écriture artiste*, of pent-up impressionist narrative, as the 1888 *O Ateneu* of Raul Pompéia" (368). The most accomplished of the Brazilian naturalists, Azevedo also promoted the emancipation of women that David Bailey finds to be characteristic of Luso-Brazilian Naturalism. For Bailey, this new movement incorporated women into "the means of production" and in the process increasingly freed them from "dependency and exploitation" (4). This is precisely the social, economic, and sexual context in which Azevedo's novel *O cortiço* stands out the most.

The Brazilian naturalists regarded the works of Zola and Eça de Queirós more as models to exceed than as texts to merely ape or imitate. A basic human drive, sex is quickly seized upon as a theme, and as even a cursory survey reveals, its most representative texts feature it: Azevedo's *O cortiço, O mulato,* and *Casa de pensão*; Domingos Olímpios's *Luzia-Homem*; Inglês de Sousa's *O missionário*; Júlio Ribeiro's *A carne*; and Adolfo Caminha's *Bom-Crioulo*. Haberly is of a similar mind, adding of Brazilian Naturalism that "its almost obsessive focus on, and detailed description of, sexual relationships" can be seen as "both a thematic and stylistic continuation of romantic Regionalism—but with a new and very different ideological basis," one proclaiming "three central truths": that the changes wrought by naturalist theory would be negative both for individuals and for society as a whole; that "sexual desire is the single most powerful and controlling human emotion"; and that "genetic heredity and environmental conditioning entirely determine character and behavior" ("The Brazilian Novel from 1850 to 1900" 147–48).

The lesbianism in *O cortiço* can be read as simply salacious, fodder for the male gaze, or as a serious exploration of female sexuality, agency, and solidarity. While both interpretations are possible, it is the latter one that in the course of the novel comes to the fore, offering both the most textual evidence and the most convincing (see E. Fitz, *Machado de Assis and Female Characterization* 60–69). Brazilian Positivism, very influential at the time, held that women generally were stronger than men, able to endure pain better, and all in all superior human specimens. It would not be illogical, therefore, to suppose that Azevedo simply wrote into his novel what was being propounded by Brazil's best minds. Applied, as it is in *O cortiço,* to human sexuality as well as to political power and social mores, this theory about the superiority of women could have been read as a direct attack on Brazil's repressively patriarchal social structure, and, as the sections that relate to its lesbianism suggest, the novel leans that way. Far from decrying the union between Léonie and Pombinha, the many women who are not lesbian applaud the power the two have over their bodies and their lives, including their economic fortunes. They are, the text implies, doing exactly what two superior creatures would naturally do. And their sisters salute them for it. In the late nineteenth century it was difficult, if not impossible, to find another novel like *O cortiço* anywhere in the Americas.

Modernism in Spanish America (1882–1910/1915) and Brazil (1922–1945)

Spanish American *Modernismo* is a rich and heady mélange of the exotic and the sensual. It was "the first literary movement to have arisen in Latin America," but it was also, as numerous critics have pointed out, part of the fin-de-siècle malaise that many believe infected Western culture and civilization during the final years of the nineteenth century (González Echevarría, *Oxford Book of Latin American Short Stories* 105). In this sense alone, the modernist revolt in Spanish America demonstrated its inherent cosmopolitanism. No longer limited to the national and the regional, or to its old themes, tropes, and images, Spanish American literature was now part of a global trend. But Spanish American *Modernismo* was also the victory of the beautiful over the didactic, of the ethereal over the real, and of the musical over the plodding. It marked the birth of a new kind of poetry for the Spanish-speaking world, first in Spanish America, then in Spain.

For Cathy Jrade, "Modernism is the linguistically rich and formally innovative literary movement that began in Spanish America in the late 1870s and that lasted into the second decade of the twentieth century. Its recourse to European artistic visions and poetic models—primarily French Parnassian and symbolist verse—reflected a dissatisfaction with the restrictive Spanish poetics of the day, a longing for cultural autonomy, and a desire to achieve a sense of equality with the great cultures of Western Europe" ("Modernist Poetry" 7; see also Jrade, *Modernismo, Modernity*). The movement's creative epicenter, Rubén Darío believed *Azul* (1888) to be an exemplar of French Parnassianism, and, in 1894 he, along with Bolivia's Ricardo Jaime Freyre, founded the *Revista de América,* which was heavily oriented toward replicating French Symbolist poetry in the Hispanic New World.

Jean Franco suggests that as envisioned by the movement's acknowledged master, Rubén Darío, Spanish American *Modernismo* had three main characteristics: it rejected the need to teach, instruct, or impart a message or moral; it stressed beauty as the highest achievement to which the poet could aspire; and it insisted on freeing the new poetry it espoused from the traditional poetics of Spanish-language verse (119). And in the view of Rodríguez Monegal, the "Spanish American modernists discarded completely the ponderous, 'uncouth,' traditional manner in Spanish [prose and poetry] and began to write in a more direct, elegant, supple style," one that blended the "Parnassians in their quest for perfection of form and sculptured imagery and the symbolists in their exploration of musical possibilities in verse" (*Borzoi Anthology* 1:338; see also 1:353).

In a more inter-American context, we can easily understand why a North American poet, Edgar Allan Poe, was also influential for the Spanish American *modernistas.* They were especially drawn to Poe's contention that a poem existed and functioned as an object of art in and of itself and to his distaste for the didactic in poetry. The appeal of Poe, including his passion for musicality in verse, to the Spanish American modernists is clear. Generations of readers have, for example, heard Poe's poem "The Bells" in José Asunción Silva's "Día de defuntos," which Franco finds to be "far superior" to its US model (128).

In retrospect, we can see that Spanish American *Modernismo* underwent a clear trajectory. Although it began in the late 1870s and early 1880s as an ivory-tower kind of writing, it ended up, in the early years of the twentieth century, much more a part of the real world. This same evolution is reflected in the career of Rubén Darío, the movement's leader and most representative figure. While his celebrity began with exotic and sensuous poems like his *cisne,* or swan, pieces, it concluded with politically charged poems like "To Roosevelt" and the more conciliatory "Salutación al Águila." A unifying force in Spanish America, *Modernismo* transformed the literature of Spanish-speaking America into a global force. But only to a degree. Unfortunately, Spanish American *Modernismo* did not receive the widespread international appreciation it merited. Indeed, it still has not, though a new generation of critics is correcting this long-standing oversight. While Darío and his cohorts changed the way poetry was written and read in Spain, and although Darío was known and respected in other centers of European culture, especially Paris, he did not strike fire as much as he and his new poetry should have. Why this was the case remains a moot point, though Ignacio Infante has some provocative ideas.

Modernismo in Spanish America (which began c. 1888) corresponds chronologically to Parnassianism in Brazil, where it too was an established and well-defined school. This comparison is apt, chronologically speaking, but although Brazilian Parnassianism produced some excellent poems (those of Bilac, for example, and a few others), it was not revolutionary in the ways Spanish American *Modernismo* was. It is also important to remember that while Spanish American *Modernismo* blended the theories and practices of both French *Symbolisme* and Parnassianism into a harmonious new kind of poetry,[10] Brazilian poetry during the same period did not practice this same kind of synthesis. Instead, it hewed closer to the models provided by French literature and so developed three very distinct schools, Romanticism, Parnassianism, and Symbolism, each with its own definition and each with its own practitioners. "Brazilian poetry of this period [roughly 1880 to 1922] was both less innovative and more closely tied to European models than that of Spanish America," write González Echevarría, Pupo-Walker, and Haberly (7). The same scholars also hold that Brazil's remarkable Symbolist João da Cruz e Sousa ranks among "the most powerful and unique New World voices" and can be regarded as "perhaps the greatest black poet of Latin America" (7).

Québec's Émile Nelligan merits comparison with both Darío and Cruz e Sousa as a great renovator of American poetry and with Machado de Assis as a writer possessed of a new understanding of language (see New 122–24). A member of L'École littéraire de Montréal, which began in 1895 and continued to 1925 and beyond, Nelligan resided, as Darío did, in "a literary world," exploring, as Machado was doing, the nature of language, the "power of the symbol," and the gulf between language and the world it seeks to re-present (New 125). The Montreal school resembled other American modernist movements in that it was pulled in two directions, toward the more avant-garde trends appearing in Europe but also toward American native traditions (see Hayne 154; and E. Fitz, *Rediscovering the New World* 121–45). Nelligan, "the first Québec poet able to bear comparison with his contemporaries in France," merits being read in the same context as Darío, Machado, and Cruz e Sousa (Hayne 155).

We need to be careful with our nomenclature here. In Brazil, it was the Symbolist school, and not the later movement of the same name, that corresponded chronologically to Spanish American *Modernismo*. As I will show, what the Brazilians called *Modernismo* would be paralleled in Spanish America with what was called there *vanguardismo,* which is known in the English-speaking world as something akin to postmodern verse. As we move into the early decades of the twentieth century, the terminology does get confusing. If, as many have argued, Spanish American *Modernismo,* which we associate with the dislocation and trauma of the late nineteenth century, was the Hispanic world's response to the crisis of modernity, the Brazilian modernist movement, dating officially from 1922, could be taken as the antidote to it, that is, as an engagement with the real world rather than a retreat from it. For Brazil, a nation with a strong scientific tradition, the dislocation of tradition by science and technology in the late nineteenth century was not as disruptive as it was in Spanish America. It was not entirely smooth, of course, as the tragedy of Canudos shows, but overall, Brazil was better prepared to respond favorably to the scientific and technological breakthroughs of the early twentieth century than its Spanish American neighbors. Discussing the scientifically trained Brazilian writer Euclides da Cunha, the author of the seminal study of the Canudos rebellion, *Os Sertões* (1902, published in English as *Rebellion in the Backlands* in 1944), González Echevarría writes that "Euclides reflects Brazil's commitment to science in the nineteenth century, which for various reasons outstripped that of the rest of Latin America" (*Myth and Archive* 128).[11] Although the two movements shared a name, and although they did have some things in common (a certain revolutionary fervor, for example), they were far from being the same and must not be regarded as such. They offer very different worldviews and their literature reflects this.

Where the Spanish American *modernistas* sought harmony and balance, the Brazilian modernists, coming to the fore after Saussure and his new linguistics, after Einstein had promulgated his theory of relativity, and in the aftermath of World War I (in which Brazil, the only Latin American nation to do so, had participated as one of the allies), accepted change, instability, and uncertainty as inherent to the human condition. One of Brazil's greatest writers, Machado de Assis (who died in 1908), explored the semantic fluidity of language during the final thirty years of his career. Thanks to Machado, readers in Brazil were well accustomed to dealing with ambiguity, in language but also in life. For the Brazilian modernists, the idea of harmony, so prized by Spanish Americans like

Darío, was an illusion. Neither art nor anything else could deliver it; even in the worlds of physics, as Einstein theorized, and mathematics, as Gödel would prove, uncertainty prevailed, and as Machado had demonstrated, it was human beings' task to recognize this basic truth, to accept it, and to deal with it. As a result, Brazilian *Modernismo* has a much stronger connection to the real world, and to everyday human reality, than Spanish American *Modernismo* does.

In looking at the innovative poetry being produced by the Spanish American modernists and at the iconoclastic new narrative coming out of Brazil during the same period, it is important to remember that this was not all; many interesting novels and stories were appearing in the varied countries that together form what we think of as Spanish America, and much excellent poetry was being written in Brazil. In this latter case, the Mallarmé-like yet racially charged verse of João da Cruz e Sousa stands out. This fusion of symbolist poetics and an anguished political consciousness had no equal anywhere in turn-of-the-century America. For Merquior, "Cruz e Sousa, the finest Brazilian lyricist since Gonçalves Dias, wrote with a Novalis-like depth far removed from the verbal coquetry and the technical fireworks that were the trademark of Modernismo" (368). The poetry of Cruz e Sousa stands quite alone. It is worth noting as well that Machado, his underappreciated contemporary Lima Barreto, and Cruz e Sousa were all Black or of mixed blood. Given the deeply miscegenated nature of Brazilian society and literature, their similar heritage is not an anomaly.

Then too, as Aníbal González reminds us, modernist narrative from Spanish America deserves more critical attention than it has so far received (69–73, 95). At the same time, there is the long-standing critical opinion that in contrast to its Brazilian counterpart, the Spanish American novel of the late nineteenth century suffered from a lack of technical innovation. As a creative art form, it has long been judged to be too imitative, too orthodox; well written and dealing with serious issues, yes, but formally not very daring. Yet, as Coonrod Martínez, who discusses only texts from Spanish America, reminds us, there were exceptions.

Gallagher, nevertheless, speaks for the majority when he writes, of the nineteenth-century Latin American novel, that "with the exception of the Brazilian novelist Machado de Assis (1839–1908), Latin American writers . . . were usually too immature and too derivative to merit the serious consideration of anyone not specifically interested in the Latin American context as such" (1). The celebrated Spanish American writer and critic Guillermo Cabrera Infante also noted the singularity of Machado when, in response to an interviewer's question about how it was that only with the Boom period of the 1960s Latin America had begun producing "readable" novels, he responded, "Not true. There is no more 'readable' novel in Latin America than those written by Machado de Assis in Brazil almost a century ago" (quoted in Guibert 423). The scholar Benítez-Rojo sums up the status of the nineteenth-century Spanish American novel this way: "Trapped in the narrative mechanisms of the newspaper serial, oratory, *Costumbrismo,* allegory, and melodrama, the novels written in Spanish America used up in a few decades the simple programmatic outlines to which they subscribed without, for the rest, showing much artistic concern" (434). Taking a comparative turn, he concludes with this thought: "One must agree that" Spanish American novelists of the time "did not," in contrast to Machado de Assis, "achieve a deep understanding of the genre and, as a consequence, they did not contribute to its development" (434). Even Carlos Fuentes, who celebrates the innovative brilliance of Machado and who hails him as the greatest Latin American novelist of the nineteenth century, laments "la mediocridad de la novela hispanoamericana del XIX" (9).

Whether one is a Latin American comparatist or one's operating base is the literature of the United States, it is worth noting that both Machado and Darío were largely ignored by the rest of the world. For those who study Spanish America and Brazil, being ignored by North American critics is the norm. Tiresome, yes, and vexing, unfortunately this is something Latin Americanists have long been accustomed to. The times, however, are changing. Departments of English and American literature in the United States are being staffed these days with more open-minded scholars, young people who do not automatically look down upon literary production from Latin America. Ignacio Infante, a professor of comparative literature and Spanish at Washington University, for example, has recently argued that the work of Darío and the other Spanish American *modernistas* has been vastly undervalued by Anglo-American intellectuals. Building on the work of Alejandro Mejías-López, Infante writes that "even though" Spanish American *Modernismo* "is generally regarded as the first modern poetic movement consciously connecting and bridging both sides of the Atlantic," its "critical impact" in the English-speaking world has been "completely negligible" (180). "Until now," Infante contends, the *Modernismo* of Darío and his cohorts "has not been deemed worthy of critical consideration and translation within the hegemonic Anglo-American modernist canon produced by scholars and critics of Anglo-American literature" (181). Most distressing of all, Infante and

Mejías-López suggest, the dismissive attitude toward Spanish American *Modernismo* "is related to the rise of Anglo-American modernist poetics as a key component of the new canon of English studies" (Infante 180).

Why, one might ask, is it so difficult even now for enthusiasts of Anglo-American Modernism to recognize the important contributions Spanish American *Modernismo* made to the modernist revolution? Have English-language writers and critics been so disdainful of literature written in Spanish that they still ignore or devalue the poetry of Silva, Darío, or Lugones? Have these denizens of the Anglo-American academy been so imprisoned by their East/West training and orientation that they fail to consider North/South lines of influence? One wonders. Or is this simply yet another example of the "blind literary prejudice" against Latin American literature that Rodríguez Monegal spoke of in 1969 ("New Latin American Literature in the U.S.A." 3)? A new cohort of scholars, led by Infante and Mejías-López, is working to change this and in the process to show the entire world the value of modernist writing from Spanish America and Brazil.

In the light of Infante's argument, we can better appreciate Tapscott's observation that a "fascination with the tension of the Image" stands as "perhaps the single greatest Modernist inheritance pervading Latin American poetry since Darío" (10). To carry this thought into the inter-American perspective, one can see interesting studies involving the Imagism of Pound, Hilda Doolittle, and Amy Lowell. For the US Imagists, as for the Spanish Americans, the image was both referential and iconic, pointing to something else but also calling attention to itself. It simultaneously revealed and concealed. But always it generated meaning and inspired the imagination.

Machado too has suffered from this same Anglo-American culture of arrogance and disdain toward all things Latin American. It is why so few people outside the kens of Spanish or Luso-Brazilian literature have even heard about Latin American writers and texts. And it is why even today the Princeton scholar Michael Wood feels compelled to explain that when he chats with people about Machado de Assis, he has to first tell them who he is. As Wood, having noted that Machado has existed in good English translations for more than fifty years now, writes, "Everyone who reads him thinks he is a master, but who reads him, and who has heard of him? When I talk to people about Borges, I often have to say the name carefully, but I don't always have to say who he is" (297). Going on to note that upon reading Machado for the first time Susan Sontag was, as she put it, "astonished that a writer of such greatness does not yet occupy the place he deserves," Wood then wonders, "Have we become less provincial" in the past decade or two (297)? I believe we have.

In Latin America, the nineteenth century was the age of independence. But it was also the period when literature engaged, directly and indirectly, with political concerns. Romanticism, inspired by the French model, was fundamental to this engagement. But in Spanish America and Brazil, where Romanticism evolved in almost opposite fashion, politically charged literature produced some exceptionally innovative narrative and poetry. In both Spanish America and Brazil, the novel form, always associated with the society around it, began to be cultivated. This fusion of politics and art produced an abundance of marvelous literary texts. If in the early years of the century independence was the prime concern in Spanish America, in Brazil it was the status of the Indian and, a few years later, abolition. Cultural emancipation was also on the agenda for Latin American writers (more so for the Spanish Americans than for the Brazilians), as it was for writers in the United States, where the question of political independence had already been settled. And while Spanish America would have to fight a long war to gain its freedom from Spain, Brazil would gain its independence bloodlessly, by the signing of a piece of paper.

7   Rubén Darío, Machado de Assis, and End-of-Century Brilliance

It is squarely within this same reformist approach to American literary history, then, that I propose the following argument: That in the final two decades of the nineteenth century, the most innovative poetry and prose fiction being written in the Americas, North, Central, and South, were coming from Spanish America and Brazil. And the two most representative *craques*[1] of this two-pronged literary revolution were, in poetry and from Spanish America, Rubén Darío[2] and, from Brazil, the great novelist and short story writer Machado de Assis. In the Americas of this period, they had no peers. From the comparative and inter-American perspective, the emergence of Machado and Darío constituted a major event, one that changed our view of the state of poetry and fiction in Latin America and in the Americas during the final two decades of the nineteenth century.

The elder of the two, "Machado de Assis was born in 1839, in Rio de Janeiro. His father, a poor house painter, was the son of freed slaves. His mother was a servant from the Azores who worked in a wealthy household on the outskirts of the city. She died when her son was nine years old. Machado's father was remarried to a poor black woman and then died a few years later. Machado de Assis, therefore, grew up a poor, mulatto orphan, the grandson of slaves in a country where slavery would continue officially to exist until he was fifty years old. He had no formal education and probably never attended school" (Sá Rego). Machado was also "frail and shy," epileptic, myopic, and a stutterer (xix). Nevertheless, he persevered. "He acquired French and English, read voraciously in several languages," and "worked as a typesetter" while pursuing his passion for literature. "He wrote nine novels, a few plays and volumes of poetry, some literary criticism, many journalistic columns, and also published a few excellent translations from French and English" (xix). Along the way, he also found time to pen some 226 short stories, several of which stand as masterpieces of the genre. About Machado, one of the enduring questions has always been how "a man who was born in poverty, had no formal education, and faced so many physical and social disadvantages was able to become such an impressive writer" (xix). However one looks at it, Machado's is a great American story.

Rubén Darío was born in 1867 in Metapa, a small Nicaraguan town known today as Ciudad Darío. His parents separated soon after he was born, and so Darío was reared by his aunt, who was able to send him to a Jesuit school for his early education. Darío was a precocious child, writing poems very early on. His talent was spotted by people in the capital city, Managua, where he was invited to come as a lad and given a post at the National Library. At age fifteen, Darío traveled to San Salvador to work with the scholar Francisco Gavidia, who, seeing his charge's potential, tasked him with studying French literature, concentrating on Victor Hugo. Later, in 1886, Darío would journey to Chile for further study, reading, and writing. *Azul* (1888) would be composed during this fruitful Chilean sojourn. Its author was nineteen.

An intriguing difference between the two men is that while Darío's eminence would breed swarms of imitators, Machado "stood isolated, respected yet misunderstood," the creator of a new and, for his contemporaries, baffling kind of Realism, one that would not generate a following until much later, when his innovative narrative theories and iconoclastic style were better understood and appreciated (Merquior 369; see also Gledson, *Deceptive Realism*).

This chapter will explore five major points of comparison between these two authors.

1. Progress and the Human Condition

To begin with, both Darío and Machado rejected the prevailing concept of material progress that reigned supreme in Western culture in the closing decades of the nineteenth century. The power of this vision of progress was that there was some truth to it. It *is* beneficial, and to everyone, that we have progressed in certain areas: better medicines to combat disease, for example. But it is less beneficial when, after creating these medicines, we rig our social, political, and economic systems so that only a select few have access to them. Yet this is exactly what we have done. People who uphold this outlook call themselves capitalists. And capitalism is based on the pursuit of self-interest. And while Adam Smith argued in *The Wealth of Nations* (1776) that the pursuit of self-interest would benefit everyone, history has proven that it does not. From Smith's time, through the time of Darío and Machado, and even today, when economic globalism has caused so many social, political, economic, and environmental problems for so many, the record of unfettered capitalism shows that societies built around the worship of self-interest end up causing terrible problems and abandoning more people than they benefit. This is what we can learn from history. But we can also learn it from reading the poetry of Rubén Darío and the fiction of Machado de Assis.

Then too, both the Nicaraguan poet and the Brazilian narrativist detest *egoísmo,* which, defined as selfishness or the pursuit of self-interest above all else, stands as the fundamental premise of capitalism. And capitalism functions as the driving force behind the idea of progress, at least of the material kind, so despised by the Spanish American *modernistas* and Machado. Behind this position, however, lies the real problem, which is that if we worship at the altar of selfishness and materialism, then what kind of society do we construct? As Darío writes, "Hay que declarar la guerra al egoísmo. Hay que rehabilitar el ensueño y la fé" (*Obras completas* 4:772; We must declare war on egoism. We must rehabilitate fantasy and faith). While we cannot say for certain that Machado would have agreed entirely with Darío's statement here, we do know that from very early on in his career as a writer he abhorred egoism. For Machado, love of self was always a problem, and this sentiment permeates his work. On this point, the toxicity of selfishness, Machado and Darío would surely have concurred.

Egoism plays a key role in Machado's iconoclastic 1880 text *Memórias Póstumas de Brás Cubas* (*The Posthumous Memoirs of Brás Cubas*), which is narrated by a dead man. It appears literally in chapter 7, entitled, suggestively enough, "The Delirium," where egoism is identified as a basic law of the universe and of all human activity. And it is accepted as such by our narrator. In its original 1880 Portuguese, the narrative itself actually uses the term *egoísmo* three times, lest the reader miss its critical importance to the tale being spun out. The decisive moment comes when Brás Cubas, our self-conscious narrator-protagonist, accepts egoism, or selfishness, as the principle by which he will live out his life. Our at this point still trusted hero, the deeply bourgeois Brás Cubas, finds himself astride a flying hippopotamus who is transporting them both back to the beginning of time. On the way, they meet a huge and awe-inspiring female figure who introduces herself as Nature, or in a sop to the human belief in hope, Pandora. This mysterious figure, equating herself with some vital life force, then, via William L. Grossman's 1952

English translation responds to a credulous Brás, who has just challenged something Nature/Pandora has said she finds absurd and risible, "Egoism, you say? Yes, egoism. I have no other law. Egoism, self-preservation . . . this is the universal law" (Machado de Assis, *Epitaph of a Small Winner* 34). In Gregory Rabassa's 1997 translation this exchange comes out a bit differently: "Selfishness, you say? Yes, selfishness. I have no other law. Selfishness, preservation. . . . that's the universal law" (*Posthumous Memoirs of Brás Cubas* 18–19).

Like Darío, Machado (through the mouth of his character Brás Cubas) sets egoism in conflict with first imagination and then art. "The history of man and the earth," reports Brás, as he watches the ages of humankind fly past him with little or no progress in the human condition being attained, "had an intensity in that way that neither science nor imagination could give it," with the end result that the human comedy was "all sewn together" through the ages "with a precarious stitch by the needle of imagination" (*Posthumous Memoirs of Brás Cubas* 19). One feels here that Darío's belief in the ability of art and the imagination to redeem us is greater than Machado's, and indeed it is probably worth noting that Machado has long been regarded as an inveterate pessimist, as one of the most disillusioned writers of all time. The last sentence of his extraordinary *Posthumous Memoirs of Brás Cubas* speaks of human existence not as a joyous adventure in learning and the doing of good deeds but as "our misery," a reference clearly intended to include the reader as well as the characters in the book (203). Whether Brás's rather bleak assessment of human existence is true or not remains a moot point, though in comparing Machado with Darío the reader does get the feeling that our ability to imagine a better, more just world, or that by imagining it we can bring it about, is greater for the Spanish American poet than it is for the Brazilian novelist.

Then, and dismissing Nature/Pandora as "the chimera of happiness" and "an illusion," Brás, more drawn, one feels, to the second part of her dual name, delivers the telling line: "Come on, Pandora, open up your womb and digest me." "It's amusing," he says, referring to the tiresome and, finally, monotonous human spectacle he has been witness to, "but digest me" (20). We humans do have the capacity to hope, and imagination and art do help us frame this hope and visualize what a better, more just existence could be like, but human history shows us that we are agonizingly slow to make our hopes a reality. Perhaps we are loath to do so; perhaps we prefer to allow our baser instincts, such as egoism, win out. Whatever the reason, every age, every generation, ends up being about like the earlier ones; it's science that "scrutinizes" and it's "art that elevates," but numbingly, our old, mutually offsetting urges—to create and to destroy, and to permit injustice when we claim we want justice—prevent the true progress that our imaginations and our art allow us to see (20). As Machado and Brás take the reader on what turns out to be a rather dreary and depressing survey of human history, what we take from the spectacle is that we humans never seem to learn. We never learn anything. We are our own worst enemies; we continue to do the same dumb, self-defeating things generation after generation.

This same thought is reiterated at the very end of chapter 141, where Brás, in thrall of his mad philosopher companion, Quincas Borba, and having just witnessed the savagery of starving dogs fighting over a meat-less bone, agrees with his mentor that "in some parts of the world the spectacle is on a grander scale: human beings are the ones who fight with dogs over bones and other less appetizing tidbits." "A fight," Brás is led to conclude, "that becomes quite complicated because entering into action is man's intelligence along with the whole accumulation of sagacity that the centuries have given him, etc." (186). It is this "etc.," which is present in the original Portuguese, that delivers the devastating evisceration of the happy, self-satisfied idea about "progress" that we love to cling to. After centuries of thought and reflection, our accumulated "sagacity" has led us no further than this—fighting with dogs for scraps of food. We are still doing it. Whether engaged with the poetry of Rubén Darío or the narratives of Machado de Assis, the reader of 2023, living in the third decade of the twenty-first century, knows this is true. In garbage dumps around the world, men, women, and children are fighting with one another and with dogs for something to eat. Is this what progress means, today's reader asks herself? Although it has made a few fantastically wealthy, global capitalism has not eliminated the twin scourges of poverty and hunger for the many, so why are we constantly exhorted to pray at its altar?

Although we commonly think of the term *global capitalism* as applying to our intensely interconnected life today, in one form or another it existed in earlier generations. And it was in play during Machado's time as well, a period when the kind of thinking known as "savage capitalism" was being imported into Brazil from the United States. In chapter 117 of *The Posthumous Memoirs of Brás Cubas,* the then current form of global capitalism, one shored up by the international institution of slavery, goes under Machado's microscope. On the surface this chapter, titled "Humanitism," has long been read as a withering satire of Comte's Positivism, a science-based line of thought hugely popular in Brazil. To this day the

Brazilian flag bears the defining words of Positivism—*Ordem e Progresso* (Order and Progress). But there lies buried within this critique of Positivism, with its unshakable faith in science, a scene that lays bare the utterly amoral, if not immoral, workings of global capitalism, the manner in which the few are benefited by the sacrifice and abuse of the many. What is most chilling about this little scene, tucked away in this larger evisceration of Positivism, is how easily the few who benefit from the exploitation of the global "other" find ways to justify the systematic enslavement that sustains the global economic order. This scene is likely even more powerful today, when we know more about how global systems operate, than it was in 1880, when it was first written.

Importantly, the person espousing the mad "philosophy" of "Humanitism" is not Brás Cubas (who, as in chapter 7, again simply agrees, without thinking about it, with what he is being told) but his compatriot Quincas Borba, who may or may not be insane. Ambiguity rules supreme in the world of Machado de Assis, and it is up to the reader to decide. Tellingly, in Quincas's system of thought, which he finds superior to all others, "there is a need" for each man "to worship himself" (162). The more cloistered egoism lurking behind this argument echoes the egoism more literally advanced in chapter 7. And in both cases the uncritical Brás, representing Brazil's ruling class, is only too happy to embrace it. But this is not the end of it. And in fact, it is, as the attentive reader sees, the system that is at fault, and not merely the handful of people who, untroubled by all the harm it does others, profit from it.

This scene is built around the global problem of want. In a moment of delicious irony, Quincas discourses on the problem of hunger while happily chewing on a delicious chicken wing. "Gnawing on" his tasty tidbit, our great theoretician of the unquestioned benefits of global capitalism opines, with the "philosophic serenity" of someone whose hunger will be taken care of, "I don't need any other documentation of the sublimity of my system than this chicken right here. It nourished itself on corn, which was planted by an African, let us suppose imported from Angola. That African was born, grew up, was sold. A ship brought him here, a ship built of wood cut in the forest by ten or twelve men, propelled by sails that eight or ten men sewed together, not to mention the rigging and other parts of the nautical apparatus. In that way, this chicken, which I have lunched on just now, is the result of a multitude of efforts and struggles carried out with the sole aim of satisfying my appetite" (163). For Quincas and for Brás, who accepts what Quincas is saying, even a global system based on slavery (as Quincas implies) is fine—as long as it benefits someone. For those who benefit from it, in 1880 or in 2023, the slavery part of such a system is not a problem.

The added value, as an economist might say, that Machado imparts to this shameless and self-centered apology for slavery (and for other forms of exploitation) is that it is delivered here not by a member of the ruling class, from whom one would expect it, but by a madman. It is madness, Machado is telling us, through the mouth of Quincas Borba, to set up and maintain such a monstrous system. Yet then as now, the global elite do exactly that. And the justification is always the same: if I get what I want out of it, nothing is amiss. One cannot read this chapter without thinking about how the pursuit of self-interest is the beating heart of capitalism.

The ethic Brás, our narrator, embraces, then, is that of selfishness. All of his decisions about life, love, and happiness will be filtered through the lens of selfishness. "How will this benefit me?" becomes the question that will guide his life. Born to upper-middle-class money and privilege as he was, and aspiring rather idly to power, Brás's decisions reflect those of the Brazilian elite, and by extension those of the elite everywhere. And this is why his novel is as relevant today as it was in 1880. Perhaps more so, as in 2023 the deleterious effects of global capitalism are widely known and discussed.

But as the alert reader of Machado's novel gradually discovers, Brás, for all his affability and charm, and for all that he claims he is going to tell us the truth, reveals himself to be an unreliable narrator. So too, then, is the Brazilian ruling class, whose interests and attitudes Brás so completely embodies. Smart, glib, and capable of great things but also an indolent parasite, Brás has spent a lifetime using other people. Thus it is that in the final chapter the reader realizes that if she and people like her continue to accept Brás's utterly self-centered outlook, human life itself will come to an end. Totally wrapped up in his own self-interest, Brás takes pride in having produced no progeny. How does the reader, who may well have been taken in so far by our wry and seductive narrator, respond to this rather dunning realization? That is the question, the one the reader-citizen has to answer.

If Darío frames the problem of egoism in terms that are more aesthetic and philosophical, Machado sees it in more political terms, as a question of how and why we make the sundry decisions we do and, as a consequence, how and why we structure our societies as we do. Darío is not oblivious to this, but owing in part to the nature of lyric poetry, he does not plumb it as openly as Machado the narrativist does. Machado and Darío both wanted to reenergize our imaginations. Both practiced innovation in their respective art forms, and both believed in the value of art. Where they differed was on the role art would play in society. For Machado, the novels and short stories he produced were most definitely a form of artistic creativity, and he took pride in them as such, though there is also reason to believe that he viewed his narratives as an instrument of social change.

Then too, it is quite possible to think, reading his post-1880 work especially, that Machado saw the attentive, engaged reader he so assiduously cultivated, and occasionally chastised, as the kind of new citizen he wanted as well. A new readership and a new citizenry for a new Brazil. From the very texts he wrote, one can conclude that Machado wanted his new readers, both male and female, to function as citizens. The training of the former was invaluable to the latter; that is, both had to learn to examine the facts and the words carefully, to consider their possible meanings, and to then arrive at a logical conclusion, which, for the citizen who could vote (and for those who could influence others about how to vote), might well take the form of exactly that—voting. The skills needed by the reader are clearly needed by the citizen as well. While one feels that Darío would not disagree with this hypothesis concerning the role of his reader, he does not develop it in his poetry as overtly as Machado does in his fiction. At the same time, Darío might well say, what Machado shows the reader proves the truth of his contention that egoism must be controlled, in literature by the reader (who can learn, via the negative example, not to endorse or emulate it) and in life by the citizen (who can learn not to vote for candidates who indulge it).

The problem of egoism goes back even further in American literature. Hawthorne regarded it as the taproot of misadventure, an evil to be avoided at all costs. For the author of *The Scarlet Letter,* the indulgence of selfishness led to ruin, for the individual and for any society built around it. The antidote to it was putting the welfare of others before one's own interests. For Hawthorne, the primary virtue of human existence was service to others, not self-indulgence. For the robber barons, such an idea was risible. So it was that in the United States of the postrevolutionary period, when geographic and economic expansion were unrestrained and the basic principles of US-style capitalism were being solidified, Hawthorne's position was increasingly regarded as a quaint reminder of a rapidly fading past, one in which honorable conduct and service to others were virtues not merely preached but practiced and so quickly shunted aside in the race for commercial expansion. Spanish America, having just passed through its own bloody and traumatic revolutionary period, and monarchist Brazil were alarmed at how easily the United States could abandon its founding principles. The unrestrained pursuit of economic self-interest had come to define the United States, and Latin Americans, all too aware of their vulnerable positions, knew that meant trouble for them.

Do unto others, Brás and the power brokers of the world like to say, and do it quick, before they do unto you. This admonition, though not literally present in the work of either Machado or Darío, might well sum up the attitudes of these two great late nineteenth-century Latin American writers. And it would capture their opposition to the Social Darwinism and the survival-of-the-fittest philosophy so prevalent in many quarters (those with money and power) of the United States and Latin America. Whether the response to this kind of thinking should be to retreat into an ethereal world of art for art's sake or to attack, trying to make reader-citizens aware of the choices they must make, is a moot point. We can see Darío and Machado offering us these two very different responses. It is not insignificant that Latin Americans knew they were about to be systematically exploited and abused by the kind of "progress" being pitched by US Big Business and its political lackeys.

Latin Americans could see that in the post–Civil War United States venality was crushing the spirit of democracy, and they understood that this stemmed from the corrupt wedding of Big Business and right-wing politics. They also knew that this unholy alliance of WASP culture and money would inevitably condemn the people of Spanish America and Brazil to chattel if not outright slavery. The signs were everywhere, and Latin Americans saw them. Followers of Darwin in the United States—and there were many—maintained that their supposed racial superiority over what they took to be a half-breed (and therefore inferior) Latin America "had already rendered inevitable the expansion of the United States over large portions of the globe" (Carman and Syrett 288). A white, Anglo-Saxon, and Protestant God had, in the view of US expansionists, already justified their racism and religious bigotry. For WASPish true believers, the takeover and occupation of Catholic and racially mixed Latin America was preordained by US "exceptionalism" and was going to be carried out whether the people of Spanish America and Brazil liked it or not. So much for liberty and justice for all. Its political instrument would be the self-serving doctrine of Manifest Destiny. "From 1880 to 1900," argue the historians Carman and Syrett, "the United States developed into an intensely nationalistic nation, and the preachers of expansionism . . . both promoted and reflected the growth of [US] imperialism" (288). And although other cultures were involved, the Hawaiian Islands and the

Philippines, for example, Latin America (especially Spanish America) would bear the brunt of this imperialism. And the people of the Caribbean would be the first to get it. This was the larger American context in which Darío and Machado lived and wrote.

This question of progress, whether we, the American people, were truly moving toward something better or whether we were regressing, done in by the materialism that had improved our lives in so many ways, was also a question that linked Darío and Machado to the US writer Henry Adams. Published in 1905, Adams's book *The Education of Henry Adams* is less an autobiography of its author than it is an autopsy of what was for him the already visible decline of Western civilization. In a dispassionate dissection of what many refer to as the modern malaise, Adams, born to wealth, position, and power, writes that he feels that life no longer has any clear purpose, that there are no longer any absolutes one can cling to in a changing time, and that the human quest for meaning is now doomed to failure. The quest for money and power, which had come to define the United States, was not enough. Indeed, it was degrading. True progress, the kind that advances civilizations and improves human life, was, Adams fretted, falling prey to greed and to a new and relentless thirst for power, one that could not be slaked. The old verities were being undermined just as surely as the old virtues were.

Adams's pessimism about the future has a parallel both in Darío's verse and in what the great majority of critics believe to be Machado's pessimism. Long regarded as one of world literature's most disillusioned writers, Machado, it could be argued, would understand Adams's lament and, to a degree at least, feel a kinship with him, a kindred spirit, as it were. It is easy to imagine Machado's reading *The Education of Henry Adams* with some concurrence, though the Brazilian's perspective would have been more than a little different because it was not from the heart of the beast but from the periphery, the margins of capitalist society, one of the places that got the wrong end of the Wall Street whip. Machado saw this as early as 1880 and *The Posthumous Memoirs of Brás Cubas,* and Darío wrote about it in "A Roosevelt" (1905).

The difference is to be found in the response of these two great American writers. For Darío, it lies in the retreat into the unsullied world of art and beauty, of art for art's sake, while for Machado it is more a matter of putting art at the service of checking selfishness and egoism and of promoting a commitment to civic duty, to getting the reader-citizen to think more critically about what needs to be done to improve things. For those who know Machado's work in depth, this reading can seem overly and, some will say, undeservedly optimistic, but I believe that in the transition from *The Posthumous Memoirs of Brás Cubas* to *Counselor Ayres' Memorial* there is a ray of hope.

For those familiar with the less than rosy *Weltanschauung* of Machado de Assis, a thorough reading of *The Education of Henry Adams* leads one to contemplate a number of parallels and comparisons with the still egregiously underappreciated Brazilian writer. Chapter 15, "Darwinism," for example, brings to mind, in *The Posthumous Memoirs of Brás Cubas,* Machado's skewering of the survival-of-the-fittest doctrine (chapters 14–15, 17, 32) as well as the pillorying of Comte and Positivism (chapter 117). Adams's chapter 28 describes human history not in terms of the growth of knowledge and how it might be of benefit to all but, as Machado does in chapter 141 (where the words come from the mouth of a madman), in terms of endless struggle between individual egos and rigid, imprisoning systems of thought. In Adams's book, chapters 29 through 34 reiterate this outlook, emphasizing humanity's record of not progressing very much except in material terms and instead choosing to fight endlessly over the same tired issues, a point driven home in chapter 7 of *The Posthumous Memoirs of Brás Cubas* and then even more poignantly at the very end of chapter 141. For both Adams and Machado, or at least the Machado of *The Posthumous Memoirs of Brás Cubas* and the novel that followed it, *Quincas Borba* (1891), there is an eerie sense of exhaustion, paralysis, or stasis being emitted by their writing. Adams, of course, was writing nonfiction, and Machado fiction, but a similar sentiment pervades the writing of both.

Both Machado and Darío were skeptical about this end-of-century idolatry of material progress, though in reading what they produced after 1896 it is possible to conclude that Darío felt the sting of failure more than did the more resigned yet still hopeful Machado. With *Prosas Profanas,* which appeared in 1896 (five years after *Quincas Borba*), Darío and his brand of Spanish American *Modernismo* reached their zenith. Here, late in the nineteenth century, Darío's world of myth, fantasy, exotic realms, and the exquisite reached its maximum expression.

In between the beautiful images and the musical lines, a note of failure begins to seep into what is for some an escapist world, where art and the artist have valance they would not have in the rest of society, a crass, material, and pedestrian place not characterized by a faith in beauty and harmony. One discerns in the *Prosas Profanas* the creeping fear that a belief in art, no matter how sincere, no matter how fervent, is not enough. But the same anxiety also permeates, now more strenuously, the *Cantos de vida y esperanza* (1905), written seven years after the disastrous Spanish-American War, two years after the US intervention in Panama, and one year after Machado's penultimate novel, *Esau and Jacob,* appeared. Here, in the *Cantos,* Darío's production of escapist or exotic verse saw its end. Still beautiful, but now purged of the exotic and infused with a note of the elegiac, the *Cantos* marked an end to the most transformative strain of Spanish American *Modernismo.* The real world was starting to subsume it. Embracing the Hispanic tradition more than the French, which had so empowered his earlier breakthroughs in *Azul,* the *Cantos* show us a resigned, if not defeated, Rubén Darío.

"Lo fatal," perhaps Darío's most anguished poem, dates from 1904. Not even art, its lines seem to say, can save us from the despair of being human. A not entirely dissimilar response can be gotten from reading Machado's *The Posthumous Memoirs of Brás Cubas* (1880). Of his novels, his final one, *Counselor Ayres' Memorial,* seems to place considerable hope in idealistic and committed young people, especially young women like Fidélia. Far from being any kind of Pollyanna, Machado, as bleak as his vision for human progress can be, as in chapter 7 of *The Posthumous Memoirs of Brás Cubas,* still holds out the possibility of hope, the chance that his reader-citizen will move from reading books to political action and actually vote to improve human existence, not just for the wealthy and privileged but for everyone. While in poems like "A Roosevelt," "Salutación al Águila," and a few others Darío showed that he was indeed politically aware, one concludes that of the two it was Machado who was more consistently aware, socially, politically, and economically. He manifested this awareness by writing about Brazilian political trends and such urgent issues as slavery and its aftermath, abolition, the formation of the republic, and the rights of women. Yet to be fair, one must also conclude that the Brazilian master, like the Nicaraguan, couched all these extraliterary concerns in the cultivation of his art. In sum we might say that while Darío revolutionized Spanish American poetry by creating an "artificial paradise," as Stavans puts it, Machado did the same thing for Brazilian narrative, but he did it by inventing a "new narrative," one that seems on the surface to be a realistic portrayal of his society but that on closer observation undercuts it all, showing the inherent semantic instability of language (liv).

Although both Darío and Machado prized art, only one, Darío, staked out the art-for-art's-sake position. Olavo Bilac, the author of "Profissão de Fé" (1886) and *Via Láctea* (1902), is his Brazilian counterpart on this point (see Moisés, "Brazilian Poetry from 1878 to 1902" 85–95). Machado's commitment to the art of narrative, as his contemporary Henry James saw it, was more muted and a function of the audacious new narrative he was writing after 1880 and talking about not in the form of critical essays but almost entirely within the confines of the texts themselves, where his own characters, Brás Cubas being the prime example, would discuss it.

2. From the Sensual to the Sexual

Both Darío and Machado embrace a theme hitherto much tiptoed around, human sexuality, and both recognized the value of sensuality in their work. In examining their work, it would seem that Darío especially understood the sexual impulse to be directly linked to both imagination and creativity. Although Machado clearly viewed sexuality as exerting a powerful influence in human affairs, it is less obvious that he saw its spurring of creativity as clearly as Darío did. Yet the work of both writers shows that few forces in human existence are as dissolving of rigid barriers, narrow definitions, and hegemonic structures as is sexual desire. The social historian Emília Viotti da Costa discusses how common it was in that portion of nineteenth-century imperial Brazil most interesting to Machado de Assis for elegant prostitutes and women of high social standing to mingle easily with each other at public events (184–85). According to K. David Jackson, Carl Schlichthorst pointed out the same phenomena. The German visitor concluded that in Brazil both society women and expensive courtesans regularly attended the theater and that far from presenting obstacles to this behavior, Brazil was "a paradise for these creatures," a fluid and highly sexualized space where there were "no differences between the two classes" (Schlichthorst, quoted in K. Jackson, *Machado de Assis* 157).

In reading the history and literature of Brazil, one can easily come to feel that Brazilian society has been rendered uniquely flexible at least in part because of the destabilizing role sexuality has played in its development. This was true from the very beginning, as Gilberto Freyre contended in *Casa-grande e senzala* (1933), and it has continued on. Numerous Brazilian writers have explored this theme as well, including from the colonial period Gregório de Matos and from the nineteenth century such canonical figures as José de Alencar (*Senhora*, 1875, for example), Machado de Assis (see E. Fitz, *Machado de Assis and Female Characterization* 26–27, 60–69), and Aluísio Azevedo, whose 1890 novel *O cortiço* (*The Slum*) features lesbianism as an alternative to patriarchy and female solidarity. Adolfo Caminha's 1895 novel *Bom-Crioulo* puts the issue of male homosexuality, involving a Black man and a young white man, at the center of his text and develops it not as an aberration but as a love story, one undone by prejudice (see Mundell). In the twentieth century, we have Jorge de Lima, whose "Êssa Negra Fulô" ("That Black Woman Fulô"), of 1928, wove together issues of slavery, sexuality, gender, class, and power to produce one of the most intriguing poems of the time. We also have José Lins do Rêgo's *Menino de engenho,* which depicts how Black women often provided young white men with their early sexual education. By 1943, and *Near to the Savage Heart,* Clarice Lispector was advocating not only for the liberation of women, socially, psychologically, and sexually, but for that of men as well. And in her deeply inter-American novel *A república dos sonhos (The Republic of Dreams),* Nélida Piñon contrasts the sexual profligacy of the Portuguese colonizers of Brazil and their female African partners with the sterile and rigid Puritans of North America. More recently, Lamonte Aidoo has argued that even in the often very hierarchical "big house," where the plantation master and mistress resided, female sexuality routinely eroded barriers of gender, class, and race (see Aidoo). The issue here is not whether sexuality is a theme in the literature of Spanish America, the United States, and Canada; we know, of course, that it is. The question is whether, as seems to be the case, Brazilian literature's examination of human sexuality is a constant, recurring theme, a motif, as it were, of its national development. It seems plausible. If one accepts this possibility, then Machado's cultivation of human sexuality would not be as startling, or as transgressive, as is the case with Darío and Spanish American literature.

Either way, we can agree that by focusing anew on issues of human sexuality, both Darío and Machado freed their readers to think differently about everything, including what had long been masculine-oriented ideas about what constituted this thing called "progress," what it meant, and who benefitted from it. If, moreover, sexuality had to do with the quest for pleasure, rather than utility and the accumulation of wealth, then it was in direct opposition to the veneration of material progress that dominated the late nineteenth century. Then too, one can see how both writers—though again Darío takes the lead—envision the unencumbered pursuit of sensual pleasure, which in turn points to the attainment of sexual pleasure, as a kind of antidote to the world weariness, *Weltschmerz,* or alienation that characterized this end-of-century period, when science had undercut religion and there seemed to be little to cling to. Like so much of Darío's poetry, Oscar Wilde's biblical tragedy *Salomé* (1893) deals with this same clash between religious propriety and human sexual desire. Satisfaction was hard to come by. This particular sense of the value of sexual release, its supposed curative properties, is not nearly as prominent in the novels and stories of Machado as it is in the poetry of Darío, where it is all but an omnipresent force. It may well reflect as well the degree to which Darío's best poetry was in some ways a reflection of a deeply personal struggle he himself was experiencing between his religious faith and his sexual desires.

Reading Darío, one is led to ask, Why is sexual pleasure so relegated to the status of sin? Is this some bizarre quirk of our Judeo-Christian heritage? Are there no human cultures that regard sex as something other than sinful and depraved? Darío believed, or wanted to believe, that yes, such cultures did exist. And to judge from much of his imagery, he seemed to believe that they could be found in ancient Greek mythology. This was the basis for his extensive cultivation of the myth of Leda, Jupiter/Zeus, and the swan. For Darío, the fact that the divine (Jupiter/Zeus) and the human (Leda) could, via art and the imagination, be brought together in sexual congress whose result was the creation of great beauty (Helen of Troy is their offspring) was sufficient to justify his decision to merge the sensual, the sexual, and his Christian beliefs. By doing so, Darío hoped to overcome the conflict between the latter and the former. He hoped, in short, to harmonize his life by writing a new kind of poetry, one in which the experiencing of sexual pleasure was not inimical to religious belief.

The first poem of *Azul,* "Primaveral," whose title is translated by Lysander Kemp as "Springtime" (see Tapscott 31), builds on images of a female beloved being summoned, flowers opening up, the scent of fragrant honey in the air, and nude nymphs playing together in the crystalline water. Yet the entire scene is pervaded not by a sense of sin or perversity but by an innocent and natural sensuality. Also from *Azul,* two stories, "El palacio del sol" and "Palomas blancas y garzas morenas," similarly quiver with sexual pleasure, or the promise of it. So too does the swan-related verse in which Darío, contemplating not Leda's reaction but the "celeste melancolía" (celestial melancholy) of the swan (Jupiter/Zeus), whose "luminoso cuello estirado" (luminous extended neck) has placed itself "entre los blancos muslos de Leda" (between Leda's white thighs). While Darío wants his reader to feel the "melancholy" of the swan, who, as Jupiter/Zeus, chose to abandon his divinity in order to come down from his celestial perch and enjoy the pleasures of sex with an earthly woman, Leda, the emphasis here is on what is clearly phallic, the "cuello estirado."[3]

The poem ends at this point, and nowhere in it is there any mention of what Leda, the human female, feels about what has taken place.
Did she derive the same kind of pleasure from their sexual encounter
that Darío did? Could the descriptor *melancolía* apply both to Jupiter/
Zeus and to Leda? Could it not be that she too feels melancholy at being
taken sexually by a greater force, even that of a god? Although this reading seems quite plausible, we do not know. The poem is entirely about
male satisfaction and power; Jupiter/Zeus, the dominant god, can transform himself into a swan in order to copulate with a human woman he
desires, but this same woman cannot transform herself into a god in order
to have sex with Jupiter/Zeus even if she desires him. On both counts,
Leda's response is missing. We are told nothing of it, and she does not
speak. While unity is undoubtedly a goal of Darío's, and while the sexual
union between males and females is a key manifestation of it in his poetry,
the fact that Leda has no voice tends to undercut this very same desire for
unity. Unless, of course, and as would be typical for men of Darío's time,
this unity were imagined as achievable even between people of unequal
status. Either way, however, there would seem to be a power relationship
here that is troubling to the modern reader. This is an aspect of Darío's
poetic universe that has not worn well.

In another of the Leda poems, the swan, described in the most erotic
of terms, again "viola" (violates) Leda:

Tal es, cuando esponja las plumas de seda,
olímpico pájaro herido de amor,
y viola en las linfas sonoras a Leda,
buscando su pico los labios en flor.

(Thus he is, when he strokes his silken plumes,
An Olympian bird wounded by love,
And, in the sonorous waters, he violates Leda,
His beak seeking her flowering lips.) (Franco 145)

For the translators Greg Simon and Steven White, this line comes
across somewhat differently:

Grand, as he ruffles his silken feathers,
this bird from Olympus bearing love's wound,
ravishing Leda in roiling waters,
thrusting at petals of her sex in bloom . . .

(Quoted in Darío, *Rubén Darío* 21)

Here, however, in Darío's utilization of the myth, Leda expresses a word of complaint, though only in the vaguest and most resigned of terms, the terms of one who suffers eternal violation:

> Suspira la bella desnuda y vencida
> y en tanto que al aire sus quejas se van
> del fondo verdoso de fronda tupida
> chispean turbados los ojos de Pan.

> (The beauty, nude and conquered, sighs,
> And her complaints are born away by the breeze.
> From the green depths of the thick foliage
> Pan's eyes glint with agitation.)

Simon and White render the same lines thusly:

> When at last her sobbing is heard no more,
> the stripped, mastered beauty lets out a sigh.
> From the tangled green rushes by the shore,
> Sparkle-eyed Pan watches, and wonders why.
>
> (Quoted in Darío, *Rubén Darío* 21)

Once again, the emphasis of Darío's poem is on the male; though Leda does here sound a note of displeasure, an objection perhaps, it is lost in the poem's focus on the swan, the male figure. For Darío, Leda's lament at being ravished is subsumed by the distress Jupiter/Zeus, a powerful god, feels by dint of having debased himself by descending to the level of mere humans in order to satisfy his lust.

Reading Darío today, one is led to ask several other questions as well: How close are the concepts of beauty, sensuousness, and eroticism? Is the sexual urge part and parcel of our creative urges? Does the study of aestheticism also entail the study of morality? Some have believed it does. In the Western tradition, the story of aesthetics goes back to the ancient Greeks. In more modern times, its most powerful advocate has been, in fact, the German philosopher Immanuel Kant. For Kant, "the beautiful is the symbol of the morally good, and . . . it is only in this respect . . . that it gives pleasure" (Hofstadter and Kuhns 341). Part of that pleasure derives from sensual stimulation, but part of it, taking the form of erotic attraction, is more explicitly sexual in nature. Sensuous but never pornographic, Darío's poetry equates human sexuality with creativity, the bringing forth of beauty. Much of Darío's best verse oscillates between sensuousness and sensuality. At times it even becomes lustful, leading to images of "violent possession" (Stavans xxxviii). This Kantian belief that morality resides in beauty and that beauty, as created by the artist, produces various forms of pleasure provides Darío with a solid basis for his aesthetic needs. Solidly rooted in the aesthetics of the Western tradition, Darío is able to connect beauty, eroticism, and morality with the highest form of artistic expression.

And yet there are problems. While the reader of the late nineteenth century might have found Darío's focus on the sexual satisfaction of the male partner to be entirely normal, today's reader, more attuned to greater equality between the sexes, even in sexual matters, and unaccepting of sexual assault in any form, is less accepting of his perspective here. Nor does the concept of the artist as exclusively male hold sway any more. Time and experience have, on this point, changed how we respond to Darío today. The modern reader is more skeptical of the one-sidedness of his handling of human sexuality and human creativity. She understands Darío's quest to bring the experience of sexual pleasure into a state of harmony with Christian theology and so overcome the Christian equating of sexuality and sin, but she finds it more challenging to be content with the exclusion of women and their sexual pleasure from his poems and to conclude that classical mythology provides a clear solution to this dilemma. Rape, to return to the myth of Leda and the swan, is still rape. The verb *violar* makes the salient point. And its meaning is inescapable. Nevertheless, Darío, coming at it from a male perspective and seeking always to reconcile his embrace of sensuality and sexuality with Christian culture, believed that he, at least, had found in the underpinnings of Western civilization a way to do it. He was a man of his time and place, and his work must be apprehended in this context. As readers and critics, we know this is true. But on this point is Darío limited to his time and place?

Machado, also interested in human sexuality as a force fundamental to the human experience and a writer much less burdened by Christian doctrine,[4] took a different approach to plumbing this topic, one that centered not on male sexuality, as was the case with Darío, but on female sexuality. The passivity of Darío's women—Leda, for example—gives way in Machado's world to females who assert themselves. This is what stands out in Machado's post-1880 work as far as a comparison with Darío is concerned. In *The Posthumous Memoirs of Brás Cubas*, for example, the character Eugênia is fully aware of her deformity but quite willing to use her other charms to get what she wants in life. No shrinking violet, she is about as far from Leda's characterization by Darío as one can get. In Darío's world there are no female characters who delight in their own sensuality, or who explore it as much as several of Machado's memorable women do. In this Machado was a pioneer.

Male sexual desire is certainly present in Machado's narratives; Brás Cubas's easy lechery toward a variety of women is recognizable and readily apparent. What stands out, however, is Machado's steady exploration of female sexuality and sexual desire. The fascinating Sofia, of *Quincas Borba* (1891), heads this list, which also features such memorable characters as the adulterous Virgília (also from *Posthumous Memoirs of Brás Cubas,* 1880), the erotically transgressive Dona Severina (from "A Woman's Arms," 1885), and the repressed Conceição (of "Midnight Mass," 1894). There are many other examples. In charting this hitherto unknown territory, Machado can be thought of as anticipating Freud (K. Jackson, *Machado de Assis* 118).

Machado's commitment to female sexuality became especially prominent after 1880, the date usually given as the beginning of his mature period. In *The Posthumous Memoirs of Brás Cubas,* as suggested above, the reader finds a spate of female characters who come to life at least in part because of their sexual natures. One of these is the delightful Spanish working girl Marcela, who, our narrator (summing up their relationship) tells us, "loved me for fifteen months and eleven *contos,* no more, no less" (*Posthumous Memoirs of Brás Cubas* 38). As far as her sexuality is concerned, Marcela is about as far from Leda (with whom she is fleetingly and ironically compared) as one can get (35). Not burdened by the truth but keenly aware of the need to close the deal, Marcela, we learn, "didn't have any rustic innocence and hardly understood the morality of the law. She was a good girl, cheerful, without scruples, a little hampered by the austerity of the times, . . . fond of luxury, impatient, a friend of money and young men. That year she was madly in love with a certain Xavier, a wealthy and tubercular fellow—a pearl" (33). An exemplary entrepreneur in the new capitalism that the Brazil of this period was busy importing from the United States, Marcela specializes in the buying and selling of sex. And she is good at her business.

At no point, moreover, does the narrator condemn her or decry what she does for a living. For Marcela, a successful capitalist, sex is simply another commodity. There are buyers and there are sellers. And the price, a function of supply and demand, is set accordingly. As in Darío's use of classical mythology to harmonize the Catholic theology of his upbringing with his decidedly un-Catholic sexual desires, questions of morality have nothing to do with Marcela's development as a character. For her, and for her customers, morality and business are unrelated, except of course in the context of hypocrisy, where some creative spin on morality is necessary for purposes of making a sale. For Machado, Marcela is a successful businesswoman, not a "fallen" woman, and she comes to life as such. There are no Marcelas in Darío's beautiful and rarefied but still male-oriented world.

For David Jackson, Machado's view of "female sexuality was contingent on class and social restrictions but undoubtedly motivated by the double standards of a patriarchal society in which males had unrestricted access to courtesans and lovers" (140). His was a society in which women were expected to repress their own erotic desires and to feel guilty about having them. Aware of this, Machado chose a different approach to their representation. This cannot be said of Darío. Machado, who creates female characters who exult in their sexuality, rattles the patriarchal cage; Darío, for all his erotic play and inventive daring, does not. If both Darío and Machado cultivated questions of sexuality and desire, Machado, with his probing of female desire, would have to be considered the more revolutionary of the two.

In Europe, Oscar Wilde was arguing that art and morality had to be separated, that the one had no obligation to the other. Darío, perhaps more openly than Machado, played with the tension between eroticism and bourgeois notions about rectitude, with the former often draped in references to Greek and Roman mythology, thus bestowing on it an acceptability it would not otherwise enjoy. The myth built around Leda's rape by the swan is often tilled by Darío for exactly this reason. For Machado, as for the later Freud, the erotic impulse was simply more fundamental a part of the human psyche and did not need to be justified. What was new for the Brazilian writer, however, was his exploration of female sexuality, or female desire. Sofia, of *Quincas Borba,* is the great example of this, though there are several others.

The case of Sofia is further engaging because it shows that like Darío, Machado could avail himself of classical mythology to frame his erotic characterizations. Sofia's characterization in fact is presented in the context of the wife of King Candaules, who ruled ancient Lydia. In chapter 35 the narrator, describing Palha, writes, "Thus, he was a sort of King Candaules, exhibiting less to be sure, but to a larger public" (Machado de Assis, *Philosopher or Dog?* 46). For the reader who is not aware of the story of King Candaules but looks it up, the reward is that she sees how the process of comparing one thing with another thing inevitably involves both similarity and difference. Semantic change occurs. There are no fixed, eternal meanings; all is relative. Typical of the mature Machado, the narrator also injects a touch of levity and informality here so as to throw off the reader or lessen the impact of the allusion on her consciousness. Rarely, if ever, does Darío do this; for him, the use of classical mythology is couched in an artistically serious context. For Machado, who was fond of treating serious issues in a comic mode and comic issues in a serious mode, thus keeping the reader off-balance and forcing her to arrive at her own conclusions, the contextualization provided by King Candaules is no less serious an issue; it is, however, less ostentatiously structured and more open to interpretation.

In Sofia's presentation, she is dressed in *décolletage* by her capitalist husband, Palha, the parasitical "friend" of Rubião, the novel's protagonist, and as we learn, she takes pleasure in being so displayed. Sofia allows herself to be dressed in this fashion to please her husband, who orders her to do so to entice possible business clients for him. She knows this. The surprise is that, as the text makes clear, she admires her body and takes delight in showing it off. In the myth of King Candaules, he too puts his wife on display, forcing her to appear nude in the presence of one of his chief ministers. In an unexpected consequence of this act, the king's wife conspires with the minister and persuades him to kill the king and take up with her. While Sofia may well be carrying on an affair with a member of their social circle (the text titillates the reader with this possibility just as Sofia titillates herself and others), it is not Rubião, who, gradually losing the ability to distinguish between madness and sanity, thinks she is flirting with him. She is not, as the reader sees. Or is she? One of the novel's basic subtexts for the reader-citizen is that we must take care not to misinterpret the welter of signs that constantly surround us. But as Kafka would later become famous for showing, it is difficult, if not impossible, to succeed in doing this, in understanding what things mean. More than anything else, Machado suggests, life is a process of stumbling along in the dark, constantly making mistakes and then dealing with the consequences, which involve making more decisions, whose outcome we can never be sure of. We live in an unalterable state of confusion and uncertainty. This, for Machado, is the human condition, and it is his primary subject matter.

The crucial difference between Darío's and Machado's use of classical mythology to sharpen characterization and advance basic themes is that the Brazilian master was more interested in female sexuality than the Nicaraguan. And the King Candaules myth is far from the only one

Machado makes use of. There are many others, and they come from all parts of the world.

In the case of Palha and Sofia, however, it is interesting for the modern reader, who is well aware of how the market uses sex to buy and sell things, to observe Palha taking the actions he takes and to consider why he, the husband and businessman, does so. But while Palha's story is emblematic of capitalism and so rather banal, what holds the reader's interest in terms of their relationship is not him but her. As a character, she is more captivating than he is. Although undoubtedly lusting after the hatching of new financial schemes (one of which will ensnare poor, unsuspecting Rubião), Palha also lusts after his wife. What surprises the reader, however, is that Sofia likes being used in this fashion, exhibited, as it were, as a sexualized and therefore powerful woman. Coming to understand this, Sofia takes pleasure in flaunting her charms and in making men—and, one can suppose, women as well—desire her. Sofia can be regarded as a woman whose sexuality grants her a kind of agency she would otherwise never have had.

3. Innovations in Form, Structure, and Style

In their own distinct ways, and allowing for differences of genre (poetry versus narrative), both Darío and Machado initiated a revolution in terms of form and structure. From his French models, Mallarmé and Verlaine, Darío learned of the need to create new rhythms and to instill them with music. And to demonstrate its viability, his new poetry must create a new language with which to work. In addition to renovating many traditional verse forms, Darío, writes the poet and critic Stephen Tapscott, "invented" both new forms and a new diction "to record a new mode of consciousness for Latin American poetics" (31). This talent for blending the old with the new imparted to Darío's poetry a sense of hybridity and innovation. His metrifications evoke the past while departing resolutely from it. As a result, Darío's work amounts to a true watershed moment in the history of Spanish American verse. Importantly, his creative reception of nineteenth-century French poetics is truly liberating. Far from merely imitating his French models, Darío invented a hitherto unknown form of poetic expression, one unique in Spanish America and in the Americas generally.

It is this new poetic style that most sets Darío apart. Focusing on diction, syntax, and euphony, he invented a new poetic language, one that, as in "Era un aire suave," was sensual, rhythmic, and intensely musical. Darío's language is not that of everyday life, or reflective of Spanish

American history, culture, or literature. Rather, it is the language of exotic places and other times, and it is language that produces a fantasy world.

> Calla, calla princesa—dice el hada madrina—
> en caballo con alas hacia acá se encamina,
> en el cinto la espada y en la mano el azor,
> el feliz caballero que te adora sin verte,
> y que llega de lejos, vencedor de la Muerte,
> a encenderte los labios con su beso de amor.

> ("Hush, Princess, hush," says her fairy godmother;
> "the joyous knight who adores you unseen
> is riding this way on his winged horse,
> a sword at his waist and a hawk on his wrist,
> and comes from far off, having conquered Death,
> to kindle your lips with a kiss of true love.")
>
> (trans. Lysander Kemp; Tapscott 17)

Elegant, refined, and seductive, Darío's language is rarefied to the point of seeming otherworldly. In the annals of Spanish American poetry it is startlingly new. With Darío and the other *modernistas,* there were no longer any *gauchos* or *caudillos,* any great *cordilleras,* any teeming jungles, vast savannas, or Indians. Responding to *Azul* in 1888, the reader could not be but keenly aware that she was entering into a rarefied and challenging world, one hitherto unknown in Spanish American literature and one that would require (as Machado's new narrative would) new readers and new norms of evaluation and appreciation.

Already in *Azul,* whose title pays homage to Victor Hugo's maxim *L'art, c'est l'azur,* the reader is treated to a poetry unexpectedly charged with an abundance of untraditional contexts, new sound patterns, and exotic images. Enjambments and caesura are employed in unexpected ways, and the reader, accustomed to the forms and tropes of traditional Spanish and Spanish American verse, is led into a new and mellifluous world of color, sound, sight, and sense. In the opening pages of *Azul* the reader senses this liberating break with the past. A hallmark of Symbolist poetry, synesthesia is, in fact, a basic building block of Darío's modernist verse. If the Mexican Gutiérrez Nájera pioneered the use of colors and color imagery in Spanish American poetry, Darío, likely influenced by both Baudelaire and Rimbaud, went further, merging colors with other sensory capabilities and with emotional and intellectual states. As in Baudelaire's famous sonnet "Correspondances" (1857), a staple of

French Symbolism, Darío's rarefied images could now flow freely into one another without the cumbersome apparatus of formally comparative constructions. The universe, as apprehended by the senses and the intellect, became, via this innovative injection of synesthesia, vastly more fluid and interconnected, with each shimmering image giving rise to another. That he could achieve this as successfully as he did was Darío's genius, and it transformed his similes and metaphors into daring and unexpected relationships with other words and with their now multiplying meanings. In his globalized symbolism, and in the obliqueness of its referents, Darío featured the iconic nature of language rather than its traditionally representative nature, its use as a tool by which the people and objects of the real world are given names and referred to. This new sense of language, of its semantically unstable nature, where words refer more to other words than to any exterior reality, offers a key parallel with the post-1880 narratives of Machado.

As we compare and contrast Darío and Machado, it is useful to take into account Steiner's observation that "the principal division in the history of Western literature occurs between the early 1870s and the turn of the century. It divides a literature essentially housed in language from one for which language has become a prison" (176). Before this critical period, which coincided with the work of our two Latin American masters, "poetry and prose were in organic accord with language" (176). There existed "a pact," a belief in an unbreakable bond "between word and world," but this ancient belief shattered with the new thinking about language and reality that began in the last three decades of the nineteenth century and found its linguistic validation in the work of Saussure in the early years of the twentieth century (177). If, as I believe to be the case, the poetry of Darío and the prose of Machado both illustrate Steiner's point, then that means that two American writers were at the forefront of the sea change that Steiner sees as characterizing late nineteenth-century Western literature.

Darío, profoundly influenced by the French poets Verlaine, Baudelaire, Mallarmé, and the others cited by Steiner, experimented with a great many poetic forms and techniques. But especially after 1896 and the *Prosas Profanas* he began to question language's ability to represent reality. As we have seen, he modified traditional forms of Spanish language verse, many of which he found stiff and unaccommodating, but thanks to his catholic reading habits and language training, he was also able to create wholly new ones. Darío was open to the literary and artistic universe, drinking in the ways writers from other cultures did things. His awareness of language less as a system for the representation of other things than as an artistic medium in and of itself enabled him to create an exotic and refined, intensely poetic language and to cultivate a distinctly poetic diction. His use of the rarefied word *linfa,* for example, instead of the more common word *agua,* or "water," is but one occasion of this. There are many others. This tendency has led some to decry what is, for them, a certain preciousness to Darío's poetry, a feature that has no counterpart in Machado's prose fiction. Yet readers more appreciative of certain international trends in Western poetry at this time can point to this as a laudable and easily discerned feature of the Nicaraguan's work, not as a criticism. Far from being a defect, *préciosité* is a defining characteristic of this kind of versification and not a weakness. And on this score Darío ranks high. He was a master of it, in the Americas and globally. But there is much more to it than this.

It is clear now, for example, that the "question of the status of language as sign or semantic revelation in tension against its function as symbol or an agent of concealment is . . . at the heart of the *modernistas'* Symbolist program" (Tapscott 10). Boyd Carter, pointing to what is innovative about the poetry of Darío, cites his choice of themes, forms, and techniques. In all this he breaks with the past, of which he is very much aware. Then too, there is this from González Echevarría: "In Spanish America, the modern arrived with Modernismo, a late nineteenth-century poetic movement derived mostly from French models. Nicaraguan Rubén Darío was its chief figure and the first Latin American author to enjoy star status throughout the Spanish-speaking world. He was the best poet in the Spanish language since the poets of the Golden Age in the sixteenth and seventeenth centuries. No one since Góngora had so clearly revolutionized the language of poetry as Darío did beginning in the 1890s. The modern was essentially that which was not Spanish but was instead linked to the world of international commerce of goods and ideas made possible by new modes of communication. The *modernistas* created a discourse that cut itself off from tradition, and they did so by writing in an exquisite, elegant, and euphonious style that described not nature but a world of luxury created by the products of human industry. Theirs is an indoor, decadent milieu cluttered with exotica from the farthest reaches of the world, like the statue in Darío's 'The Death of the Empress of China,' and redolent of a languorous kind of forbidden eroticism" (introduction 16).

On one point of language use Darío and Machado are very close. It has to do with the ability of language to represent, or re-present, reality.

In the 1896 poem "Yo persigo una forma . . ." ("I Seek a Form . . .")
Darío finds, much to his discontent, that words and their referents cannot be linked. What is sought can never quite be attained. "Yo persigo
una forma que no encuentra mi estilo," he writes, only to discover, after
endless attempts, that "Yo no hallo sino la palabra que huye" (I seek a
form that my style cannot discover . . . And I find only the word that runs
away; trans. Lysander Kemp, Tapscott 33, 34). Although he does not
pursue this frustration, here or in any of his future work, its confrontation
here shows Darío touching on the root problem of the global modern,
this vague but gnawing sense that nothing is permanent and that even the
old values, so ardently held, were transitory. The traditional center, to
paraphrase, cannot hold. Machado too would address this sense of dis-
placement and alienation, but he would approach it from the perspective
of language itself, showing in text after text that if meaning in language
is relative and a function of one word in relation to all the other words
in the same semantic structure, whether this is a poem, a short story, or a
novel, then meaning in literary texts must also be relative and a function
of multiple readings and interpretations. If we think of Saussure as the
last of the great European modernist thinkers, then Machado, who anticipated his work on how language works and how it generates meaning by
some twenty-plus years, must be considered one of the great American
modernists as well.

Machado too was a literary revolutionary. Beginning in 1880 with
The Posthumous Memoirs of Brás Cubas he changed forever the ways
prose fiction would be written (and read) in Brazil. And as with Darío,
language training and foreign influences were essential to his creation
of a new narrative, for Brazil and, for those who prefer a more comprehensive approach, for all of Latin America. Indeed, not until the time of
Borges would a writer as visionary and as radically inventive as Machado
de Assis be seen in Spanish American narrative theory. Major influences
on Machado include Shakespeare (whom he read in the original), Dante,
and all of French literature, French being another language he had mastered. Although these (and other) influences are discernible in his work,
his poetry and theater as well as his prose fiction, we see the widely noted
influence of Laurence Sterne's *Tristram Shandy* in *The Posthumous Memoirs of Brás Cubas,* the omnipresence, conspicuous in *Quincas Borba,* of
French literature and history, the creative use of Shakespeare's *Othello*
in *Dom Casmurro* (1899), the importance of Dante in *Esau and Jacob*
(1904), the strategic employment of Shelley in *Counselor Ayres' Memorial,*

the frequent referencing of *Don Quixote* and Goethe, particularly *Faust,* in several of Machado's short stories and novels. These are the most commonly invoked foreign sources, but many others come into play as well.

While it is a commonplace to say that Darío created a radically new language for his poetry, the same can be said of Machado. But it was of a different sort. Or to be more precise, its impetus was different. Machado, as I have argued elsewhere, came up with a new theory of language (E. Fitz, *Machado de Assis and Narrative Theory*). Although Darío did give birth to an extraordinarily new kind of poetry, sensual, fluid, and intensely musical, he does not offer us what Machado does. Machado's post-1880 new narrative presaged the revolutionary linguistics of Saussure and in this sense anticipated the work Borges would do in the 1930s with his *ficciones.* For those who accept the integrated approach to Latin American literature I propose in this study, the new narrative of Latin American literature began, in truth, with Machado de Assis. We can, I believe, refine this conclusion even further; if the Borges *ficciones* were hailed in France (via French translation) as being exemplary of what Structuralist theory would look like if it took the form of fiction, then we could easily think of Machado's post-1880 work, which cultivates the unstable relationship between language, reality, and meaning, as epitomizing the principles of Post-Structuralism. With this new and more integrated understanding of American literature, we can conclude that both Structuralism and Post-Structuralism find their literary progenitors in the work of Jorge Luis Borges, of 1930s Argentina, and Machado de Assis, of late nineteenth- and early twentieth-century Brazil.

Machado's language, moreover, is by no means plain—far from it—but neither does it employ ultraliterary words like *linfa, liróforo, parlar,* or *ánfora.* It is rarely exotic, particularly in his fiction. His poetry, however, offers a notable exception. On the question of exotic imagery, Machado's "Blue Fly" has an orientalist cast, while another poem, "Vicious Circle," built on Greek imagery, emits a radical skepticism that exceeds anything Darío ever wrote, going beyond the doubt expressed in *Prosas Profanas.* Machado's skepticism would have meshed easily with Saussure's linguistics, which the Brazilian master presaged. For Machado as for Saussure, meaning was not stable and eternal. To the contrary, it was fluid and relative, dependent on context, individual perception, and the particular verbal structure that produced it. Borges would arrive at a similar position in the 1930s as he began to write his *ficciones.* In Machado's case, the result was ambiguity, an uncertainty about the meaning of things that would stem from his doubt about epistemological shortcomings and about the semantically unstable nature of language itself.

Although Machado was never a consistently brilliant poet, he did compose some truly excellent verse (see García). And a comparison with the Nicaraguan has already been noted. At its best, argues Torres-Ríoseco, Machado's poetry "resembles . . . that of Rubén Darío, the great poet of Spanish America" (231). In "Mosca Azul," with its "elegant diction and imagery," the Chilean critic continues, Machado has given us "a composition that recalls the best of Darío's immortal *Prosas Profanas*" (231). "A model of Machado's parnassian style, 'The Blue Fly' combines formal precision and clarity of image with both exoticism and philosophic disillusionment" (81). Then, citing "Círculo Vicioso," Torres-Ríoseco concludes that Machado surpassed Darío in two aspects: in his intellectual divagations and his "penetrating sense of humor," one that some readers have found cynical in nature (232).

But no poem of Machado's is bleaker or more unsparing of the human creature than "Suave Mari Magno," which forces the reader to confront the disturbing degree to which we are enthralled by the suffering of others. A dog is dying on the street, in the hot summer sun, and as people pass by, not one fails to stop and gawk at the agony of the dying animal. It was, as Machado writes, with clinical detachment, "Como se lhe desse gôzo/ Ver padecer" (*Obra Completa* 3:161; As if it gave each one pleasure/To see it suffer). It is with the irony-drenched subjunctive that Machado here sticks in the stiletto. It *does* give us pleasure to see the suffering of the dog, and much to our dismay we know it. Worse, one can conclude, we are perfectly willing to let the suffering of others continue, whether it is that of animals or of other human beings. Shocked by our own capacity for cruelty and apathy, it is the reader who, mulling it over, brings to life the chilling human tragedy inherent in this superficially serene but ultimately devastating little poem.

Smooth, elegant, and cool, Machado's language, though revolutionary in its own semantically unstable and quizzically self-referential fashion, would never, with the possible exception of "Blue Fly," be mistaken for that of Darío. They cultivate two different linguistic systems, designed to do different things and achieve different ends. But in Latin America and in the Americas more broadly conceived, Darío and Machado achieved breakthroughs in terms of literary language and how we need to think about it. We do not see their equal until later in the twentieth century and the *ficciones* of Borges.

Finally, Machado's mature style is ironic, comic (often sardonically so), and metafictive. Often built around various manifestations of unreliable narrator-protagonists (like Brás Cubas or, from *Dom Casmurro*, the bitter, self-centered, and perhaps guilt-riven title character), this work constantly seeks to create a new reader as well, one who, as in her role as a citizen, must learn to pay close attention, to consider all possibilities, and to make decisions—knowing all the while that no decision is perfect or permanent and that other interpretations are always possible. Still, in literature as in life, decisions must be made, even in the face of unrelenting ambiguity, confusion, and prevarication.

In contrast to other writers of this time, including Darío, Machado cultivated extensively what I have called his "metaphoric method," a technique by which he advances both the story and the plot not by explaining things to the reader, as in the traditional novel, but by presenting her with an interlocking series of metaphoric scenes, which, when considered collectively, as self-referential parts of a single semiotic system, lead her to possible conclusions. Before we are even set, Machado, that is to say, his narrator-protagonist Brás Cubas, starts us off with one of these story-summarizing metaphors on the opening page, in the "To the Reader" section. Explaining that the text we are reading was written by a dead man—him!—Brás then tells us, in full comic mode, that he wrote this narrative "with a playful pen and melancholy ink" (*Posthumous Memoirs of Brás Cubas* 5). What this frivolity masks, and what his tale, his life story, does not tell us, is that by the end of the narrative we will look back at this moment and realize that we were not just laughing at verbal jests involving dead authors, playful pens, and melancholy ink; we were engaging with something far more serious, life itself, and how we, the living, try to deal with it. Approaching the text from this perspective, one achieved only at the end of the book, the reader sees that she can take the "melancholy ink" as a metaphor for life and the "playful pen" as a metaphor for the artist's representation of it.

Later, more prototypical examples of this same technique, the use of metaphors to advance the story and the plot, are chapters 21, on the muleteer, and 117, on Quincas Borba's grand master plan for human existence, or, from *Quincas Borba,* when the Black Brazilian cook is shunted aside in his own kitchen in favor of an imported, and white, European chef (chapter 3). Such scenes as these, tiny in terms of how much space they take up but mighty in terms of their significance, show us what we might want to ponder, or be aware of, but they do not tell us what we are supposed to think. Machado never does. This is a key part of his modernity.

The reader of the scenes about the muleteer and Quincas might well consider the morality of selfishness and of capitalism itself, while the reader of *Quincas Borba* might find herself mulling over the nature of race in Brazil and the impact on a culture of needlessly importing from abroad. Rubião, the novel's protagonist, is informed by his capitalist "friend," named, interestingly enough, Cristiano, about the necessity of "having white servants" in his house if he wants to move into their society's higher echelons (*Philosopher or Dog?* 5). The clue is there, as is the social history behind it, but it is up to the reader to make the connection. We are led to the trough but not made to drink. Or even told to do so. Yet everything is there for us to see and think about. Like the citizen, Machado's reader, challenged by what appears to be a welter of often conflicting facts and opinions, must make a decision. The active, engaged reader, which is what Machado wants, will, like the active, engaged citizen, do this. Being a good reader, Machado's narratives suggest to us, is good preparation for being a good citizen. Nothing similar takes place in Darío's world. But neither is there any reason that it do so. Art is its own justification. But some art can have an importance and a value beyond itself.

This is how and why, in contrast to the also intense world of Darío, with its nymphs and satyrs and its quest for harmony and beauty, Machado's texts, their own kind of art, lead to a critique of his society. While Darío's poetic world is beautiful and resonant, it is not, with only a handful of exceptions, socially engaged in the ways Machado's novels and stories are. The alert reader can extrapolate this kind of social engagement if she wishes to, but she is not led, albeit indirectly, to do so as is the case in Machado's artistic world.

Because Machado is much less well known, even to Latin Americanists, than is his contemporary Rubén Darío, a few words are in order so that we can more completely understand his importance. Haberly writes of Machado that he "stands apart from all other Brazilian writers of prose fiction in the nineteenth century. Indeed, there are no comparable writers in all of Latin America before Jorge Luis Borges—a writer whom Machado in many ways resembles, particularly in his use of certain symbolic structures (the mirror, for example) and of highly unreliable and self-conscious narrators" ("Brazilian Novel from 1850 to 1900" 153). Like Borges, Machado seems to have read everything—and to have used it as grist for his mill.

This sets him apart, to a degree, from Darío, whose utilization of foreign sources and influences seems, on balance, more conventional. Immensely effective, to be sure, and both beautiful and powerful in the extreme, but not as ironic, as critically engaged, or as divergent. It is probably also useful to remember that while it was Darío's marvelous new use of language that, already in 1888, most distinguished his brand of *Modernismo,* Machado too created a new language for his own literary revolution, which began in 1880 with his astonishing narrative *The Post-humous Memoirs of Brás Cubas.* The difference is that for the Brazilian, the change from the old to the new is more apparent at the level of structure than at the level of diction, as is more the case with his Nicaraguan counterpart. While far from perfect, this basic distinction, parlous though it may be, is nevertheless a useful one to keep in mind. Often ironic, and leavened with ambiguity, the language of Machado's prose fiction is never exotic or rarefied.

As far from preciosity as a writer can get, Machado, writes González Echevarría, "is the premier nineteenth-century Latin American [prose fiction] writer and one of the best of all time anywhere. Had he been born French or English, there is little doubt that his works would be prominently featured in the Western canon. In the Americas he is certainly on the level of Melville, Hawthorne, and Poe. No one in Spanish comes close to his polish and originality. . . . He anticipates and equals Borges's penchant for ironic detachment and authorial self-effacement, but his skepticism was less corrosive and more compassionate" (*Oxford Book of Latin American Short Stories* 95). Beyond any doubt, Machado stands as "one of the greatest writers produced by the Americas," and it is high time he was recognized as such (K. Jackson, *Machado de Assis* 6). For Putnam, comparing Henry James and Machado, the US writer lacks the "*sabedoria,* the great, deep life wisdom" that the Brazilian writer has (178; see also 183–84).

The Posthumous Memoirs of Brás Cubas gives rise to a formal question as well. Is it even a novel? Should we term it an "anti-novel"? Should we consider it Latin American literature's first *nueva novela,* or *novo romance?* For me, the answers are yes, yes, and yes. In our newly comparative literary history of early Latin American literature, how can we deny that the *Posthumous Memoirs* invents, in fact, a new form—I would say a radically new form—of the novel genre? So, how will we classify it?

As we consider this question, here's another thought to remember concerning the nineteenth-century Latin American novel: "Trapped in the narrative mechanisms of the newspaper serial, oratory, *Costumbrismo,* allegory, and melodrama," writes Benítez-Rojo, "the novels written in Spanish America used up in a few decades the simple programmatic outlines to which they subscribed without, for the rest, showing much artistic concern. One must agree that their authors—unlike Machado de Assis (1839–1908) in Brazil—did not achieve a deep understanding of the genre and, as a consequence, they did not contribute to its development" (434).

Benítez-Rojo is not alone in his praise. González Echevarría, Pupo-Walker, and Haberly have this to say: "Machado was the first world-class Latin American writer; he enjoyed a reputation whose only worthy predecessor may have been Sor Juana Inés de la Cruz in colonial Mexico" (1). The same scholars then say this: "By 1900 Machado was already the finest Latin American novelist, though few knew his work outside Brazil" (5). The hemispheric and global reception of Machado de Assis is slowly changing, however, and for the better. In 2015 K. David Jackson asserted that while Machado ranks as "one of the greatest writers produced by the Americas," he is fast establishing himself "as one of the fundamental authors of world literature" as well (*Machado de Assis* 6, 7).

It is important for readers in the United States and the rest of the world to know that Machado de Assis was a writer, and a great artist, who had Black blood running in his veins. He is gaining a new and revitalized reputation as a Black writer in Brazil, where the white elite has long found it more comfortable to praise him, and to present him to the world, as being more white than Black. Thankfully, this old, racist attitude is changing. But here in the United States, because of his groundbreaking theoretical positions, coupled with his dazzling innovations as a novelist and short story writer, Machado is not what readers and critics have long been accustomed to labeling a "Black writer." To be a "Black writer" in the United States means something very different from what Machado de Assis is, so that his reception here is a deeply complicated and tangled matter (see Valdés and Fitz). With all attendant differences—the infamous "one drop rule" in the United States,[5] for example—Machado's reception in his native Brazil offers a parallel case (see Seixas Guimarães). Questions of influence and reception are always complex, of course, but the case of Machado de Assis is particularly so, I believe. This deplorable milieu was the one into which this brilliant writer, a man of mixed race, the grandson of freed slaves, and a great Brazilian and American writer would be received. Rubén Darío, who encountered his own forms of prejudice, did not have to bear Machado's extra burden.

The heightened, refined sense of art championed by the art-for-art's-sake crowd permeated Spanish American *Modernismo,* as it did Brazilian Parnassianism, and set it apart from what had come before. The aesthetic roots of this particular brand of American Modernism are found in the preface to Théophile Gautier's *Mademoiselle de Maupin* (1835), which argued that true art has no utility other than its own existence (E. Fitz, *Rediscovering the New World* 121–45). For writers who believe in it, for example, Gautier and Leconte de Lisle, the principle of *l'art pour l'art* posits that beautiful, melodious poetry need not be socially conscious. It is its own justification. In the United States, Edgar Allan Poe would lay out a similar position in *The Poetic Principle* (written 1848, published 1850). Poe's vision ran counter to the long tradition of Spanish and Spanish American poetry, which tended to be realistic and oriented toward the issues of the real world. What the Spanish American *modernistas* proposed with their new poetry was a radical departure from the past, indeed from their own heritage. And it was the influence of the French poets Baudelaire (especially his *Les fleurs du mal*), Rimbaud, Verlaine, and Mallarmé that carried the most weight.

While the influence of the French *Symbolistes* and Mallarmé on Darío is well known and well documented, an arguably similar influence was exerted by them on the post-1880 prose fiction of Machado de Assis (E. Fitz, *Machado de Assis and Narrative Theory* 162–65). Machado knew French Symbolist poetry and read it in the original. He understood the complex and protean relationship between language, meaning, and reality, and beginning in 1880 with *The Posthumous Memoirs of Brás Cubas* he explored what this kind of thinking might mean for narrative fiction.

Both Machado and Darío defied traditional genre differences. If we approach their work thinking that fiction tends to be centrifugal while poetry tends to be centripetal, we will soon be frustrated. While these two tendencies are certainly there, they are regularly undercut by their opposites; Machado's metafictive narratives can be as specific, intense, and concentrated as one would expect from the best lyric poetry, while Darío's verse can (in a very few words) be as expansive as the best fiction.

4. Cosmopolitanism in an Age of Burgeoning Nationalism

Darío and Machado were both cosmopolitan writers. Darío took his reader to distinctly exotic realms, while Machado brought the entire world to his readers. This move to cosmopolitanism was more notable for Darío and Spanish American literature than it was for Machado and Brazilian literature, which had long been engaged with a variety of global systems, from the economic to the intellectual. From the beginning, in 1492, Spanish America had been a more closed society, one that did not prize intercourse with the rest of the world, as was the norm in Brazil. In terms of a nation's literary history, this difference is of enormous importance, as it directly affects how a national literature grows and develops through time. A major portion of Darío's immense importance to Spanish American letters is that he liberated it from the narrow confines of nationalism. But he also liberated its poetry from the straitjackets of those traditional forms he found too staid, too inflexible, and unmusical. With Rubén Darío and the other *modernistas,* Spanish American literature went global, becoming a force to be reckoned with. While it has taken a long time for the importance of Spanish American *Modernismo* to be as widely appreciated as it should be, today, thanks to the work of scholars like Ignacio Infante and others, it is finally gaining the global respect it deserves.

Darío takes his sources largely as they are; he does not alter them much, except for poetic effect. The myth of Leda and the swan, for example, is used just the way it is in its own context. His goal was to gain a legitimacy for sensuality as a positive, creative human condition by allying it with classical myths and figures. If he was to succeed with this project, he could not drastically change any of these imported references. Machado, who also makes use of classical mythology, is prone to changing his sources, including his quotations, to meet his needs. His references, which are many and varied, constitute a kind of running dialogue with world literature. We do not see this as much, or approached in the same way, in the work of Darío, who comes across as being less engaged in a critical dialogue with his sources than in a straightforward utilization of them. Machado's novels, stories, poems, dramas, and nonfiction are "crisscrossed with references and allusions to and quotes from dozens of authors and works" from around the world (K. Jackson, *Machado de Assis* 107). And in most cases, they show Machado using world literature to make a place for himself and, as he proposed in his 1873 essay "The Instinct of Nationality," for Brazilian literature as well. This strategy appears to have paid off for the Brazilian writer since today Machado is rapidly gaining stature himself as a staple for World Literature advocates. Although Darío too is gaining status as a global writer, as one of the earliest members of the Western tradition to spot the disruption and anxiety that lay behind the façade of what was being pitched as the glitter of material progress in the final years of the nineteenth century, his global reputation has not grown as rapidly as Machado's. Today we think of Machado de Assis as a world writer in ways that we do not yet think of

Darío. At the end of the nineteenth century, however, and in the context of the Americas, these two great Latin American writers were showing what a new poetry and a new narrative could look like.

Both Darío and Machado exuded a strong sense of being in the world, of participating in it, and of not being limited to their respective cultures. For nineteenth-century Spanish American literature, and for its poetic tradition especially, this was something of a novelty, though the poetry of Sor Juana Inés would be the notable exception. This note of secularism seems less anomalous and more standard for Brazil, which, thanks to its maritime Portuguese heritage, had from its origins been a player in a global system of circulation and exchange. At the same time, reading Darío leads one to feel that his very authentic and innovative cosmopolitanism was, on balance, more restricted to global mythology, and to the cult of art for art's sake, than was Machado's more diverse and often more politically perceptive fount of international influences. Although he could, and did, avail himself of mythology, Machado's influences came from a plethora of other sources as well. Even more than Borges would do decades later, Machado took these multitudinous authors, texts, philosophies, and mythologies and put them to use, often in altered form, according to his needs. Machado's narratives, his poems, and his comedies are larded with an astonishing array of global authors and works. Darío, by way of contrast, tended to select sources that were more of a kind and to modify them less. For Jackson, this literary and philosophical worldliness on Machado's part stems from his creative absorption and re-presentation of what in his time constituted what was regarded as the world's best literature and thought (K. Jackson, *Machado de Assis* 104–22). More than Darío, "Machado takes his reader on a tour . . . of world literature," relentlessly subjecting the texts he selects for use to myriad modifications, deliberate misreadings, strategic misquotations, ironic comparisons, and subtle parody (106).

Machado de Assis, on the other hand, was merely enhancing, and deepening, the already extant cosmopolitanism that had long defined Brazil. In considering this question, it is important to remember that beginning in its colonial era, Brazilian ports were open to global traffic. New ideas from abroad could enter Brazil and be disseminated among its artists and thinkers. This was as true for science and politics as it was for literature and art. Indeed, a large part of Machado's synthesizing genius stems from his deep reading of world literature and his ability to apply it to the Brazilian scene. This Brazilian tradition of "cannibalizing" foreign influences in order to then transform them into something uniquely and identifiably Brazilian would, in fact, become the basis for the more formal movement, beginning in 1922, known as Brazilian *Modernismo*. This is precisely the context in which David Damrosch discusses Brazilian *Modernismo* in his seminal *What Is World Literature?* But the inclination to do this, to hybridize, had been a guiding principle in Brazil since its founding by the Portuguese, themselves a globalized people, in 1500. A prime example of this process, Machado was steeped not merely in the literature and philosophy of the Western tradition but in the global tradition. While Machado's base was always Brazil, his outlook was global. In this he reminds the reader of Shakespeare, who was quintessentially English even as he often wrote of other times and places. The ethos was the same. This affinity helps explain, perhaps, why Shakespeare plays so prominent a role in Machado's writing. Finally, it is also worth noting that Machado's cosmopolitanism was infused with humanity's best social, political, and intellectual thought. He knew how to bring disparate ideas together in the creation of something new and unique. Machado and his work exemplify what it means to be American. Out of many, one.

Although he was not known in the United States, by the time of his death in 1908 Machado was already becoming a celebrity in other parts of the world. Feted in France by no less a figure than Anatole France, Machado was "the first truly great novelist to have written in Latin America" (Gledson, *Misplaced Ideas* xv). He was almost certainly the greatest American novelist up to his time, and he may quite plausibly be one of the greatest American novelists ever (K. Jackson, *Machado de Assis* 4, 6). Machado's importance as a Brazilian writer, a Latin American writer, an American writer, and a global writer is undisputed.

5. Art and the Artist in Society

Both Darío and Machado venerated art and the role of the artist in what they regarded as a shallow, numbingly materialistic society. This is particularly obvious in the case of the Spanish American master and his *modernista* colleagues, but less overtly, traces of the same sentiment can be found in the Brazilian's fiction. And it may well explain why, in contrast to his contemporary, the much more militant Lima Barreto, Machado was not more open and direct about his political opinions. Machado's political consciousness is there for anyone who wants to see it, in the early works as well as the later ones, but it is never the overriding concern; art is. As Jackson puts it, Machado "wrote for profoundly literary reasons" (*Machado de Assis* 110). He was not a propagandist nor an advocate, in his work, for any particular cause. He was an artist, one whose medium of expression was language. And as a man of color from the margins of society, Machado was possessed of an incisive social awareness. His 1905 story "Father versus Mother," coming long after slavery was abolished in Brazil and leading US readers to review their own runaway slave laws, is as searing an indictment of slavery as anything in American literature. It is, however, less a condemnation of slavery outright than a devastating portrait of how good, hardworking people can find ways to rationalize this odious institution and, as long as it makes them money, justify it. As Maria Nunes puts it, Machado "was more concerned with the perfection of his art than with taking a militant role in social causes. . . . He did not wish perhaps to be known as a black, white, or mulatto artist but as an artist" (x). On this score, Machado and Darío shared common ground.

If, however, on both the personal and the professional level art exculpated Darío from the guilt and shame he felt at being a religiously Catholic man with very carnal desires, then for Machado we can say that art can redeem us, that it can remind us that we are capable of doing better. It needs always to be there, exhorting us to less egoistic and more altruistic actions. Although slight, a difference perhaps of emphasis, this point is important because it suggests that Machado's sense of art was less personal and more public than Darío's. Machado, in fact, might well have given us a fascinating discourse on "the art of the novel," as his US contemporary Henry James did. Instead, Machado's views on the nature of language, imitation, and narrative as an art form are embedded in his post-1880 novels and stories.

If it is true, as many believe, that Darío's motivation stems in part from a personal crisis of faith, then we can better understand how his new poetry would seek to expiate the guilt he would have felt at being a devout Catholic with erotic desires (see Stavans, xxxiv–xxxv, xliv). Art would be his redemption. It alone would reconcile what otherwise could not be reconciled. Seen from this perspective, art, for Darío the man, serves much the same purpose as it did for those who feared modernity had destroyed the old order and its systems of belief and stability. Although more specific in nature, Darío's personal need to harmonize what must have been for him the agonizing clash between his religious beliefs and his erotic impulses would reflect the concerns of the many who felt at the end of the nineteenth century that science and technology had replaced the old verities of life.

The main difference between the two writers on this point is this: Darío, perhaps because he was religious and because he was more indebted to Hugo, Gautier, and Leconte de Lisle than Machado, was much more closely tied to the art-for-art's-sake school. Machado was not tied to it. Although art functioned as his lodestar, his organizing principle, he did not flaunt the value of art and its tempering importance to a self-centered, materialistic, and pedestrian society as Darío did. Machado did not *need* art in the way Darío did. He clearly saw its value, but he was not so personally linked to it. Whether this was good or bad is a moot point; what is important is that both these Latin American masters viewed art in much the same way, as a way of redeeming ourselves, of showing that we do, in fact, know what is truly important in life and what is not.

To understand how Darío and Machado compare, we must take into account the generic differences between them. Poetry and prose fiction are written, and read, differently, and these differences must be considered in trying to come to grips with how these two writers regarded art, the artist, and their place in society. Machado's novels especially are more capacious, and more open, than Darío's poetry. This might be taken as an example of the differences between narrative and poetry, but there is something more involved here, something that has to do with worldview. Darío's poetry, though refined and at times exotic, tends to be more limited in scope. Brilliant and exquisitely focused, but tightly focused. At the risk of a bad generalization, I will suggest that while Darío's poetry looks inward and conveys a personal urgency, Machado's novels and stories look outward, exuding a sense of impersonal, impassive objectivity. Like Nature/Pandora in chapter 7 of *The Posthumous Memoirs of Brás Cubas*. We have here, in a sense, two ways of looking at the malaise of modernity, the personal and the objective, the resigned. In the Americas of the late nineteenth century, Machado and Darío stand alone.

While Machado viewed the harmony of art as the antidote to the chaos of life, which he understood as aleatory and full of pointless repetitiousness, there is scant evidence that he regarded the artist with any particular reverence, as Darío and others of his time did. For the Nicaraguan as for Hugo (whom he had translated and who was one of his main influences), the artist was a divine being, someone who could create harmony, so lacking in human life, out of disharmony and discord. As we have seen, Darío hoped to assuage his religious anxiety through his art; thus he needed this harmony, this resolution of conflict, on both a personal and an artistic level. If a parallel existed with Machado, and if Machado did entertain notions of the artist as a divine being, it is difficult to discern. His personal involvement in his work seems to have been much less than Darío's, as does his advocacy of the artist in society.

Machado's belief in art, on the other hand, seems undeniable. One is tempted to go a step further and venture that if Darío saw the poet as a seer, Machado, the great doubter, probably did not. Instead, one can feel that, as Brás Cubas lays out human history in chapter 7 of Machado's novel, we never seem to learn, not even when a seer tells us how to live our lives in better, more equitable and more just ways. We are, Machado might tell us, too selfish, too deluded by visions of power, and too bedazzled by what we mistakenly think is our importance to listen to seers. Still, like Pandora's box, hope springs eternal, even in the risible train wreck that for Brás Cubas is human history, and so art and in a certain way the artist do have value. They remind us that there is hope. We humans could do better, individually and collectively, if we wanted to, if we wanted to learn. This is the point of believing in the poet as a seer. If Darío finds a way to harmonize his personal religious beliefs, his sexual desires, and his art, Machado doubts that as a species we will ever find such harmony.

There is no solid evidence that Machado ever believed that art could really change anything. Yet as the allusion to Pandora in chapter 7 of *The Posthumous Memoirs of Brás Cubas* shows, the possibility of doing better is always before us. And that is the job of art in society. For Machado, one might say, art is that always badly pummeled last thing—hope—to stick its head out of Pandora's urn, the one that contains all the ills of the human race. The artist, then, would be Pandora herself. As in the original Greek myth about Pandora, Machado's artist, imbued with the female life force, would be a creator, she would be possessed of great gifts, and she would be alluring, attractive to the human race even as its men and women largely ignored her entreaties.

Late in life, in a July 7, 1907, letter to his friend and compatriot the statesman Joaquim Nabuco, Machado noted three salient qualities he admired in the work of a mutual colleague of theirs; his work, Machado writes, is "profundo, fino e bem dito," and through time it "conservará o seu grande valor" (*Obra Completa* 3:1084; profound, fine/of high quality and well said/expressed . . . [it] will conserve its great value). He intimates here that all truly great art is of deep and lasting significance, it is meticulously crafted according to what amount to the rules of aesthetics, and it is carefully wrought (see K. Jackson, *Machado de Assis* 298). Aristotle, one feels, would approve. Then, as if to seal the deal, he says to Nabuco, "Sabe como eu sempre apreciei essa espécie de escritos" (1084; You know how I have always prized that kind of writing). Given the date of this missive, the reader can assume that, as obliquely as always, Machado is giving us a clue as to how he wants his own works of literary art to be remembered.

For the Latin Americanist, it is interesting to compare Machado's principles of great art as laid out in this letter to Darío's work. How does it stack up? Exceedingly well, I would say. The only stumble might be in the category of Darío's utilization of sexuality, which, as we have seen, tends to be overwhelmingly male in orientation. Women are just not much a part of it, as they are in Machado's fictional universe. Among Darío's female creations only the enigmatic Eulalia, from *Prosas Profanas,* gets to utter a few words. Even then, we do not understand what she is telling us because she only laughs, "y es cruel y es eterna su risa de oro" (and her golden laugh is cruel and eternal; trans. Lysander Kemp, Tapscott 36.). Otherwise, what comes to light in this comparison is that in the late nineteenth and early twentieth centuries Latin America produced two of the greatest, most innovative American writers.

For Darío, a cosmic harmony known only to the artist ordered the universe. For Machado, the question was more complicated. He rejected even the concept of a single, totalizing system, but he did value art, with its insistence on selectivity, coherence, and proportion. This is apparent enough in all his work, though it is most tellingly expressed, as we will see, in *Quincas Borba.* For Darío, however, this cosmic harmony was divine in nature and transcended the human world, which was fraught with egoism, deceit, contradiction, and conflict. The artist, in his case the poet, was that rare and gifted being who resided on earth (and who was beset with earthly desires of the flesh) but communicated with the gods. Among mortals, only the artist touched the divine and, as the vehicle by means of which the precious transformation took place, allowed it to give birth to art and beauty. In so doing, the artist alone could achieve the harmony that existed for the gods but did not exist in the flawed world of ordinary men and women.

In the poem "Era un aire suave," from *Prosas Profanas,* Darío references this divine harmony by writing:

Era un aire suave de pausados giros;
el Hada Harmonía ritmaba sus vuelos,
e iban frases vagas y tenues suspiros,
entre los sollozos de los violoncelos.

(It was a gentle air, with turns and pauses;
the sprite Harmony guided all its flights;

and there were whispered words and tenuous sighs
among the sobbings of the violoncellos.)

(trans. Lysander Kemp; Tapscott 34)

In Darío's hands, the harmony of the heavens, of the sacred, is transformed into the harmony of art, music, and sensation. From the perspective of the text itself, harmony predominates, in thought and form. In
attaining this sacred goal, the poet becomes an elevated being, one who
sees society not in terms of temporality, bourgeois values, and rank materialism but in the timeless, eternal values of the divine. If one takes this
revulsion at middle-class life and mores as political in nature, then it is
quite possible to interpret the work of Darío and his acolytes as reflecting
a social awareness to their work. In fact, it would be an oversimplification
to think that the *modernistas* lacked a social consciousness, for they did
not. And this fact ties Darío, especially, to a certain type of European and
even North American modernist.

With "Yo soy aquel que ayer no más decía," from *Cantos de vida y
esperanza (Songs of Life and Hope)*, Darío seems to reflect on what art
can and cannot achieve. Doubt appears to be creeping into his formerly
secure vision of art's potential. Still finding it a star that can guide us even
in the crassest of times, he here maintains that only "la sagrada selva" (the
sacred forest), that is, "el Arte puro" (pure Art), can achieve the cruelly
elusive "armonía" (harmony) that we humans seek (Chang-Rodríguez
and Filer 249). Prefiguring by fifteen years Eliot's vision of the "sacred
wood," Darío's *sagrada selva* gives birth to an artistic balance that trem-
bles with desire and fever and vibrates with life, though only within the
controlled confines of art. Via its special status as "el Arte puro," Darío's
poetry transforms itself into a timeless, eternal force that, in victory over
death, materiality, and repression, can proclaim: *"Ego sum lux et veritas
et vita"* (249; I am light, truth, and life). But this sacred transformation
by means of art is never guaranteed; nor is it even certain, for all the
poet's efforts, that humankind will seek it out or take it seriously, even
though Darío explicitly tells us, in this late poem, that it is his "sincere . . .
intent," his "sincere . . . intention," to harmonize the "éxtasis" (ecstasy)
of desire with life, with art, and with his Christianity, which is represented
by the reference to how the human "caravana" (caravan) passes through
"Belén" (Bethlehem) (249–50).

As suggested above, Darío's use of "la sagrada selva" is not entirely
dissimilar to the ethos of Eliot's *The Sacred Wood* (1920). That highly
influential work, Eliot's first stab at literary criticism, served as the basis

for the New Criticism, which called for exegetes to focus their attention on the text itself, and how it works, as opposed to the author's life, circumstances, or beliefs. This approach to literary criticism works very well when applied to Darío's often arcane and mythologically based poems, although it is also thought to be true that much of Darío's poetry is personal, an expression of his effort to reconcile his sexual desires with his Catholic faith. And *The Sacred Wood* does call for the control of emotion, not its unfettered expression, though it can also be argued that part of the appeal of Darío's verse is, in fact, its emotional power, but only as this is controlled by poetic form. *The Sacred Wood* also afforded Eliot an opportunity to define his concept of the "objective correlative," a word, phrase, image, or other device by which a poem encapsulates its main emotions. In the case of Darío, this could be seen in his recurring use of the myth of Leda and the swan, which allows him to harmonize his own, very human and very carnal desires with those of the gods, who felt no shame about fornicating with earthly women. Sexual pleasure thus portrayed, draped in the context of the amoral Greek gods, was not a sin but a celebration of life, love, and art.

Harmony is key to Machado's artistic vision too, though for him, a deep-dyed ironist, order is often expressed via disorder, or what seems at first glance to be disorder. In his novels, the first text to demonstrate this was *The Posthumous Memoirs of Brás Cubas,* followed some ten years later by *Quincas Borba,* a novel built around the concept of art's relationship to the disorder of life. Much of the action takes place on Harmonia Street, a place not of harmony but of confusion and conflict. "Let it not surprise you," says the novel's narrator, speaking directly, if misleadingly, to the reader, that the things that happen here, as in real life, resist clear, certain, and systematic explanations (*Philosopher or Dog?* 134; see also 129–30, 150ff.). There is no harmony; there is only the absence of harmony. As an artist, one who works with words, Machado here faced the problem of how to depict, or re-present, this state of affairs in a work of art. The text we read reflects his struggle to do precisely this. In *Quincas Borba,* the psychologically splintered Rubião only reflects what Machado casts as the similarly fragmented and contentious world around him. It is a world populated by smooth but rapacious businessmen like Palha, who, like a leech, attaches himself to Rubião as soon as he discovers that the latter has come into a sizeable inheritance. It is no accident, one feels, that the character who preys on Rubião is precisely Cristiano Palha, a man whose desire for money leads him to disregard all ethical concerns. A kind of vulture capitalist, Palha, like so many, concerns

himself only with the pretense of respectability, and when he has taken
Rubião for all he can, with his sketchy but self-serving financial schemes,
he abandons him. Cristiano Palha is Machado's portrait of what capitalism in action looks like.

Aesthetically speaking, Machado's problem begins with the nature of
his protagonist, Rubião, a simple man of unstable mind who misconstrues
what the people around him say and do. Or, to come at this from another
perspective, he is trusting and thus easily taken advantage of by people
like the unscrupulous but very successful capitalist Cristiano Palha.[6] And
increasingly unable to deal with reality as it is, he retreats into, or, if the
reader prefers, is driven into, a fantasy world, one from which he will not
be able to escape.

Quincas Borba ranks, arguably, as Machado's most challenging novel.
More than any of his others, this 1891 text pits the fundamental mutability
of life against the artist's desire to impose form on it. Thus does Machado
engage with the very basic question of mimesis, how art, specifically art
in which language is the medium of representation, imitates reality. Commenting on the human desire for order and on the nature of *Quincas
Borba* as a novel (or yet another anti-novel), Haberly writes that the "singularity of *Quincas Borba* lies in its denial of the validity of the text as a
version of reality" (introduction xxv). The narrative we read as *Quincas
Borba* is in fact a "fiction," as Borges would term the new kind of writing with which he was experimenting in the 1930s. Deliberately an open,
self-interrogating text that constantly challenges and cajoles the reader,
Machado's 1891 novel offers up a plethora of possible interpretations, all
of which undercut one another. But the reader, driven by her desire for
order, nevertheless creates her own meaning, though now fully aware that
it too may be in error. In yet another experiment with the nature of the
unreliable narrator, our anonymous guide in *Quincas Borba* lets us know
that the narrative we are reading is nothing more than a stitched together
version of the "tatters of reality" and that if we wish to take meaning
from it, or to impose a meaning on it, we are free to do so (*Philosopher
or Dog?* 150). But we can never be sure of our determinations. Finally,
as Haberly points out, each possible reading ultimately fails "to capture
an ultimately unknowable reality, since our human vision of our own
lives, of the lives of others, of the world in which we live, is vague, frag-
mentary, and formless" (introduction xxv–xxvi). After 1896 and *Prosas
Profanas*, Darío came to a similar conclusion. Language, no matter how
artfully it is used, is not the reality it seeks to represent or re-create; a
gap, as Saussure would put it a few years later, separates language from

its referents. The sense of isolation and instability that this realization produces constitutes the restive heart of global literary modernism, and it was being plumbed simultaneously by two Latin American writers.

Art, no matter how refined or carefully wrought, will not save Rubião. Indeed, as he falls deeper and deeper into the pit of insanity, art comes to mock him. We identify with Rubião, and we think of him as an average, middle-class citizen of the time. He is a basically good man. A humble teacher by profession, Rubião is kind and generous and seeks love in his life. He wants to love another and to be loved in return, yet he is denied both. Failure, confusion, and frustration are his lot. In contrast to Cristiano Palha, who gets from life more than he deserves, Rubião gets much less than he deserves. While the reader feels only disgust at Palha, in the end she feels if not catharsis then at least the injustice of what has happened to Rubião. His is a small tragedy, or rather a tragedy in a minor key, a prelude to the next novel, *Dom Casmurro*.

Yet in spite of their recognition of the role the artist plays in society, both Darío (whose work openly venerates the artist and art more than does the work of his Brazilian counterpart) and Machado exhibited an acute political consciousness. With Machado, it was there all along, though it became sharper and more focused after 1880, whereas with Darío it emerged late in his career. The surfacing of this realpolitik awareness is therefore most startling in the case of Darío, after Poe the strongest American advocate of the art-for-art's-sake school of thought. In contrast to Poe, however, the later Darío had a perceptive and undeluded understanding of what were, toward the end of the nineteenth century and the beginning of the twentieth, fast-changing inter-American relations. And Spanish America, Darío and others knew full well, would not be the better for it, for in the wake of the Spanish-American War they were about to feel the consequences of the United States' newly acquired taste for political and economic imperialism. This was when the inter-American perspective really began to heat up.

Two poems in the Darío canon stand out in this inter-American regard, "A Roosevelt," which offers a rebuke and a note of warning to the increasingly expansionist Colossus of the North, and "Salutación al Águila," which was written by Darío at the Third Pan-American Conference, held in Rio de Janeiro in 1906. In the earlier poem, written with the full experience of the Spanish-American War behind him and its consequences happening all around him, Darío cautions the United States to honor its own founding principles and abandon its exploitive policies toward Spanish America. More indignant than angry, "A Roosevelt" is measured in its objections to what the US government and business sector are doing. But it is also lacerating in its observations. How, Darío asks, can the United States, the land of Washington, Whitman, and Lincoln, of the Declaration of Independence and the Bill of Rights, betray its grand vision with such predatory business tactics and political interventions in other American nations? Calling the United States "el futuro invasor" (the future invader) and denouncing its marriage of raw power with "el culto de Mammón" (the cult of Mammon), Darío accuses the United States of shameful conduct, of using the torch of "Libertad" (Liberty) to light not the path to the emancipation of others but to their political and economic servitude (trans. Lysander Kemp; Tapscott 39). Although the word itself does not appear in the text, the stench of hypocrisy wafts through it.

More resigned to what now seemed to be the inexorable fate of Spanish America at the hands of a United States newly aflame with a racist imperialism masquerading as Manifest Destiny, the second poem walks back the more sharply critical posture of the first: "Bien vengas, oh mágica Águila, que amara tanto Walt Whitman." Choosing instead to celebrate the energy of the United States, "Salutación al Águila" nevertheless smolders with a certain shade of resentment. And in certain lines this resentment boils over into a barely concealed warning:

Águila, existe el Cóndor. Es tu hermano en las grandes alturas.
Los Andes le conocen y saben que, como tú, mira al Sol.
May this grand Union have no end, dice el poeta.
Puedan ambos juntarse, en plenitud de concordia y esfuerzo.

(But, Eagle, don't forget the Condor. He's your brother on the great heights.
The Andes know him, and know, like you, that he looks at the Sun.
May this grand Union never end, says the poet.
Let the two of you join in a plenitude of harmony and strength.)
                    (trans. Simon and White; Darío, *Rubén Darío* 124–25)

"Los cisnes" ("The Swans") also sounds a similar concern. Fully aware, especially after 1898 and the Spanish-American War, of the threat a newly aggressive United States represented to Spanish America, Darío writes:

Nos predican la guerra con águilas feroces,
. . . .
Seremos entregados a los bárbaros fieros?
Tantos millones de hombres hablaremos inglés?

(People say we'll be at war with the eagles that are fierce,
. . . .

Are we to be overrun by the cruel barbarians?
Is it our fate that millions of us will speak in English?)
                    (trans. Simon and White; Darío, *Rubén Darío* 18–19)

Overall more conciliatory in nature, the 1906 poem was composed in response to the pragmatic wishes of many Latin American attendees at the conference who saw their futures, their social, political, and economic fates, inextricably linked, for better and worse, to the future actions of the United States. For them, the only real question was, How much could they prevail upon the leaders of the United States to hew more closely to the lofty principles of their nation's founding and eschew the greed of its corporations, financiers, and bankers?

A third poem, also the product of this conference, is Darío's "A Machado d'Assis." At some point during the proceedings, these two great American writers were able to find time to meet and chat. Although the exact content of their conversation is not known, one can imagine that it dealt with a wide range of topics, including literature and inter-American relations. Darío's poem graciously describes his Brazilian host as "todo modestia y gracia," "moreno," and possessed of an "aspecto mandarino" and hails Machado as a "sabio griego" (Biblioteca Nacional Digital de Chile website).[7]

In Canada too, literary breakthroughs were being made. Published in 1882, just after Machado's *Posthumous Memoirs of Brás Cubas* and just before Darío's *Azul,* Laure Conan's *Angéline de Montbrun* deals with the social and emotional restrictions that scarred the healthy growth and development of women in Canadian society. Regarded as French Canada's "first psychological novel," Conan's narrative is also notable for its formal originality (Urbas 7). Appearing in the same year as *Azul,* the underappreciated (outside Canada, that is) *Strange Manuscript Found in a Copper Cylinder* (1888), by James De Mille, often steps away from the story being told to offer metafictive discourses on the writing of narrative and on what is involved in the act of interpretation. Seen from this perspective, the connections between De Mille's novel and the work of Machado de Assis are obvious. The story that forms the heart of De Mille's tale, however, the discovery of a strange Antarctic people who offer an alternative view of life and what is truly valuable in it, makes one think of Poe's *Narrative of Arthur Gordon Pym,* which Borges would later find influential for his theory of magic in narrative (see "El arte narrativo y la magia" 1932).

One could be forgiven for thinking that the reason the United States of this expansionist period felt free to target Spanish America rather than

Canada is twofold: Canada was white, English-speaking, and Protestant (and, to be sure, a part of the British Empire), while Spanish America was Black or racially mixed, Spanish-speaking, and Catholic. Advocates of Manifest Destiny even believed they would be doing the poor, backward people of Latin America a favor by taking them over. It is true that at the time there were those in the United States who promoted the idea of invading Canada and assuming dominion over it, but their numbers pale in comparison with the numbers of those who saw no problem with invading Spanish America and (to a lesser degree) Brazil, which were further away and considerably less known by the majority of US citizens. From the perspective of Wall Street and the politicians who did its bidding, the small, island nations of the Caribbean, like sugar-rich Cuba, were easy pickings.

In the genre of poetry, the Americas brought the nineteenth century to a particularly high note. Three figures stand out: Nicaragua's Rubén Darío, Brazil's João da Cruz e Sousa, and Canada's Émile Nelligan. All three combined the formal elegance of French Parnassianism (with Parnassianism becoming a powerful school in Brazil; see Moisés, "Brazilian Poetry from 1878 to 1902" 85–98) with the evocative seduction of Symbolism. The poetry of Cruz e Sousa is particularly driven by religious fervor, an unbridled originality, and "his status as a black man in a racist society" (100). Late in the century, Darío gained renown as an established master. Nelligan, a prodigy, did his most brilliant work between the ages of 16 and 19, when he succumbed to mental illness and was institutionalized (Hayne 155).

Toward the end of the nineteenth century, Spanish America and Brazil gave birth to a pair of transformative literary revolutions. One, centered in Spanish America, focused on poetry, while the other, less known one, emanating from Brazil, dealt with narrative. For the inter-Americanist, both movements transformed not only Latin American letters but also our understanding of American literature. Rubén Darío, the defining figure of Spanish American *Modernismo,* and Machado de Assis, the Brazilian whose post-1880 novels and stories changed forever how we think of language, reality, and narrative art, stand out as Latin American literature's two towering giants from this period. The appearance in 1880 of Machado's *Posthumous Memoirs of Brás Cubas* was a watershed event in Latin American literary history, as was the publication eight years later of Darío's *Azul.* Darío's fame has long been recognized, but in the comparative Latin American context I espouse here the groundbreaking work of Machado de Assis has not. While his genius is well known, an evaluation of Machado as a Latin American writer and an American writer remains to be done. Taken together, Darío and Machado show Latin American literature to be the brightest star in the late nineteenth- and early twentieth-century American literary firmament. Although there are many other outstanding Latin American writers from this fecund period, Darío and Machado stand unmatched.

Conclusion

"THOUGH COGNATE, Brazilian and Spanish American literary traditions are distinct," and while they "have an obvious and profound kinship," "Brazil's is, with that of the United States, the richest national literature in the New World" (González Echevarría, preface xi–xii, xi).

When the editors of volume 3 of the *Cambridge History of Latin American Literature* wrote that "Brazil's is the most independent, and perhaps most original, national literature in the New World," they were postulating that while the United States and England were still in some sort of cultural synchrony, and while something similar could be said of Spanish America and Spain, Portugal had long before "ceased . . . to be a significant literary presence in Brazil" (González Echevarría, Pupo-Walker, and Haberly 1). In the Americas, Brazil was very much the product of its own singularity. Endorsing the comparative study of Brazilian and Spanish American literature, these same scholars emphasized that these two diverse and fecund American literary traditions were far from identical, that *Latin America* meant not just Spanish America but Portuguese-speaking Brazil as well, that what was true of Spanish America was often not true of Brazil, and that the many differences between Spanish America and Brazil stemmed from their also different Iberian roots and from their different New World experiences (1, 2).

Those interested in a comparative approach to the literatures of Spanish America and Brazil would do well to keep the above words in mind, for they speak both to the potential rewards of such an enterprise and to the methodological pitfalls involved. Commonalities in theme, genre, and period, for example, must be recognized, for they tie our two great literary traditions together. But the all-important differences that exist between them, which are many and deep, must be respected too. Indeed, they must be understood in all their manifold complexities. Failure to do this will result in the failure of the comparative Latin American project. While, as we have seen, Spanish American and Brazilian literature have much in common, they are far from identical, and what can be said about one may well not be true of the other. As is always true of the comparative method, difference is the key issue.

Some of the essential differences are already known:

1. During their respective colonial periods, the Spanish forged trails into the American hinterlands, while the Portuguese, who did not encounter indigenous civilizations that were as advanced as those the Spanish met with, were content with clustering along the beaches.
2. Colonial Spanish America was much more closely managed by Madrid than the Luso-Brazilians were by Lisbon.[1]
3. Spain was much quicker to establish institutions of higher learning and printing presses in its American colonies than the Portuguese monarchs were.
4. In contrast to Spanish America, which, by Spanish edict, was closed to the rest of the world, Brazil, whose ports were open to ships of all nations, benefitted immensely from connecting with new ideas from abroad. One result of this openness to the rest of the world was that colonial Brazil, unlike Spanish America, was never fearful of the outside world and indeed was receptive to it.
5. Unlike Spanish America, which suffered from political Balkanization after its wars for independence (1810–1825),[2] Brazil did not suffer political disintegration. While Spanish America was breaking up, Brazil was able to grow and develop cohesively, a social and political process that was greatly enhanced when, in 1808 (and the arrival of the Portuguese royal family, in flight from Napoleon), it gained status by becoming, first, a kingdom and, second, the heart of the entire Portuguese Empire, which was already global in nature. "Obviously," González Echevarría, Pupo-Walker, and Haberly point out, "such an extraordinary turn of events has no equivalent in the history of Spanish America" (3).

Comparative studies of Spanish America and Brazil are the future of scholarship involving Latin America. The importance of Spanish America has long been recognized. The importance of Brazil, socially, politically, and economically, to the Americas and to the world can no longer be ignored. Its time has come, as has the integrated approach to Latin America and to the Americas generally that it brings with it. Regardless of their specific areas of specialization, today's Latin Americanists have to be knowledgeable about both Spanish America and Brazil. Both traditions must be known, understood, and appreciated, their similarities as well as their differences. In 1889 the US secretary of state, James G. Blaine, an advocate of greater trade with Latin America and of a more unified inter-American community of nations, presided over the first Inter-American Conference, held in Washington, DC, in 1889–90. The Cuban writer and journalist José Martí spoke about the need for hemispheric solidarity and cooperation.[3] But "while cordiality characterized the sessions, it became increasingly obvious that the Latin Americans were less interested in placing orders for the new industrial products" being produced in the United States "than they were in containing the expansion of an ambitious neighbor," the United States (Burns, *Latin America* 148). The Spanish Americans, whose dominion included much of the Caribbean, especially wanted their sovereign status noted and respected. Brazil supported this principle but also sought to parlay its own intention to become Latin America's leader and chief intermediary between Washington and Spanish- and Portuguese-speaking America.

Two years later, in 1891, Martí would, as we have seen, coalesce his ideas about America's future into an essay titled "Nuestra América," which first appeared in print in the Mexican journal *El partido liberal.* Martí knew the United States well, having spent the years 1881 to 1895 there. Although known as an early advocate of inter-American relations, Martí was an ardent Cuban patriot and openly decried the possibility that the United States might take control of his homeland. For the scholar of inter-American literary study, Martí's essay is now required reading. The problem is that it does not mention Brazil or include it in the larger hemispheric vision of "America" that it offers. Thus, for English-only readers Martí's stirring argument makes inter-American study seem to be only a matter of English and Spanish. Portuguese and Brazil are completely elided, as if they did not exist. Since Brazil is the largest and most populous nation in Latin America, and since, as we have seen, scholars such as González Echevarría have praised the richness of Brazilian letters—he, Pupo-Walker, and Haberly, in their introduction to volume 3 of *The Cambridge History of Latin American Literature,* term it "the most independent, and perhaps most original, national literature in the New World" (1)—this omission of it constitutes a serious impediment to better inter-American understanding. Students and scholars who seek a comparative approach to the combined study of Brazilian and Spanish American literature read Martí's essay, which is widely consumed in the US academy, with considerable dismay as well, and for much the same reason: Brazil and its language are rendered invisible. This badly skews the understanding of "Latin America" that US readers need to have.

Of more use to comparative Latin Americanists, and to comparative inter-Americanists in a more hemispherically inclusive sense, is José Vasconcelos's *La raza cósmica,* which appeared in 1925. A native of Mexico, Vasconcelos posits here a view of what he calls "Ibero-America" that includes Brazil as well as Spanish America. In terms of his praise of miscegenation, he anticipates the similar arguments of the renowned Brazilian anthropologist Gilberto Freyre in *Casa-grande e senzala.* Vasconcelos understood and appreciated Brazil to the point that he could argue, in his book, that Latin America's "cosmic race" was inherently mixed and that it had emerged first and foremost in Brazil. By seeking to unify Latin America around what, for him, was the very positive idea of mixing—not just biological but social, political, and economic mixing as well—Vasconcelos further contended that Spanish America and Brazil would become complementary to the culture of the United States and that, looking toward the future, the two Americas, North and South, would be able to work together in mutually beneficial ways. This was his hope, as it had been the hope of Rodó and many other Latin American intellectuals and political leaders.

This idea of inter-American cooperation has a long history. Vasconcelos would undoubtedly have been aware of it from his knowledge of Latin American history. He would have known, for example, that as early as 1815 Simón Bolívar, the liberator of South America, had proposed a kind of union, or association, of Ibero-American states, one that might one day include even the United States (Pagden 195–98). Even Alexander Hamilton and Thomas Jefferson had envisioned a "pan-American hegemony" (199). Hoping to transform his vision of a unified America into a fact, Bolívar had called for the first Inter-American Congress to be held in Panama during the summer of 1826. The United States, alarmed at what many of its conservative leaders felt was a too rapid rush to share power with its fellow citizens from Latin America, many of whom were Black or of mixed race, was invited but temporized about attending. Against the wishes of Bolívar, both Brazil and the United States were ultimately invited. Brazil declined to attend, and the United States, because of illness afflicting its representatives and delay, arrived too late to attend any of the sessions (see C. Fitz 226).

Three end-of-century narratives stand out: Graça Aranha's controversial novel *Canaã* (1902), Euclides da Cunha's *Os Sertões,* and José Enrique Rodó's still provocative study *Ariel* (1900). Aranha, focusing on the venerable theme of miscegenation, presents Brazil as a unique American nation. Although he envisions it as the land of milk and honey, he also sees the challenges it faces. Da Cunha, as we have seen, is also concerned with miscegenation, though he, with his scientific training, has been taught that racially mixed people are destined by the iron laws of biology to regress. For a nation like Brazil, with its long history of racial mixing, this amounted to a death sentence. Less concerned with miscegenation and more concerned with questions of political and economic power involving Latin America and the United States, Rodó gives the comparative Latin Americanist a different take on both Latin American and inter-American affairs.

Quite distinctive in their approaches to the question of Brazilian and Spanish American identity, these three works, all canonical (and therefore influential), serve "to illustrate both the gap between Brazilian and Spanish American self-definitions at the turn of the century and the important differences between Brazilian literature during this period and Spanish American *Modernismo*" (González Echevarría, Pupo-Walker, and Haberly 6). Rodó, in particular, wrote at a time when a more reality-based reaction against Spanish American *Modernismo* began to set in. Concerned, as the late Darío and others had been, about the growing interference of the United States in the internal affairs of Latin American nations, Rodó was more realistic in how he saw relations between Latin America and the United States at the dawn of the new century. And like Martí and a great many other Spanish American intellectuals, Rodó also imagined giant, Portuguese-speaking Brazil to be essentially an odd and slightly problematic extension of Spanish America (see Newcomb 57–86). While he appreciated the economic might of the United States, and while he admired its at least nominal commitment to democratic self-rule (which he saw being eroded away by the rapaciousness of Wall Street and the hypocrisy of political leaders), he also believed that North and South America could not merely coexist but actually benefit each other. Each, he felt, could supply the other with what it lacked. Making use of a Shakespearian image, he argued that the Latin American Ariel could complement the North American Caliban. The more idealistic Ariel (among other things devoted to the highest principles of democracy) would remind the increasingly materialistic and aggressive Caliban of his own commitment to democracy. And that one does not practice democracy by taking advantage of other, weaker nations that are struggling to nurture their own democracies. Rodó saw it as his duty to remind the United States that lest it be judged hypocritical, it needed to practice what it preached. Like many other Latin American writers, intellectuals, and political leaders of this time, he was keenly aware of the problem the United States was grappling with: would it be defined by the noble principles of its found-ing, or would it be owned and operated by Wall Street and its Big Money power brokers?

Three political events mark this period: One, Brazil abolished slavery in 1888 and in 1889 became a republic, one modeled very much on the United States (see Eakin). It then began assiduously to promote itself to the United States as the intermediary between it and Spanish America. Two, the United States launched its war with Spain (1898), which gained it control of a coveted market in the Caribbean as well as the enmity and distrust of Spanish America. And three, Brazil, seeing its arguments pay dividends, saw itself established as the "cornerstone" of US Secretary of State Elihu Root's Latin American policy and, so enabled, commenced with the nurturing of its "special relationship" with the United States (Burns, *History of Brazil* 329). The largely trumped-up Spanish-American War had an adverse impact on inter-American relations. From the per-spective of Latin America, the United States had "seemed for a while" earlier in the century "to offer" productive "models—Protestant disci-pline, prosperity, democratic freedoms—but admiration for the United States was quickly enough compromised by an imperial sense of Manifest Destiny and gunboat diplomacy" (Tapscott 6–7).

In the United States of the racially inflamed 1920s, however, when incorrect but still widely popular ideas about the "white" race being supe-rior to all others were accepted as scientifically proven, the ideas being promulgated by such Latin American thinkers as Vasconcelos and Freyre would not have been well received. And they were not. Faulkner's discus-sions of miscegenation, as in *Absalom, Absalom!* and other of his works, did not sit well with a great many readers and critics in the United States of the 1920s and 1930s, though they were easily understood by Latin Americans (see Fitz and Fitz). The entire concept of racially mixed socie-ties as being anything but detrimental to racially "pure" societies was the standard thinking of the time, and it got a big boost in the United States from F. Scott Fitzgerald's *The Great Gatsby,* wherein the character Tom Buchannon emphatically makes this very mistaken point.

With its scientific basis, da Cunha's *Os Sertões* reflects this same dev-astating error—even as its author, racially mixed himself, begins to doubt what he has been taught about race and the biology of race. The cour-age and tenacity of the racially mixed *sertanejos,* or backlanders, he sees defending their homes are not the qualities of a weak, degenerate people, as he has been led to believe they are. This tension, reflecting da Cunha's own inner struggle about what was true and what he should believe, imparts to his narrative a personally compelling conflict that parallels the larger struggle that he chronicles, between impoverished and backward northern Brazil and wealthy and progressive southern Brazil. A trained scientist and a confirmed Positivist, da Cunha had been taught by the best minds of his day, people who had themselves been trained by the best scientific minds of Europe and the United States, that racial mixing was deleterious and retrograde and that certain races were inherently inferior to others. "An intermingling of races highly diverse," da Cunha informs his reader, "is, in the majority of cases, prejudicial. . . . Miscegenation carried to an extreme means retrogression" (*Rebellion in the Backlands* 84–85). This terrible mistake would give rise to Aryanism and the Holocaust. World War II would be fought largely to save the world from its awful consequences, one of which was the rise once again of white power movements. Doubt about the validity of what he had been taught permeates da Cunha's attempt to explain, to himself and to his national audience, the tragedy of the violent and bloody Canudos uprising, from December 1896 to October 1897, in a hitherto forgotten corner of northeast Brazil. The events at Canudos rocked Brazil to its core and, only a few years after it had proclaimed itself a federative republic, forced it to fear for its future. Today, thanks to our better understanding of human genetics, we know that what da Cunha had put his faith in was simply wrong, the product of bad science. But at that time this truth was not known and so not available to him. Yet in observing the events at Canudos, da Cunha knew something was terribly wrong.

In this book, I have argued that Latin American literature and history provide a uniquely productive basis for the work of Richard Morse. A visionary thinker, Morse, a historian, argued that we should conceive of Latin America as encompassing both Spanish America and Brazil and that both Spanish and Portuguese needed to be mastered. Of all the European-based American literatures, those of Spanish America and Brazil are the oldest and most evolved as far as the American experience is concerned. But contrary to what many think, they are far from being the same. In my view, there were three basic differences between early Spanish America and Brazil: First, they came from Iberian experiences and traditions that were quite distinct; Portugal was not Spain. Second, the early Spanish and Portuguese encountered profoundly different Native American cultures; the Tupi-Guarani were not the Aztecs, the Mayas, or the Incas. And third, colonial Spanish America and Brazil would develop along different social, political, and economic lines. Colonial Brazil was more loosely run, it featured more officially sanctioned mixing, sexually and socially, and it was more global in nature, more open to the traffic of international ideas.

In literary terms, the above meant that colonial Brazil was more receptive to new ways of thinking from abroad. It was more malleable and not fearful of influence from other cultures. It developed a nascent sense of nationalism, of being "Brazilian," before the several Spanish-speaking nations of America developed any sense of being "Spanish American." It did not have strong indigenous cultures to draw upon, as did Spanish America. Its epic tradition was less martial and more political in nature; its eighteenth century was more flourishing and original; and its nineteenth century was more unified and self-referential. Brazilian writers drew inspiration both from foreign sources and from their forebears and their own national traditions. This created a national literature that was notably cohesive.

I have also tried to show that by the end of the nineteenth century Spanish America and Brazil produced not one but two literary revolutions: one, from Spanish America, in poetry; the other, from Brazil, in prose fiction. These were nonpareil in the rest of the Americas, and taken together they proved the originality and excellence of Latin American letters. Far from being "a placid backwater of world literature," nineteenth-century Latin America was, in point of fact, a fully informed bastion of it, a locus of energy, creativity, and intellectual seriousness. For early Americanists, to know the foundings and the foundations of Spanish America and Brazil is to know the foundations of America itself. It is for this reason that Latin America—its languages, its people, its history, and its traditions—provides such an excellent platform from which to study the rest of the Americas. From the beginning, "America" was an idea, an opportunity to start again and this time to do things right. For its European players at least, America offered a chance to create a Utopia. How this has so far worked out is very much the ur-theme of American literature, and it has long tied us all together. It still does.

Notes

Introduction

1. For purposes of chronological perspective, it is useful for the comparative Latin Americanists, and for Americanists in general, to remember the pertinent dates of the arrivals of the Europeans to the New World. The Spanish arrived in 1492 and would stay, but John Cabot (a.k.a. Giovanni Caboto), sailing under the flag of England, dropped anchor in North America only five years later, in 1497, though no permanent settlement was established. Portugal made landfall in 1500 and established its colony, Brazil. Not to be left out of the scramble for New World possessions, France made its claim in 1534.

2. For more on this, see Skidmore; also Cândido; Perrone; Newcomb; Brune; Sadlier; K. Jackson, "Introduction"; and Oliveira Lima. On the basis of work done by these and other scholars, it is possible to regard Brazil—its history, culture, and literature—as the linchpin of the inter-American project.

3. Unless otherwise noted, all translations are mine.

4. In her introduction to *Comparative American Identities*, Hortense J. Spillers discusses the importance of Martí and "Our America" but does not note that it leaves out Brazil and Canada. See also K. Jackson, "Introduction" 4.

5. For more on Martí and his failure to discuss Brazil, see Newcomb 27–32.

6. For more on how contemporary views of Latin America are changing, see Valdés and Valdés; also Santiago.

1. The Iberian Origins

1. The Jews were afforded legal protection from discrimination in 1507, when discrimination against them was formally abolished. Payne 230.

2. Earlier, in 1139, King Afonso had defeated the Moors in a decisive battle and reduced them to "tributary status." Payne 117.

3. The prudent scholar will read these pronouncements skeptically. The assertion of Luso-Brazilian racial and cultural tolerance, while accurate in the main, is more complicated than suggested here.

4. An exception was the US government, which after 1960 (in Cuba) and 1964 (in Brazil) had become acutely conscious of political events in Latin America.

5. In *Writing and Reading Differently,* a collection of essays published in 1985 and devoted to the teaching of literature and composition in the United States, only one piece deals with writing in Spanish, and none deal with Portuguese or Brazil. See Atkins and Johnson.

6. Thanks to modern genomic science, we now know that there is only one "race" of people on our planet, the human race. What we used to imagine were the various "races" are nothing but variations on our single, human family. Studies have now proven that there are as many genetic differences within a single group of people supposedly of the same "race" as there are between the so-called races. Thus the whole idea of there being multiple "races" is entirely spurious.

7. Bosi, to cite one critic, contends that Freyre does not sufficiently address the violence that accompanied the Portuguese colonization of Brazil. "Why should we idealize what occurred?," he asks. "Should Brazilian scholars compete with other colonized peoples to decide who was *best colonized?*" Bosi 48; see also 14–15, 49.

8. I consider Skidmore's essay required reading for any inter-Americanist interested in the importance of miscegenation in the Americas.

3. The Literature of Discovery and Conquest

1. For my approach to the chronological development of Spanish American literature, I am guided by Englekirk et al., *Anthology.*

2. In Latin American literary history, the term *realismo mágico* pertains overwhelmingly to Spanish America and not Brazil, where even its existence is a much debated point and where it is regarded as a foreign influence.

3. See also Henríquez-Ureña 12 and 207. The full text of the poem, in *Oueueres poetiques de Mellin de S. Gelais,* is available online. While Saint-Gelais's sonnet was written in praise of the *Voyages aventureux* of Jean Alfonse de Saintonge, the author would certainly have known of Colón's report, which, in various translated forms, enjoyed a wide and avid readership all across Europe. See Henríquez-Ureña 12.

4. For my chronology of the evolution of Brazilian literature, I make use of those established by Massaud Moisés in *A literatura brasileira.*

5. An escalating trade war between France and England over the question of who would control this fur trade erupted almost immediately in Canada.

6. As their ship is departing Brazil for France, several Indian maidens swim out into the sea following Correia and Paraguaçu. One of them, Moema, will drown. In Machado de Assis's 1876 novel, *Helena,* Moema is the name of the spirited little mare that the female protagonist, Helena, rides with unusual grace and control. While invoking Brazil's indigenous past, as well as referencing a classic of early Brazilian literature, the name Moema also allows Machado to tout the potential of females as leaders of Brazil.

7. Canada enjoys a strong and thriving indigenous heritage. For more information on Canada, its literature, and its culture, see New 3–24; Goldie; and McGrath and Petrone.

8. Penned by Cortés himself, they were dispatched to the Spanish Crown in 1519, 1520, 1522, 1524, and 1526. Of these "terse, soberly written yet vivid reports," scholars Englekirk, Leonard, Reid, and Crow opine that they also "possess literary merits comparable to the *Commentaries* of Julius Caesar and to the *Anabasis* of Xenophon" (*Outline* 13).

4. The Flowering of Colonial Latin American Letters

1. For a discussion of how this position has led to a skewed understanding of US history and of the relationship of the United States to the rest of the world, see Bacevich.

2. Writing a few years earlier, in 1946, Pedro Henríquez-Ureña, also concerned with the racial question in the Americas, lamented what, for him, was the "seemingly insoluble problem" the "color line" had become in the United States (34). Both Henríquez-Ureña and Herring, along with many other Latin Americanists, were seeing racial issues more and more from a comparative and inter-American perspective. World War II and the Good Neighbor Policy, implemented by the United States, which needed natural resources from Latin America to conduct the war effort, had awakened at least Brazilians and Spanish Americans to the possibility of improved relations between the United States and the nations of Spanish- and Portuguese-speaking America. We can say, then, and with pride, that Latin Americanists helped the civil rights movement in the United States.

3. From 1580 to 1640 Portugal was ruled by Spain.

4. Matos's sonnet, in which he sings the praises of his "discreta e formosíssima Maria," apes the well-known Góngora poem that begins "Ilustre y hermosíssima María."

5. At the risk of oversimplification, we can think of *conceptismo* as the intricate and provocative interplay of ideas and *culteranismo* as a form of versification, often associated with Góngora's *Soledades,* that concerns itself with matters of style, especially syntax, and vocabulary.

6. In addition to Moore's novel, the 1991 film *Black Robe* is also highly recommended.

7. It should also be noted that during the seventeenth and eighteenth centuries, the so-called lingua geral was widely spoken in Brazil, so much so that its usage may have exceeded Portuguese. Thus, it too could be taken as Brazil's unifying language. Only in 1758, when the Marquis of Pombal prohibited the use of the lingua geral, did Portuguese truly begin to unify the nation.

8. See Vieira 49–70.

5. The Enlightenment and Independence

1. As many have pointed out, for example, it is incongruous to associate Spanish American independence with the Inca Empire, which, though progressive in many ways, did not grant full liberty as the Spanish Americans of 1824 understood it to the people it conquered. And, of course, the Incans had their liberty taken away by the conquering Spanish.

2. Olmedo knew that Virginia was the home state of George Washington.

6. The Nineteenth Century

1. Brooke's novel, *The History of Emily Montague* (1769), exemplifies what the Canadian scholar Northrop Frye describes as "the garrison mentality" that, as of 1965, characterized for him a basic characteristic of Canadian literature (830).

2. Lucas's opinion notwithstanding, many scholars do not associate Azevedo with Brazil's sonnet tradition.

3. While this unity of God and Nature is certainly appropriate for Heredia's poem, Frye notes that he has "long been impressed in Canadian poetry by a tone of deep terror in regard to nature" (830).

4. In rough terms, the poetic equivalent to Realism in narrative is Parnassianism.

5. In its first English translation, by Clotilde Wilson, *Quincas Borba* is titled *Philosopher or Dog?*

6. See Machado de Assis, *Obra Completa* 3:1167.

7. Although it is a bit unnerving to think so, Borges may have also been influenced by Lewis Carroll and his character Humpty Dumpty, who espoused the belief that words meant whatever he, Humpty, said they did, nothing more and nothing less. See E. Fitz, *Inter-American Literary History* 357–58.

8. The Brazilian text that most evokes comparison with Crane's novel is Euclides da Cunha's *Os Sertões*, published seven years later in 1902. Like *The Red Badge of Courage*, *Os Sertões* is not so much about men at war as it is about men, and women, in moments of combat, in battles whose meaning and consequences they struggle to understand. And again like Crane's story, *Os Sertões* is cinematic, utilizing what seem to be both tightly focused shots and panoramic shots, and uncannily, disturbingly intense, with scenes of mind-numbing boredom interspersed with scenes of horrific violence. Finally, a stoicism pervades both narratives.

9. The term *Joanino* refers to Dom João VI.

10. According to Englekirk, Leonard, Reid, and Crow, the "*modernista* ideal was to synthesize perfectly the finely wrought sculpture of Parnassian verse with Symbolist nuances and word-music" (*Anthology* 415).

11. One of the main reasons why Brazil's commitment was greater than that of the rest of Latin America, as González Echevarría points out, is that while during the late eighteenth and early nineteenth centuries most Spanish American

nations were occupied with fighting wars of independence and disengaging with Europe, Brazil, a constitutional monarchy, intensified its relationships with European nations, especially those with a strong tradition of scientific study. This meant that "from early on Brazil established institutions for the promotion of scientific research and exploration," whereas Spanish America did not. González Echevarría, *Myth and Archive* 129.

7. Rubén Darío, Machado de Assis, and End-of-Century Brillance

1. In the world of Brazilian *futebol,* a *craque* is an exceptional player, a superstar. Pelé was a *craque.* In the United States, LeBron James is a *craque* in basketball.

2. For an additional comparison, consider Darío and the Brazilian poet Olavo Bilac. See Merquior 368.

3. For more on this, see Jrade, *Rubén Darío and the Romantic Search for Unity* 102–4.

4. Machado is believed to have been an agnostic if not an outright atheist. If this is true, then he would not have been as vexed as Darío was at somehow accommodating sexual desire and his religious training as a Catholic, according to which sexual pleasure was sinful.

5. According to this rule, long codified here in the United States by many state constitutions, any person with even "one drop" of "Black" blood in their veins was legally "Black," and so subject to discrimination.

6. His name reveals his true nature. *Cristiano,* or *Christian,* needs no further explanation, but when paired with *Palha,* which in Portuguese means "straw, dry, dead straw," it suddenly adds a dollop of hypocrisy to the mixture and to his characterization.

7. See http://bibliotecanacionaldigital.gob.cl/bnd/623/w3-article-134214 .html. In translation, these quotes would be "all modesty and grace," "dark," and with a "mandarin aspect," a "wise Greek" or perhaps a "Greek sage."

Conclusion

1. At the same time, it is important to remember that during the Iberian Union (1580–1640), Brazil was not as important to the Spanish as were its "other" American colonies. The consequences of the union were significant, especially during the seventeenth century.

2. Caitlin Fitz has speculated that one reason why the Spanish American wars for independence dragged on for so many years was that the United States, for all of its talk of support, never did for Spanish America what France had done for the thirteen colonies when they were seeking their independence from England.

3. According to Englekirk, Leonard, Reid, and Crow, Martí, already recognized as an astute observer of US culture, spoke at the International American Conference being held in New York City in 1889 (*Anthology* 376).

Bibliography

Adorno, Rolena. "Cultures in Contact: Mesoamerica, the Andes, and the European Written Tradition." In González Echevarría and Pupo-Walker, *Cambridge History of Latin American Literature*, 2:33–57.

Aidoo, Lamonte. *Slavery Unseen: Sex, Power, and Violence in Brazilian History.* Durham, NC: Duke University Press, 2018.

Aldridge, A. Owen. "Anne Bradstreet: Some Thoughts on the Tenth Muse." In *Early American Literature: A Comparative Approach*, 25–52. Princeton, NJ: Princeton University Press, 1982.

Alencar, José de. *Como e porque sou romancista.* Salvador: Livraria Progresso, 1955.

Alves, Castro. *The Major Abolitionist Poems: Antônio de Castro Alves.* Edited, translated, and with an introduction by Amy A. Peterson. New York: Garland, 1990.

Amora, Antônio Soares. *História da literatura brasileira.* 7th ed. São Paulo: Edição Saraiva, 1968.

Anderson Imbert, Enrique, and Eugenio Florit. *Literatura Hispanoamericana.* New York: Holt, Rinehart, & Winston, 1960.

Arguedas, José María. *Deep Rivers.* Translated by Frances Horning Barraclough, with an introduction by John V. Murra and an afterword by Mario Vargas Llosa. Austin: University of Texas Press, 1978.

Astrov, Margot, ed. *American Indian Prose and Poetry: An Anthology.* New York: Capricorn Books, 1962.

Atkins, G. Douglas, and Michael L. Johnson, eds. *Writing and Reading Differently: Deconstruction and the Teaching of Composition and Literature.* Lawrence: University of Kansas Press, 1985.

Atwood, Margaret. *Survival: A Thematic Guide to Canadian Literature.* Toronto: Anansi, 1972.

Bacevich, Andrew. *After the Apocalypse: America's Role in a World Transformed.* New York: Metropolitan Books, 2021.

Bailey, David J. *Naturalism against Nature: Kinship and Degeneracy in Fin-de-siècle Portugal and Brazil.* Oxford: Legenda, 2020.

Barletta, Vincent. "António Vieira's Empire of Word, Sea, and Sky." In Vieira, *Sermon of Saint Anthony to the Fish and Other Texts,* 10–19.

Barrenechea, Antonio. *America Unbound: Encyclopedic Literature and Hemispheric Studies.* Albuquerque: University of New Mexico Press, 2016.

———. "Good Neighbor/Bad Neighbor: Boltonian Americanism and Hemispheric Studies." In Parkinson Zamora and Spitta, "The Americas, Otherwise," 231–43.

———. "A Hemispheric World of Difference: Literature of the Americas (1982–2020)." In Kaup and Ochoa, *Essays in Honor of Lois Parkinson Zamora,* 3–26.

Bates, Margaret J. "A Poet of Seventeenth-Century Brazil: Gregório de Matos." *Américas* 4, no. 1 (July 1947): 83–99.

Benítez-Rojo, Antonio. "Nineteenth-Century Spanish American Novel," In González Echevarría and Pupo-Walker, *Cambridge History of Latin American Literature,* 1:417–89.

Bercovitch, Sacan. *A History of the Americas: A Syllabus with Maps.* Boston: Ginn, 1928.

———. "The Puritan Vision of the New World." In Elliott, *Columbia Literary History of the United States,* 33–44.

Bolton, Herbert E. "The Epic of Greater America." *American Historical Review* 38 (April 1933): 448–74.

Borges, Jorge Luis. "El arte narrativo y la magia." In *Discusión,* 109–24. Buenos Aires: M. Gleizer, 1932.

———. *Other Inquisitions: 1937–1952.* Translated by Ruth L. C. Simms and with an introduction by James E. Irby. New York: Simon & Schuster, 1968.

Bosi, Alfredo. *Colony, Cult, and Culture.* Translated by Robert T. Newcomb and edited by Pedro Meira Monteiro. Dartmouth: University of Massachusetts, Dartmouth, and the Luso-Asio-Afro-Brazilian Studies & Theory Program, 2008.

Braga, Thomas. "Castro Alves and the New England Abolitionists." *Hispania* 87, no. 4 (1984): 585–93.

Braz, Albert. *The False Traitor: Louis Riel in Canadian Culture.* Toronto: University of Toronto Press, 2003.

———. "Promised Land/Cursed Land: The Peculiar Canada of Mathias Carvalho." *Interfaces: Brasil/Canada* 1, no. 1 (2001): 119–28.

Brinton, Daniel G. *Ancient Nahuatl Poetry.* Brinton's Library of Aboriginal American Literature, 7. Philadelphia, 1887.

Brotherston, Gordon. *Book of the Fourth World: Reading the Native Americas through Their Literatures.* Cambridge: Cambridge University Press, 1992.

Brotherston, Gordon, and Lúcia de Sá. "First Peoples of the Americas and Their Literature." In McClennen and Fitz, *Comparative Cultural Studies and Latin America,* 8–33.

Brune, Krista. *Creative Transformations: Travels and Translations of Brazil in the Americas.* Albany: State University of New York Press, 2020.

Burgueño, María Cristina. "O Caramuru y Caramurú: Sus relaciones en la formación de un protoimaginario nacional uruguayo." *Revista Iberoamericana: O Brasil, a América Hispânica e o Caribe: Abordagens Comparativas,* nos. 182–83 (January–June 1998): 117–28.

Burns, E. Bradford. *A History of Brazil.* 2nd ed. New York: Columbia University Press, 1980.

———. *Latin America: A Concise Interpretive History.* 2nd ed. Englewood Cliffs, NJ: Prentice Hall, 1977.

Bush, Andrew. "Lyric Poetry of the Eighteenth and Nineteenth Centuries." In González Echevarría and Pupo-Walker, *Cambridge History of Latin American Literature,* 1:375–400.

Cândido, Antônio. *Recortes.* São Paulo: Cia das Letras, 1993.

Cardenas Bunsen, José A. "Consent, Voluntary Jurisdiction and Native Political Agency in Bartolomé de Las Casas' Final Writings." *Bulletin of Spanish Studies* 91, no. 6 (2014): 793–817.

Carman, Harry J., and Harold C. Syrett. *A History of the American People: The Legacy of Civil War to World War II and Its Aftermath.* New York: Knopf, 1958.

Carter, Boyd G. "Darío, Rubén." In *Encyclopedia of World Literature in the 20th Century,* edited by Leonard S. Klein, 1:543–45. 2nd ed. New York: Frederick Ungar, 1981.

Castilho, Celso. *Slave Emancipation and Transformations in Brazilian Political Citizenship.* Pittsburgh: Pittsburgh University Press, 2016.

Chaloub, Sydney. "Dependents Play Chess: Political Dialogues in Machado de Assis." In *Machado de Assis: Reflections on a Brazilian Master Writer,* edited by Richard Graham, 51–84. Austin: University of Texas Press, 1999.

Chang-Rodríguez, Raquel, and Malva F. Filer. *Voces de Hispanoamérica: Antología literaria.* 3rd ed. New York: Thomson & Heinle, 2004.

Chevigny, Bell Gale, and Gari Laguardia, eds. *Reinventing the Americas: Comparative Studies of Literature of the United States and Spanish America.* Cambridge: Cambridge University Press, 1986.

Cooke, Alistair. *Alistair Cooke's America.* New York: Knopf, 1974.

Coonrod Martínez, Elizabeth. "The Latin American Innovative Novel of the 1920s: A Comparative Reassessment." In McClennen and Fitz, *Comparative Cultural Studies and Latin America,* 34–55.

Costigan, Lúcia Helena S. "Colonial Literature and Social Reality in Brazil and the Viceroyalty of Peru: The Satirical Poetry of Gregório de Matos and Juan del Valle y Caviedes." In *Coded Encounters: Writing, Gender, and Ethnicity in Colonial Latin America,* edited by Francisco Javier Cevallos-Candau, Jeffrey A. Cole, Nina M. Scott, and Nicomedes Suárez-Araúz, 86–100. Amherst: University of Massachusetts Press, 1994.

Costigan, Lúcia Helena, and Leopoldo M. Bernucci. "O Brasil, a América Hispânica e o Caribe: Abordagens Comparativas." Organized by Bernucci and

Costigan. *Revista Iberoamericana* 64, nos. 182–83 (January–June 1998): 11–14.

Coutinho, Afrânio. *An Introduction to Literature in Brazil.* Translated by Gregory Rabassa. New York: Columbia University Press, 1969.

Coutinho, Eduardo F., ed. *Brazilian Literature as World Literature.* Translated by Thomas O. Beebee, Jizelda Ferreira Galvão, and Dr. Lisa Shaw. London: Bloomsbury, 2018.

Cunha, Euclides da. *Rebellion in the Backlands.* Translated by Samuel Putnam. Chicago: University of Chicago Press, 1944.

Damrosch, David. *What Is World Literature?* Princeton, NJ: Princeton University Press, 2003.

Daniel, Mary Lou. "Brazilian Fiction from 1800 to 1855." In González Echevarría and Pupo-Walker, *Cambridge History of Latin American Literature,* 3:127–36.

———. "Brazilian Fiction from 1900 to 1945." In González Echevarría and Pupo-Walker, *Cambridge History of Latin American Literature,* 3:157–88.

Darío, Rubén. *Obras completas.* 5 vols. Madrid: Aguado, 1950–55.

———. *Rubén Darío: Selected Writings.* Edited and with an introduction by Ilan Stavans. New York: Penguin Books, 2005.

Davidson, Arnold E., ed. *Studies on Canadian Literature: Introductory and Critical Essays.* New York: Modern Language Association of America, 1990.

De la Cruz, Juana Inés. *Sor Juana Inés de la Cruz: The Answer/La Respuesta, and Including a Selection of Poems.* Translated and edited by Electra Arenal and Amanda Powell. New York: Feminist Press at the City University of New York, 1994.

———. *Sor Juana's First Dream.* Translated by Luis Harss. New York: Lumen Books, 1986.

Demos, John. *The Unredeemed Captive: A Family Story from Early America.* New York: Vintage Books, 1995.

D'Harcourt, Raoul, and Marie d'Harcourt. *La musique des Incas et ses survivances.* 2 vols. Paris: Gallimard, 1925.

Díaz del Castillo, Bernal. *The Conquest of New Spain.* Translated by J. M. Cohen. New York: Penguin Books, 1963. First published as *Historia verdadera de la conquista de la Nueva España* (Madrid, 1632).

Dickerson, Caitlin. "Dispatches: 'It's always been about exclusion.'" *Atlantic,* May 2021, 11–15.

Donoso, José. *The Boom in Spanish American Literature: A Personal History.* Translated by Gregory Kolovakos. New York: Columbia University Press in association with the Center for Inter-American Relations, 1977.

Eakin, Marshall. *Becoming Brazilians: Race and National Identity in Twentieth-Century Brazil.* Cambridge: Cambridge University Press, 2017.

Edinger, Catherine Feldman. "Hawthorne and Alencar: Romancing the Marble." *Brasil/Brazil* 4, no. 3 (1990): 69–84.

———. Introduction to *Senhora: Profile of a Woman,* by José de Alencar, translated by Catherine Feldman Edinger, ix–xviii. Austin: University of Texas Press, 1994.

———. "Machismo and Androgyny in Mid-Nineteenth-Century Brazilian and American Novels." *Comparative Literature Studies* 27, no. 2 (1990): 124–39.

Elliott, Emory, gen. ed. *Columbia Literary History of the United States.* New York: Columbia University Press, 1988.

Englekirk, John E., with Irving A. Leonard, John T. Crow, and John A. Crow. *An Outline History of Spanish American Literature.* 3rd ed. New York: Appleton-Century-Crofts, 1965.

Englekirk, John E., Irving A. Leonard, John T. Reid, and John A. Crow, eds. *An Anthology of Spanish American Literature.* 2nd ed. New York: Appleton-Century-Crofts, 1968.

Fiedler, Leslie. *Love and Death in the American Novel.* New York: Criterion, 1960.

Fitz, Caitlin A. *Our Sister Republics: The United States in an Age of American Revolutions.* New York: Liveright / W. W. Norton, 2016.

Fitz, Earl E. "Borges as Historian of American Literature: His Theory of Our Two Realisms." *Chasqui* 49, no. 2 (November 2020): 3–12.

———. "Colonial Literature in the Americas." In Fitz, *Inter-American Literary History,* 79–124.

———. "The European Background." In Fitz, *Inter-American Literary History,* 27–78.

———. "The First Inter-American Novels: Some Choices and Some Comments." *Comparative Literature Studies* 22, no. 3 (Fall 1985): 361–76.

———. *Inter-American Literary History: Six Critical Periods.* Frankfurt am Main: Peter Lang, 2017.

———. *Machado de Assis and Female Characterization: The Novels.* Lewisburg, PA: Bucknell University Press, 2015.

———. *Machado de Assis and Narrative Theory.* Lewisburg, PA: Bucknell University Press, 2019.

———. "The Nineteenth Century." In Fitz, *Inter-American Literary History,* 125–252.

———. "Our Multiple American Modernisms." In Fitz, *Inter-American Literary History,* 253–320.

———. *Rediscovering the New World: Inter-American Literature in a Comparative Context.* Iowa City: University of Iowa Press, 1991.

———. "Spanish American and Brazilian Literature in an Inter-American Perspective: The Comparative Approach." In McClennen and Fitz, *Comparative Cultural Studies and Latin America,* 69–88.

———. "William Faulkner, James Agee, and Brazil: The American South in Latin American Literature's 'Other' Tradition." In *Look Away: The U.S. South in New World Studies,* edited by John Smith and Deborah Cohn, 419–45. Durham, NC: Duke University Press, 2004.

———. "Writing Womanhood in the New Brazil: Machado's *Lição de Botánica.*" In *Emerging Dialogues on Machado de Assis,* edited by Lamonte Aidoo and Daniel Silva, 125–43. New York: Palgrave Macmillan, 2016.

Fitz, Earl E., and Ezra E. Fitz. "Faulkner, Borges, and the Translation of *The Wild Palms:* The Evolution of Borges's Theory concerning the Role of the Reader in the Game of Literature." In "Faulkner beyond the United States," edited by Barbara Ladd, special issue, *Faulkner Journal* 24, no. 1 (Fall 2008): 29–61.

Foerster, Norman, Norman S. Grabo, Russel B. Nye, E. Fred Carlisle, and Robert Falk, eds. *American Poetry and Prose.* 5th ed. 3 vols. Boston: Houghton Mifflin, 1970.

Franco, Adela Pineda. "Darío and the Ambivalent Legacies of Western Modernity." *Review 97: Literature and Arts of the Americas* 51, no. 2 (December 2018): 188–94.

Franco, Jean. *An Introduction to Spanish-American Literature.* New York: Columbia University Press, 1969.

Freyre, Gilberto. *The Masters and the Slaves: A Study in the Development of Brazilian Civilization.* Translated by Samuel Putnam. 2nd English-language ed. New York: Knopf, 1956.

Frye, Northrop. Conclusion to *Literary History of Canada: Canadian Literature in English,* general editor Carl F. Klinck, 821–49. Toronto: University of Toronto Press, 1965.

Fuentes, Carlos. *Machado de la Mancha.* Mexico City: Fondo de Cultura Económica, 2001.

Gallagher, D. P. *Modern Latin American Literature.* Oxford: Oxford University Press, 1973.

García, Frederick C. H. "Critic Turned Author: Isaac Goldberg." *Luso-Brazilian Review* 9, no. 1 (1972): 21–28.

Gledson, John. *The Deceptive Realism of Machado de Assis: A Dissenting Interpretation of "Dom Casmurro."* Liverpool: Francis Cairns, 1984.

———. *Misplaced Ideas: Essays on Brazilian Culture.* London: Verso, 1992.

Goldie, Terry. "Semiotic Control: Native Peoples in Canadian Literature in English." In Davidson, *Studies on Canadian Literature,* 110–23.

González, Aníbal. "Modernist Prose." In González Echevarría and Pupo-Walker, *Cambridge History of Latin American Literature,* 2:69–113.

González Echevarría, Roberto. "A Brief History of the History of Spanish American Literature." In González Echevarría and Pupo-Walker, *Cambridge History of Latin American Literature,* 1:7–32.

———. "Colonial Lyric." In González Echevarría and Pupo-Walker, *Cambridge History of Latin American Literature,* 1:191–230.

———. Introduction to González Echeverría, *Oxford Book of Latin American Short Stories,* 3–22.

———. "Latin American and Comparative Literatures." In McClennen and Fitz, *Comparative Cultural Studies and Latin America,* 89–104.

———. "A Lost World Re-Discovered: Sarmiento's *Facundo* and E. da Cunha's *Os Sertões*." In González Echevarría, *Myth and Archive*, 93–141.

———. *Myth and Archive: A Theory of Latin American Narrative.* Durham, NC: Duke University Press, 1998.

———, ed. *The Oxford Book of Latin American Short Stories.* Oxford: Oxford University Press, 1997.

———. Preface to González Echevarría, *Oxford Book of Latin American Short Stories,* xi–xiv.

González Echevarría, Roberto, and Enrique Pupo-Walker, eds. *The Cambridge History of Latin American Literature.* 3 vols. Cambridge: Cambridge University Press, 1996.

González Echevarría, Roberto, Enrique Pupo-Walker, and David Haberly. "Introduction to Volume 3." In González Echevarría and Pupo-Walker, *Cambridge History of Latin American Literature,* 3:1–10.

Guibert, Rita. *Seven Voices: Seven Latin American Writers Talk to Rita Guibert.* Translated by Frances Partridge. New York: Vintage / Random House, 1973.

Haberly, David T. "The Brazilian Novel from 1850 to 1900." In González Echevarría and Pupo-Walker, *Cambridge History of Latin American Literature,* 3:137–56.

———. "Colonial Brazilian Literature." In González Echevarría and Pupo-Walker, *Cambridge History of Latin American Literature,* 3:47–68.

———. "Form and Function in the New World Legend." In Pérez Firmat, *Do the Americas Have a Common Literature?,* 42–61.

———. Introduction to *Quincas Borba,* by Machado de Assis, xi–xxvi. Translated by Gregory Rabassa, with an introduction by David T. Haberly and an afterword by Celso Favaretto. Oxford: Oxford University Press, 1998.

Hallewell, L. *Books in Brazil: A History of the Publishing Trade.* Metuchen, NJ: Scarecrow, 1982.

Hayne, David H. "The Evolution of French-Canadian Literature to 1960." In Davidson, *Studies on Canadian Literature,* 144–63.

Henríquez-Ureña, Pedro. *Literary Currents in Hispanic America.* Cambridge, MA: Harvard University Press, 1946.

Herring, Hubert. *A History of Latin America: From the Beginnings to the Present.* 2nd ed. New York: Knopf, 1961.

Hofstadter, Albert, and Richard Kuhns, eds. *Philosophies of Art and Beauty: Selected Readings in Aesthetics from Plato to Heidegger.* New York: Modern Library, 1964.

Holanda, Sérgio Buarque de. *Visão do Paraíso: Os motivos edênicos no descobrimento e colonização do Brasil.* Rio de Janeiro: Livraria José Olympio Editora, 1959.

Infante, Ignacio. *After Translation: The Transfer and Circulation of Modern Poetics across the Atlantic.* New York: Fordham University Press, 2013.

Jackson, K. David. "Introduction: *World World Vast World* of the Brazilian Short Story." In *Oxford Anthology of the Brazilian Short Story,* edited by Jackson, 3–31. Oxford: Oxford University Press, 2006.

———. *Machado de Assis: A Literary Life.* New Haven, CT: Yale University Press, 2015.

Jackson, Richard L. *The Black Image in Latin American Literature.* Albuquerque: University of New Mexico Press, 1976.

Josef, Bella. *A máscara e o enigma.* Rio de Janeiro: Francisco Alves, 1986.

Jrade, Cathy L. *Modernismo, Modernity, and the Development of Spanish American Literature.* Austin: University of Texas Press, 1998.

———. "Modernist Poetry." In González Echevarría and Pupo-Walker, *Cambridge History of Latin American Literature,* 2:7–68.

———. *Rubén Darío and the Romantic Search for Unity: The Modernist Recourse to Esoteric Tradition.* Austin: University of Texas Press, 1983.

Kaup, Monika, and John Ochoa, eds. *Essays in Honor of Lois Parkinson Zamora: From the Americas to the World.* Lanham, MD: Lexington Books, 2021.

———. Introduction to Kaup and Ochoa, *Essays in Honor of Lois Parkinson Zamora,* xi–xxvi.

Kaup, Monika, and Debra I. Rosenthal, eds. *Mixing Race, Mixing Culture: Inter-American Literary Dialogues.* Austin: University of Texas Press, 2002.

Kirkpatrick, Gwen. "Forgiving Rubén Darío." *Review 97: Literature and Arts of the Americas* 51, no. 2 (December 2018): 180–87.

Kutzinski, Vera M. "Afro-Hispanic American Literature." In González Echevarría and Pupo-Walker, *Cambridge History of Latin American Literature,* 2:164–94.

———. *The Worlds of Langston Hughes: Modernism and Translation in the Americas.* Ithaca, NY: Cornell University Press, 2012.

Landers, Jane. *Atlantic Creoles in the Age of Revolutions.* Cambridge, MA: Harvard University Press, 2010.

Lasarte, Pedro. "En torno al sujeto americano en la poesía de Juan del Valle y Caviedes." In *La Chispa '97: Selected Proceedings,* edited by Claire J. Paolini, 233–44. New Orleans: Tulane University Press, 1997.

Lucas, Fábio. "Brazilian Poetry from the 1830s to the 1880s." In González Echevarría and Pupo-Walker, *Cambridge History of Latin American Literature,* 3:69–82.

Lynn, Roa. *Brazil and the USA: What Do We Have in Common?* Washington, DC: Brazilian Embassy, Cultural Section, 1999.

Machado de Assis. *Epitaph of a Small Winner.* Translated by William L. Grossman and with drawings by Shari Frisch. New York: Noonday, 1952.

———. *Obra Completa.* General editor Afrânio Coutinho. 3 vols. Rio de Janeiro: Editôra José Aguilar, 1962.

———. *Philosopher or Dog? (Quincas Borba).* Translated by Clotilde Wilson. New York: Bard/Avon, 1982.

————. *The Posthumous Memoirs of Brás Cubas.* Translated by Gregory Rabassa, with a foreword by Enylton de Sá Rego and an afterword by Gilberto Pinheiro Passos. Oxford: Oxford University Press, 1997.

Mann, Charles C. "The Founding Sachems." Op-ed, *New York Times*, 4 July 2005.

————. *1493: Uncovering the New World Columbus Created.* New York: Knopf, 2011.

Martin, Robert K. "North of the Border: Whose Postnationalism?" *American Literature* 65, no. 2 (June 1993): 358–61.

Martins, Heitor, ed. *The Brazilian Novel.* Bloomington: Indiana University Press, 1976.

McClennen, Sophia A. "Comparative Literature and Latin American Studies: From Disarticulation to Dialogue." In McClennen and Fitz, *Comparative Cultural Studies and Latin America,* 105–30.

McClennen, Sophia A., and Earl E. Fitz, eds. *Comparative Cultural Studies and Latin America.* West Lafayette, IN: Purdue University Press, 2004.

————. Introduction to McClennen and Fitz, *Comparative Cultural Studies and Latin America,* ix–xviii.

McGrath, Robin, and Penny Petrone. "Native Canadian Literature." In Davidson, *Studies on Canadian Literature,* 309–22.

McIntyre, Loren. *The Incas and Their Timeless Land.* Washington, DC: National Geographic Society, 1975.

Means, Philipp Ainsworth. *Ancient Civilizations of the Andes.* New York: Scribner's, 1931.

Mee, Charles L., Jr. "That Fateful Moment When Two Civilizations Came Face to Face." *Smithsonian,* October 1992, 56–69.

Mejías-López, Alejandro. *The Inverted Conquest: The Myth of Modernity and the Transatlantic Onset of Modernism.* Nashville: Vanderbilt University Press, 2009.

Merquior, J. G. "The Brazilian and the Spanish American Literary Traditions: A Contrastive View." In González Echevarría and Pupo-Walker, *Cambridge History of Latin American Literature,* 3:363–82.

Merrim, Stephanie. *Early Modern Women's Writing and Sor Juana Inés de la Cruz.* Nashville: Vanderbilt University Press, 1999.

Mitchell, Lee Clark. "Naturalism and the Languages of Determinism." In Elliott, *Columbia Literary History of the United States,* 525–45.

Moisés, Massaud. "Brazilian Poetry from 1878 to 1902." In González Echevarría and Pupo-Walker, *Cambridge History of Latin American Literature,* 3:83–105.

————. *A literatura brasileira através dos textos.* 21st ed. São Paulo: Editora Cultrix, 1998.

Monteiro, Pedro Meira. "The Dialectic of Resistance: Alfredo Bosi, Literary Critic." Preface to Bosi, *Colony, Cult, and Culture,* 7–17.

————. "Editor's Notes." In Bosi, *Colony, Cult, and Culture,* 97–105.

Morison, Samuel Eliot. *The Oxford History of the American People*. Oxford: Oxford University Press, 1965.

Morisset, Jean. "La conquête du Nord-Ouest, 1885–1985: The Imperial Quest of British North America." In *As Long as the Sun Shines and the Waters Flow: A Reader in Canadian Native Studies,* edited by Ian A. L. Getty and Antoine S. Lussier, 280–87. Vancouver: University of British Columbia Press, 1983.

———. *L'identité usurpée 1: L'Amérique écartée*. Montréal: Nouvelle Optique, 1985.

———. "Louis Riel: Écrivain des Amériques." *Nuit blanche* 28 (1987): 59–63.

Mundell, John A. "Queer Miscegenation: Freedom, Fluidity, and Failure in Adolfo Caminha's *Bom-Crioulo* (1895)." *Luso-Brazilian Review* 57, no. 2 (2020): 56–79.

New, W. H. *A History of Canadian Literature*. Vol. 2. Montréal: McGill-Queen's University Press, 2001.

Newcomb, Robert Patrick. *Nossa and Nuestra América: Inter-American Dialogues*. West Lafayette, IN: Purdue University Press, 2012.

Nicholson, Irene. *Firefly in the Night: A Study of Ancient Mexican Poetry and Symbolism*. London: Faber & Faber, 1959.

Nunes, Benedito. *O mundo de Clarice Lispector*. Manaus: Edições Governo do Estado do Amazonas, 1976.

Nunes, Maria Luisa. *The Craft of an Absolute Winner: Characterization and Narratology in the Novels of Machado de Assis*. Westport, CT: Greenwood, 1983.

Oliveira Lima, Manuel de. *The Evolution of Brazil Compared with That of Spanish and Anglo-Saxon America*. Stanford, CA: Stanford University Press, 1912.

Pagden, Anthony. *Lords of All the World: Ideologies of Empire in Spain, Britain and France*. New Haven, CT: Yale University Press, 1995.

Palma, Ricardo. *Cachivaches*. Lima: Torres Aguirre, 1900.

Parkes, Henry Bamford. *The American Experience: An Interpretation of the History and Civilization of the American People*. New York: Vintage, 1961.

Parkinson Zamora, Lois, and Silvia Spitta, eds. "The Americas, Otherwise." Special issue, *Comparative Literature* 61, no. 3 (2009).

Parry, J. H. *The Spanish Theory of Empire in the Sixteenth Century*. Cambridge: Cambridge University Press, 1940.

Payne, Stanley G. *A History of Spain and Portugal*. Vol. 1. Madison: University of Wisconsin Press, 1973.

Paz, Octavio. *The Labyrinth of Solitude: Life and Thought in Mexico*. Translated by Lysander Kemp. New York: Grove, 1961.

Peixoto, Afrânio. *Panorama da literatura brasileira*. São Paulo: Companhia Editora Nacional, 1940.

Pérez Firmat, Gustavo, ed. *Do the Americas Have a Common Literature?* Durham, NC: Duke University Press, 1990.

Perrone, Charles A. *Brazil, Lyric, and the Americas*. Gainesville: University Press of Florida, 2010.

Pinto-Bailey, Cristina Ferreira. Introduction to *Úrsula,* by Maria Firmina dos Reis, ix–xxi. Translated by Pinto-Bailey. Dartmouth, MA: Tagus Press, 2022.

Priestly, Herbert I. *The Coming of the White Man: 1492–1848.* New York: Macmillan, 1929.

Putnam, Samuel. *Marvelous Journey: Four Centuries of Brazilian Writing.* New York: Knopf, 1948.

Rabassa, Gregory. "A Comparative Look at the Literature of Spanish America and Brazil: The Dangers of Deception." In *Ibero-American Letters in a Comparative Perspective,* edited by W. T. Zyla and W. M. Aycock, 119–32. Lubbock: Texas Tech University Press, 1978.

———. "Survival and Revival: The Baroque in Latin American Literature." Supplement, *Luso-Brazilian Review* 15 (Summer 1978): 59–65.

Ribeiro, Darcy. *The Brazilian People: The Formation and Meaning of Brazil.* Translated by Gregory Rabassa. Gainesville: University Press of Florida, 1999.

Riley, Isaac Woodbridge. *American Thought: From Puritanism to Pragmatism and Beyond.* New York: Henry Holt, 1915.

Rodríguez Monegal, Emir, ed. *The Borzoi Anthology of Latin American Literature.* With the assistance of Thomas Colchie. 2 vols. New York: Knopf, 1977.

———. *Jorge Luis Borges: A Literary Biography.* New York: E. P. Dutton, 1978.

———. "The New Latin American Literature in the U.S.A." *Review '68,* no. 1 (1969): 3–13.

———. "The New Latin American Novelists." In *The TriQuarterly Anthology of Contemporary Latin American Literature,* edited by José Donoso and William A. Henkin, 9–28. New York: E. P. Dutton, 1969.

Sadlier, Darlene J. *Brazil Imagined: 1500 to the Present.* Austin: University of Texas Press, 2008.

Sadowski-Smith, Claudia, and Claire Fox. "Theorizing the Hemisphere: Inter-Americas Work at the Intersection of American, Canadian, and Latin American Studies." *Comparative American Studies: An International Journal* 2, no. 1 (2004): 5–38.

Santiago, Silviano. "Interpreting Interpretations of Latin America." *Brasil/Brazil* 35, no. 20 (2007): 3–25.

Sá Rego, Enylton de. Preface to *The Posthumous Memoirs of Brás Cubas,* by Machado de Assis, xi–xix. Edited by Sá Rego and Gilberto Pinheiro Passas. Translated by Gregory Rabassa. Oxford: Oxford University Press, 1997.

Scheick, William J. "The Poetry of Colonial America." In Elliott, *Columbia Literary History of the United States,* 83–97.

Schlau, Stacey. "Stranger in a Strange Land: The Discourse of Alienation in Gómez de Avellaneda's Abolitionist Novel, *Sab.*" *Hispania* 69, no. 3 (September 1986): 495–503.

Schons, Dorothy. "The First Feminist in the New World." *Equal Rights,* 31 October 1925, 11–12.

Schulman, Ivan A. "The Portrait of the Slave: Ideology and Aesthetics in the Cuban Antislavery Novel." *Annals of the New York Academy of Sciences* 292, no. 1 (1977): 356–67.

Seed, Patricia. *Ceremonies of Possession in Europe's Conquest of the New World, 1492–1640*. Cambridge: Cambridge University Press, 1995.

Seixas Guimarães, Hélio de. "Race and Color in the Reception of Machado de Assis." *Luso-Brazilian Review* 54, no. 2 (2017): 11–28.

Shouldice, Larry. "Wider Latitudes: Comparing New World Literature." *Canadian Review of Comparative Literature* 9, no. 1 (1982): 46–55.

Skidmore, Thomas E. "The Essay: Architects of Brazilian National Identity." In González Echevarría and Pupo-Walker, *Cambridge History of Latin American Literature*,1:345–62.

Sousândrade. "The Inferno of Wall Street: An Anthology." Translated by Robert E. Brown, with the assistance of Augusto de Campos. In "Brazilian Literature," edited by Kenneth David Jackson and Yvette Miller, special issue, *Latin American Literary Review* 14, no. 27 (January–June 1986): 92–98.

Spillers, Hortense J., ed. *Comparative American Identities: Race, Sex, and Nationality in the Modern Text (Essays of the English Institute)*. New York: Routledge, 1991.

———. "Introduction: Who Cuts the Border? Some Readings on 'America.'" In Spillers, *Comparative American Identities*, 1–25.

Spitta, Silvia, and Lois Parkinson Zamora. Introduction to Parkinson Zamora and Spitta, "The Americas, Otherwise," 189–208.

Stavans, Ilan. Introduction to Darío, *Rubén Darío*, xvii–lxii.

Steiner, George. *After Babel: Aspects of Language and Translation*. New York: Oxford University Press, 1975.

Stepan, Nancy. *The Beginnings of Brazilian Science: Oswaldo Cruz, Medical Research and Policy, 1890–1920*. New York: Science History Publications, 1976.

Stolley, Karen. "The Eighteenth Century: Narrative Forms, Scholarship, and Learning." In González Echevarría and Pupo-Walker, *Cambridge History of Latin American Literature*, 1:336–74.

Stuart, George E., and Gene S. Stuart. *The Mysterious Maya*. Washington, DC: National Geographic Society, 1977.

Sutherland, Ronald. *Second Image: Comparative Studies in Québec/Canadian Literature*. Toronto: Alger, 1971.

Tapajós, Vicente. *História da América*. 3rd ed. São Paulo: Companhia Editôra Nacional, 1958.

Tapscott, Stephen, ed. *Twentieth-Century Latin American Poetry: A Bi-Lingual Anthology*. Austin: University of Texas Press, 1996.

Tedlock, Dennis. *Rabinal Achí: A Mayan Drama of War and Sacrifice*. Translated and interpreted by Tedlock. Oxford: Oxford University Press, 2003.

Tolman, Jon M. "The Brazilian Novel." In Martins, *Brazilian Novel*, 1–13.

Torres-Ríoseco, Arturo. *The Epic of Latin American Literature*. Rev. ed. Oxford: Oxford University Press, 1946.

Tosta, Luciano. *Confluence Narratives: Ethnicity, History, and Nation-Making in the Americas*. Lewisburg, PA: Bucknell University Press, 2016.

Umphrey, George U. "Spanish American Literature Compared with That of the United States." *Hispania* 26 (February 1943): 21–34.

Urbas, Jeannette. *From Thirty Acres to Modern Times: The Story of French-Canadian Literature*. Toronto: McGraw-Hill Ryerson, 1976.

Valdés, María Elena de, and Mario J. Valdés. "Rethinking Latin American Literary History." In *Latin America as Its Literature: Selected Papers of the XIVth Congress of the International Comparative Literature Association, the University of Alberta, August 15–20, 1994*, edited by María Elena de Valdés, Mario J. Valdés, and Richard A. Young, 68–85. Whitestone, NY: Council on National Literatures, 1995.

Valdés, Vanessa, and Earl E. Fitz, eds. *Machado de Assis, Blackness, and the Americas*. Albany: State University of New York Press, forthcoming.

Vasconcelos, José. *La raza cósmica / The Cosmic Race: A Bilingual Edition*. Translated by Didier P. Jaén. Baltimore: Johns Hopkins University Press, 1997.

Versiani, Ivana. "The New World's First Novelist." In Martins, *Brazilian Novel*, 15–28.

Vieira, Antônio. *The Sermon of Saint Anthony to the Fish and Other Texts*. Translated by Gregory Rabassa. Dartmouth: University of Massachusetts, Dartmouth, and Luso-American Foundation, 2007. Viotti da Costa, Emília. *The Brazilian Empire: Myths and Histories*. Chapel Hill: University of North Carolina Press, 2000.

Voight, Lisa. "Por andarmos todos casy mesturados: The Politics of Intermingling in Caminha's *Carta* and Colonial American Anthologies." *Early American Literature* 40, no. 3 (April 2009): 407–39.

Von Hagen, Victor Wolfgang. *The Aztec: Man and Tribe*. Rev. ed. New York: New American Library, 1961.

Wade, Jonathan. *Being Portuguese in Spanish: Reimagining Early Modern Iberian Literature, 1580–1640*. West Lafayette, IN: Purdue University Press, 2020.

Wagley, Charles. *An Introduction to Brazil*. Rev. ed. New York: Columbia University Press, 1971.

Wasserman, Renata M. *Exotic Nations: Literature and Cultural Identity in the United States and Brazil, 1830–1930*. Ithaca, NY: Cornell University Press, 1994.

———. "Re-Discovering the New World: Cooper and Alencar." *Comparative Literature* 26, no. 2 (Spring 1994): 130–45.

Wilkie, Brian, and James Hurt, eds. *Literature of the Western World*. 2nd ed. Vol. 2. New York: Macmillan, 1988.

Williams, Frederick G. "The Wall Street Inferno: A Poetic Rendering of the Gilded Age." *Chasqui: Revista de literatura latinoamericana* 5, no. 2 (1976): 15–32.

Williams, Stanley T. *The Spanish Background of American Literature.* New Haven, CT: Yale University Press, 1955.

Wood, Michael. "Master Among the Ruins." In "The Author as Plagiarist—The Case of Machado de Assis," edited by João Cezar de Castro Rocha, special issue, *Portuguese Literary & Cultural Studies* 13/14 (Fall 2004 / Spring 2005): 293–303.

Index

Caribbean Jewish Crossings: Literary History and Creative Practice
Sarah Phillips Casteel and Heidi Kaufman, editors

Mapping Hispaniola: Third Space in Dominican and Haitian Literature
Megan Jeanette Myers

Mourning El Dorado: Literature and Extractivism in the Contemporary American Tropics
Charlotte Rogers

Edwidge Danticat: The Haitian Diasporic Imaginary
Nadège T. Clitandre

Idle Talk, Deadly Talk: The Uses of Gossip in Caribbean Literature
Ana Rodríguez Navas

Crossing the Line: Early Creole Novels and Anglophone Caribbean Culture in the Age of Emancipation
Candace Ward

Staging Creolization: Women's Theater and Performance from the French Caribbean
Emily Sahakian

American Imperialism's Undead: The Occupation of Haiti and the Rise of Caribbean Anticolonialism
Raphael Dalleo

A Cultural History of Underdevelopment: Latin America in the U.S. Imagination
John Patrick Leary

The Spectre of Races: Latin American Anthropology and Literature between the Wars
Anke Birkenmaier

Performance and Personhood in Caribbean Literature: From Alexis to the Digital Age
Jeannine Murray-Román

Tropical Apocalypse: Haiti and the Caribbean End Times
Martin Munro

Market Aesthetics: The Purchase of the Past in Caribbean Diasporic Fiction
Elena Machado Sáez

Eric Williams and the Anticolonial Tradition: The Making of a Diasporan Intellectual
Maurice St. Pierre

www.ingramcontent.com/pod-product-compliance
Lightning Source LLC
Chambersburg PA
CBHW020110030726
47498CB00006B/2035